Mastering Windows PowerShell Scripting

Master the art of automating and managing your Windows environment using PowerShell

Brenton J.W. Blawat

[PACKT] PUBLISHING enterprise
professional expertise distilled

BIRMINGHAM - MUMBAI

Mastering Windows PowerShell Scripting

First published: April 2015

Production reference: 1210415

Published by Packt Publishing Ltd.
Livery Place
35 Livery Street
Birmingham B3 2PB, UK.

ISBN 978-1-78217-355-7

www.packtpub.com

Credits

Author
Brenton J.W. Blawat

Reviewers
Tim Amico
Christophe CRÉMON
Tomas Restrepo

Acquisition Editor
Meeta Rajani

Content Development Editor
Rohit Singh

Technical Editor
Tanvi Bhatt

Copy Editors
Hiral Bhat
Sonia Mathur
Vikrant Phadke
Alpha Singh

Project Coordinator
Mary Alex

Proofreaders
Simran Bhogal
Safis Editing
Maria Gould
Paul Hindle

Indexer
Rekha Nair

Production Coordinator
Alwin Roy

Cover Work
Alwin Roy

Foreword

We all appreciate a little simplicity when it enters our busy, complicated lives. Technology is no different. In fact, that is what we expect from technology—it should simplify our lives. But it doesn't always work that way.

Sometimes technology can introduce vexing problems we don't anticipate.

With every version of Microsoft DOS and then Windows, Microsoft included separate command-line interface shells. The shell could automate some tasks, but not all of them. Some tasks had to be accomplished manually, which is antithetical—nearly heretical—to our understanding of technology's role.

What should have been simple, automated tasks became slow, frustrating, and manual chores. That conundrum didn't go unnoticed.

Microsoft provided much-needed simplicity when it introduced PowerShell in 2006. Task automation and configuration management eliminated a great deal of time-consuming manual work. In short, PowerShell was a game changer.

PowerShell has solved many of the command-line and scripting issues that complicated our work. It introduced simplicity. It helped organizations become more agile, more productive, and save money. PowerShell is a powerful tool, and it has demonstrated its practical value many times.

Despite its utility, though, PowerShell remains a confusing tool to many IT administrators, and the need for greater clarity remains.

It is through this lens that Mr. Brenton Blawat provides an insightful new analysis of PowerShell—a valuable guidebook for those who struggle to understand PowerShell. Others have offered narratives that attempt to explain PowerShell, but they rarely provide the roadmap, background, or context that administrators need to get from Point A to Point B.

So, this is the right time for a comprehensive new analysis.

In general terms, Mr. Blawat's book will help those who struggle to manage their compute environments. It includes important guidance on programming in PowerShell, starting with basic concepts and then introducing advanced configurations.

Mr. Blawat deconstructs and demystifies this programming language, sharing his intimate knowledge in a format that demonstrates the clarity of thought and prose that a difficult subject requires. Many authors have attempted this climb, but only Mr. Blawat has reached the summit. His examination provides relevant information for administrators who work with—and sometimes struggle with—PowerShell on a daily basis.

As Mr. Blawat explains in the following pages, the rapid adoption of cloud-based technologies paralleled the never-ending need for additional computing power in data centers. This created the need to efficiently build and expand systems with extreme precision. In addition to provisioning the base systems, there was a need to dynamically customize these new systems to work in unison with current running environments.

This drove the need for the next generation system automation languages that would provide full configuration for systems on the fly. Not only do these automation languages greatly reduce time to use, but they also ensure that no mistakes are made during the configuration process. All systems are created equally.

PowerShell is a .NET-based next generation automation language that provides both systems provisioning and management functionality for Windows-based systems. Leveraging command-line like interactions, PowerShell can be compiled into scripts that can systematically execute tasks on a system. Not limited to creating new systems, engineers are leveraging PowerShell to automate mundane tasks so that they can focus on other pressing activities in their environments.

Microsoft has fully embraced PowerShell in its full software portfolio to offer full integration with its products. Not only can you dynamically install the Microsoft software, but you can also fully manage the entire Microsoft software environment using PowerShell. PowerShell has also been embraced by third-party manufacturers through the integration of PowerShell modules. These modules provide full management capabilities for products such as network devices, storage subsystems, virtualization guests and hosts, security appliances, and other third-party applications.

Like many organizations, CDW has benefitted greatly from PowerShell, so this book hits very close to home for me. We use PowerShell scripts to manage customer environments in managed services and the installation of management tools.

We use Microsoft Orchestrator to provide back-end logic for simple user interfaces for help desk activities, like user-driven password resets and user-driven software installations. We also rely on Microsoft Orchestrator to automatically troubleshoot and remediate systems.

CDW's customers also benefit from PowerShell in myriad ways. We assist a wide variety of Fortune 500 clients to develop PowerShell automation scripts to build new systems and manage their environments, including health check scripts, systems discovery, and advanced regulatory security analysis.

Clearly, PowerShell's incredible utility has made it invaluable to CDW, our customers, and countless organizations across the globe. But understanding all of its many facets represents a daunting task. Organizations are unable to leverage PowerShell if they don't fully understand its potential.

That's where Mr. Blawat excels.

Mr. Blawat's comprehensive new work will serve as a reference tool for engineers who work with Windows by taking the mystery out of common tasks that aren't easily understood and aren't always intuitive. Diligent readers will no doubt find many more reasons to give Mr. Blawat's thorough narrative a prominent place on their bookshelves.

As Mr. Blawat's coworker, I also feel proud that he is sharing his knowledge with the world—not only so others can benefit from his experience, but so they can see what those of us who work with him at CDW witness on a daily basis.

PowerShell has proven to be an incredibly useful tool for IT administrators since it burst on to the scene. Now there is a book about PowerShell that will prove equally useful.

Jon Stevens
Chief Information Officer
CDW

About the Author

Brenton J.W. Blawat is an entrepreneur, strategic technical advisor, author, and senior consultant, who has a passion for the procurement of technology in profit-based organizations. He is business-centric and technology-minded. Brenton has many years of experience in bridging the gap between technical staff and decision-makers in several organizations. He takes pride in his ability to effectively communicate with a diverse audience and provide strategic direction for large and small organizations alike.

In 2013, Brenton authored his first book, *PowerShell 3.0 WMI Starter, Packt Publishing*. This book was designed to be a starter for those interested in manipulating Windows Management Instrumentation through the use of PowerShell 3.0. This book is available in all popular book stores, including Packt Publishing's website, `http://bit.ly/18pcpGK`.

Brenton currently works at CDW as a senior consulting engineer in strategic solutions and services. CDW is a leading multibrand technology solutions provider in the fields of business, government, education, and healthcare. A Fortune 500 company, it was founded in 1984 and employs approximately 7,200 coworkers. In 2014, the company generated net sales of more than $12.0 billion. For more information about CDW, you can visit `www.CDW.com`.

I would like to thank the foreword coordination team, Mary Viola, Scott Thomas, Jimmy Thomson, Brandon King, Sondra Ragusin, Meredith Braselman, and Bill Glanz. I would like to dedicate this book to my beautiful nieces, Caliett and Evie.

About the Reviewers

Tim Amico is a consulting engineer at CDW, who specializes in Configuration Manager and Operating System Deployment. He started his career in IT back in 1998, when he worked as a configuration tech for CompuCom, learning about what is required to become an IT professional. Since then, he has climbed the ladder from hardware field support and software deployment support to his current role (for the last 10 years) as an IT consultant, designing and implementing endpoint and mobility management solutions. Apart from Configuration Manager and OSD, Tim also has experience in PowerShell, BitLocker drive encryption deployments, Intel vPro provisioning and use case design, Active Directory (both in Azure and Windows Server), SQL design and reporting, PKI design, and Microsoft Intune.

Christophe CRÉMON is a SharePoint infrastructure architect, with 10 years of experience in information technology, especially Microsoft. He has been using PowerShell since 2008, and has published useful scripts and modules for IT Administrators at `powershell.codeplex.com`. He has a personal website at `www.christophecremon.com`.

Tomas Restrepo has been writing software for over 10 years, starting with C/C++ and eventually moving to the .NET platform. He currently spends most of his time helping other developers solve complex problems and troubleshooting application performance and scalability issues.

www.PacktPub.com

Support files, eBooks, discount offers, and more

For support files and downloads related to your book, please visit `www.PacktPub.com`.

Did you know that Packt offers eBook versions of every book published, with PDF and ePub files available? You can upgrade to the eBook version at `www.PacktPub.com` and as a print book customer, you are entitled to a discount on the eBook copy. Get in touch with us at `service@packtpub.com` for more details.

At `www.PacktPub.com`, you can also read a collection of free technical articles, sign up for a range of free newsletters and receive exclusive discounts and offers on Packt books and eBooks.

PACKTLIB™

`https://www2.packtpub.com/books/subscription/packtlib`

Do you need instant solutions to your IT questions? PacktLib is Packt's online digital book library. Here, you can search, access, and read Packt's entire library of books.

Why subscribe?

- Fully searchable across every book published by Packt
- Copy and paste, print, and bookmark content
- On demand and accessible via a web browser

Free access for Packt account holders

If you have an account with Packt at `www.PacktPub.com`, you can use this to access PacktLib today and view 9 entirely free books. Simply use your login credentials for immediate access.

Instant updates on new Packt books

Get notified! Find out when new books are published by following `@PacktEnterprise` on Twitter or the *Packt Enterprise* Facebook page.

Table of Contents

Preface **v**

Chapter 1: Variables, Arrays, and Hashes **1**

Variables **2**
Objects stored in variables 4
Arrays **6**
Single-dimension arrays 6
Jagged arrays 7
Updating array values 8
Hashes **10**
Deciding the best container for your scripts **13**
Summary **14**

Chapter 2: Data Parsing and Manipulation **15**

String manipulation **15**
Replacing and splitting strings 16
Counting and trimming strings 18
The Trim method 19
The Substring method 21
The string true and false methods 22
Number manipulation and parsing **24**
Formatting numbers 25
Formatting bytes 26
Date and time manipulation **27**
Forcing data types **30**
Piping variables **32**
Summary **34**

Chapter 3: Comparison Operators 35
Comparison operator basics 35
Equal and not equal comparison 36
Greater than and less than comparison 38
Contains, like, and match operators 39
And / OR comparison operators 42
Best practices for comparison operators 43
Summary 44
Chapter 4: Functions, Switches, and Loops Structures 45
Functions 45
Looping structures 52
Switches 57
Combining the use of functions, switches, and loops 58
Best practices for functions, switches, and loops 61
Best practices for functions 62
Best practices for looping structures and switches 62
Summary 63
Chapter 5: Regular Expressions 65
Getting started with regular expressions 66
Regular expression grouping constructs and ranges 70
Regular expression quantifiers 72
Regular expression anchors 78
Regular expressions examples 82
Summary 85
Chapter 6: Error and Exception Handling and Testing Code 87
Error and exception handling – parameters 88
Error and exception handling – Try/Catch 90
Error and exception handling –Try/Catch with parameters 92
Error and exception handling – legacy exception handling 93
Methodologies for testing code 96
Testing the –WhatIf argument 96
Testing the frequency 97
Hit testing containers 98
Don't test in production 99
Summary 101
Chapter 7: Session-based Remote Management 103
Utilizing CIM sessions 104
Creating a session 107
Creating a session with session options 109

Using sessions for remote management 111
Removing sessions 113
Summary 114
Chapter 8: Managing Files, Folders, and Registry Items 117
Registry provider 118
Creating files, folders, and registry items with PowerShell 119
Adding named values to registry keys 121
Verifying files, folders, and registry items 123
Copying and moving files and folders 125
Renaming files, folders, registry keys, and named values 128
Deleting files, folders, registry keys, and named values 131
Summary 135
Chapter 9: File, Folder, and Registry Attributes, ACLs, and Properties 137
Retrieving attributes and properties 138
Viewing file and folder extended attributes 141
Setting the mode and extended file and folder attributes 143
Managing file, folder, and registry permissions 147
Copying access control lists 148
Adding and removing ACL rules 150
Summary 157
Chapter 10: Windows Management Instrumentation 159
WMI structure 159
Using WMI objects 161
Searching for WMI classes 163
Creating, modifying, and removing WMI property instances 167
Creating property instances 170
Modifying property instances 171
Removing property instances 173
Invoking WMI class methods 174
Summary 176
Chapter 11: XML Manipulation 177
XML file structure 177
Reading XML files 181
Adding XML content 185
Modifying XML content 189
Removing XML content 192
Summary 193

Chapter 12: Managing Microsoft Systems with PowerShell 195
Managing local users and groups 195
Managing local users 196
Managing local groups 198
Querying for local users and groups 204
Managing Windows services 207
Managing Windows processes 213
Installing Windows features and roles 217
Summary 221
Chapter 13: Automation of the Environment 223
Invoking programs for automation 223
Using desired state configuration 229
Authoring phase 231
Staging and remediation phase 235
Detecting and restoring drifting configurations 236
Summary 239
Chapter 14: Script Creation Best Practices and Conclusion 241
Best practices for script management 241
 # commenting headers 241
Commenting code 243
Best practices for script creation 245
Script structure 245
Other important best practices for script creation 246
Controlling source files 248
Best practices for software automation 249
Summary 250
Mastering Windows PowerShell Scripting – conclusion 251
Staying connected with the author 251
Index 253

Preface

PowerShell is a network scripting language that provides a set of tools to administer Microsoft products. While PowerShell is based on command-line interactions, it is much more powerful than what the standard command line offers. It has built-in sections of code called cmdlets. They simplify functions that you may need to perform on a system. Using cmdlets greatly reduces the number of lines of code that are required to perform actions, compared to other scripting languages, such as VBScript.

PowerShell is based on the verb-noun naming convention, which allows scripters to declare an action followed by an object to configure. For example, the get-service cmdlet easily designates that you are getting a Windows service. This literal naming convention helps readers quickly learn how to program in PowerShell, as the actions are easily remembered.

Community support for PowerShell has grown astronomically. Not only have large companies adopted PowerShell in their environments, but universities are also regularly teaching PowerShell courses to their students. PowerShell's feature set keeps growing with every release of the product. It is conceivable in the near future that you will be able to fully automate the configuration of every component in a data center. This will remove the needs of multiple engineering specialists to provision networking, storage, firewalls, operating systems builds, and high-availability configurations. It will all be done via PowerShell scripting and the systems will be able to be configured using a singular network language.

This book provides a strong foundation for learning PowerShell using real-world scenarios. You will not only be able to quickly learn how to program in this language, but also be able to produce scripts that you can use in your existing environments. This book will also be a great reference book for you to look back on and revisit as you are coding. It will provide the proper syntax and show you successful ways to implement your code. When you are done with reading this book, you will be well on your way to "mastering PowerShell"!

What this book covers

Chapter 1, Variables, Arrays, and Hashes, explores the different data and object containers that you can use in PowerShell. These containers include variables, arrays, and hashes. This chapter provides examples on how to use these containers to store objects.

Chapter 2, Data Parsing and Manipulation, dives into the different data types and how to manipulate them in your scripts. These data type examples include strings, integers, dates, XML, and many more.

Chapter 3, Comparison Operators, evaluates multiple comparison operators and displays how to use each of these comparison operators. This chapter also displays how to leverage implied true and false comparison operators.

Chapter 4, Functions, Switches, and Loops Structures, displays the use of different data structures to perform repeatable actions. It provides examples on how to parse large arrays of data through looping structures and how to include overload parameters in these structures.

Chapter 5, Regular Expressions, explores PowerShell's implementation of regular expressions. It evaluates the built-in comparison operators that provide expression validation and how to create complex expressions.

Chapter 6, Error and Exception Handling and Testing Code, shows you how to create code in a robust manner to avoid exceptions during execution. This chapter explains various built-in error and exception handling techniques, as well as support for legacy systems that don't support PowerShell cmdlet triggers. It also explains the different items to be aware of during the testing cycle of your code.

Chapter 7, Session-based Remote Management, provides an insight into session-based management through PowerShell. It displays how to leverage the built-in WinRM to execute items on remote systems.

Chapter 8, Managing Files, Folders, and Registry Items, displays how to query, create, modify, and delete items in the filesystem and registry. This includes files, folders, registry keys, registry-named values, and properties.

Chapter 9, File, Folder, and Registry Attributes, ACLs, and Properties, dives deep into the interworking of files, folders, and registries. This chapter explains how to set file and folder standards and advanced attributes. It also displays how to manipulate ACLs to set permissions on files, folders, and registry items.

Chapter 10, Windows Management Instrumentation, explains how to use Windows Management Instrumentation (WMI) to query local and remote systems for advanced system information and the different cmdlets that provide access to a system's WMI.

Chapter 11, XML Manipulation, explores eXtensible Markup Language (XML) and shows you how to interact with it using PowerShell. This chapter explains the different components that make up a proper XML document and how to interact with these individual components.

Chapter 12, Managing Microsoft Systems with Powershell, provides information on how to work with Windows users and groups, Windows services, Windows processes, and the manipulation of Windows features and roles.

Chapter 13, Automation of the Environment, explains how to invoke items for use with automation scripts. This chapter explains parent and child relationships because they pertain to linking scripts together. It also explores Desired Configuration Management (DCM) and configuration baselines.

Chapter 14, Script Creation Best Practices and Conclusion, provides best practice recommendations for utilizing PowerShell in your environment. This chapter concludes with some final thoughts from the author.

What you need for this book

To work through the examples provided in *Mastering Windows PowerShell Scripting,* you will need access to Windows 7 or a higher Windows operating system. You will also need Server 2008 R2 or a higher Windows Server operating system. The chapters in this book rely highly on Windows Management Framework 4.0 (PowerShell 4.0) and Remote Server Administration Tools. You will need to download and install both of these software packages on the systems you are running these examples on.

Who this book is for

Mastering Windows PowerShell Scripting has been designed for PowerShell scripters who can be both beginners and advanced-level coders. By reading this book, you will be able to gain in-depth knowledge of PowerShell and the best practices to develop scripts using this automation language. Previous scripting and coding experience will be helpful, though it is not required.

Conventions

In this book, you will find a number of styles of text that distinguish between different kinds of information. Here are some examples of these styles, and an explanation of their meaning.

Code words in text, database table names, folder names, filenames, file extensions, pathnames, dummy URLs, user input, and Twitter handles are shown as follows: "The `get-service` cmdlet is used to retrieve detailed information about Windows services."

Any command-line input or output is written as follows:

```
# Retrieve the service sstatus and start the service if it is stopped.
$status = (Get-service -DisplayName "Windows Audio").Status
If ($status -like "Stopped") {
start-service -DisplayName "Windows Audio"
}
```

New terms and **important words** are shown in bold. Words that you see on the screen, in menus or dialog boxes for example, appear in the text like this: "To add a firewall rule on a system using the netsh command, you need to open PowerShell with the **Run as Administrator** option"

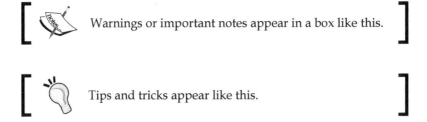

> Warnings or important notes appear in a box like this.

> Tips and tricks appear like this.

Reader feedback

Feedback from our readers is always welcome. Let us know what you think about this book—what you liked or may have disliked. Reader feedback is important for us to develop titles that you really get the most out of.

To send us general feedback, simply send an e-mail to `feedback@packtpub.com`, and mention the book title via the subject of your message.

If there is a topic that you have expertise in and you are interested in either writing or contributing to a book, see our author guide on `www.packtpub.com/authors`.

Customer support

Now that you are the proud owner of a Packt book, we have a number of things to help you to get the most from your purchase.

Downloading the example code

You can download the example code files for all Packt books you have purchased from your account at `http://www.packtpub.com`. If you purchased this book elsewhere, you can visit `http://www.packtpub.com/support` and register to have the files e-mailed directly to you.

Errata

Although we have taken every care to ensure the accuracy of our content, mistakes do happen. If you find a mistake in one of our books—maybe a mistake in the text or the code—we would be grateful if you would report this to us. By doing so, you can save other readers from frustration and help us improve subsequent versions of this book. If you find any errata, please report them by visiting `http://www.packtpub.com/submit-errata`, selecting your book, clicking on the **errata submission form** link, and entering the details of your errata. Once your errata are verified, your submission will be accepted and the errata will be uploaded on our website, or added to any list of existing errata, under the Errata section of that title. Any existing errata can be viewed by selecting your title from `http://www.packtpub.com/support`.

Piracy

Piracy of copyright material on the Internet is an ongoing problem across all media. At Packt, we take the protection of our copyright and licenses very seriously. If you come across any illegal copies of our works, in any form, on the Internet, please provide us with the location address or website name immediately so that we can pursue a remedy.

Please contact us at `copyright@packtpub.com` with a link to the suspected pirated material.

We appreciate your help in protecting our authors, and our ability to bring you valuable content.

Questions

You can contact us at `questions@packtpub.com` if you are having a problem with any aspect of the book, and we will do our best to address it.

1
Variables, Arrays, and Hashes

PowerShell provides a variety of mechanisms to store, retrieve, and manipulate data used in your scripts. These storage "containers" are referred to as variables, arrays, and hashes. They can be used as containers to store strings, integers, or objects. These containers are dynamic as they automatically detect what type of data is being placed within them. Unlike other object-oriented languages, there is no need to declare the container prior to use. To declare one of these containers, you use the dollar sign (`$`) and the container name.

An example of a container would look like this:

```
$myVariable
```

During this chapter, you will learn the following concepts:

- Variables
- Arrays
- Hashes
- Deciding the best container for your scripts

When you are creating names for containers, it is industry best practice to use names that are representative of the data they are storing. While containers are not case sensitive in PowerShell, it is a common practice to use *camelCase* when writing container names. camelCase is achieved by keeping the first letter of the container lowercase and the subsequent first letters of each word capitalized. Some variations of camelCase permit the first letter to be capitalized. This formatting aids in easy reading of the containers.

An example of a container using camelCase would look like this:

```
$webServerIPAddress
```

Variables

Variables are one of the most widely used containers in PowerShell due to their flexibility. A variable is a container that is used to store a single value or an object. Variables can contain a variety of data types including text (string), numbers (integers), or an object.

If you want to store a string, do the following:

```
$myString = "My String Has Multiple Words"
$myString
```

The output of this is shown in the following screenshot:

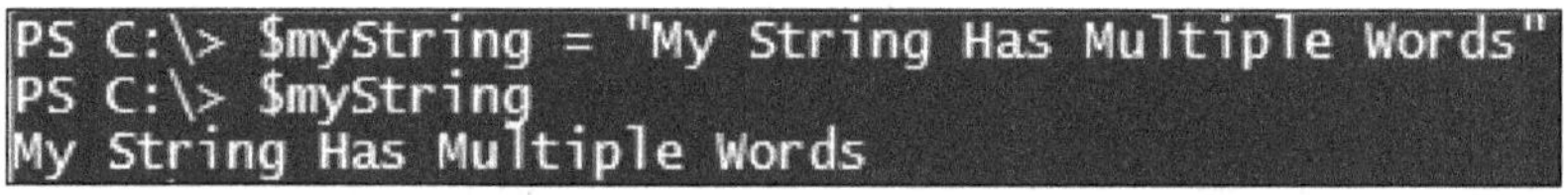
PS C:\> $myString = "My String Has Multiple Words"
PS C:\> $myString
My String Has Multiple Words

The preceding variable will now contain the words `My String Has Multiple Words`. When you output the `$myString` variable, as shown in the preceding screenshot, you will see that the string doesn't contain the quotations. This is because the quotations tell the PowerShell command-line interpreter to store the value that is between the two positions or quotations.

> You are able to reuse variables without deleting the content already inside the variable. The PowerShell interpreter will automatically overwrite the data for you.

Subsequently, if you want to store a number, do the following:

```
$myNumber = 1
$myNumber
```

The output of this is shown in the following screenshot:

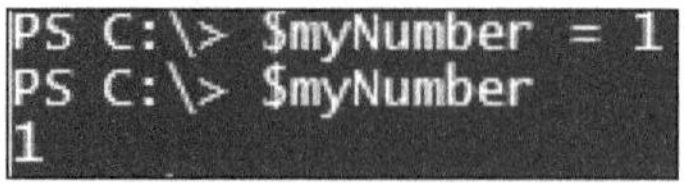
PS C:\> $myNumber = 1
PS C:\> $myNumber
1

This method differentiates while storing a string as you do not use quotations. This will tell the PowerShell interpreter to always interpret the value as a number. It is important to not use quotations while using a number, as you can have errors in your script if the PowerShell interpreter mistakes a number for a string.

An example of what happens when you use strings instead of integers can be seen here:

```
$a = "1"
$b = "2"
$c = $a + $b
$c
```

The output of this is shown in the following screenshot:

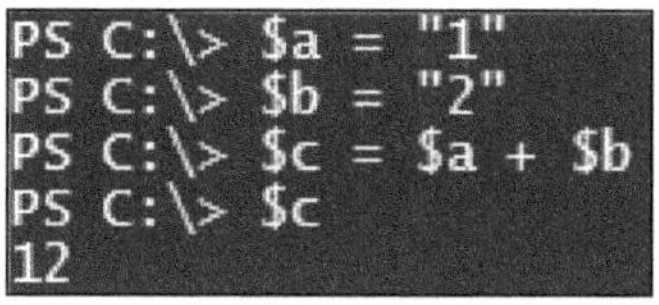
PS C:\> $a = "1"
PS C:\> $b = "2"
PS C:\> $c = $a + $b
PS C:\> $c
12

The `$c` variable will contain the value of `12`. This is due to PowerShell interpreting your `$a` string of `1` and `$b` string of `2` and putting the characters together to make `12`.

The correct method to do the math would look like this:

```
$a = 1
$b = 2
$c = $a + $b
$c
```

The output of this is shown in the following screenshot:

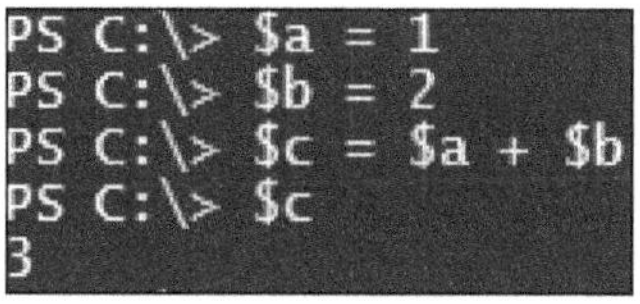
PS C:\> $a = 1
PS C:\> $b = 2
PS C:\> $c = $a + $b
PS C:\> $c
3

Since the `$a` and `$b` variables are stored as numbers, PowerShell will perform the math on the numbers appropriately. The `$c` variable will contain the correct value of `3`.

Objects stored in variables

Objects are vastly different than strings and numbers. Objects in PowerShell are data structures that contain different attributes such as properties and methods with which one can interact. Object properties are descriptors that typically contain data about that object or other related objects. Object methods are typically sections of code that allow you to interact with that object or other objects on a system. These objects can easily be placed in variables. You can simply place an object in a variable by declaring a variable and placing an object in it. To view all of the object's attributes, you can simply call the variable containing the object, use a pipe character `|`, and use the `get-member` cmdlet.

To place an object in a variable and retrieve its attributes, you need to do this:

```
$date = get-date
$date
$date | get-member
```

The output is shown in the following screenshot:

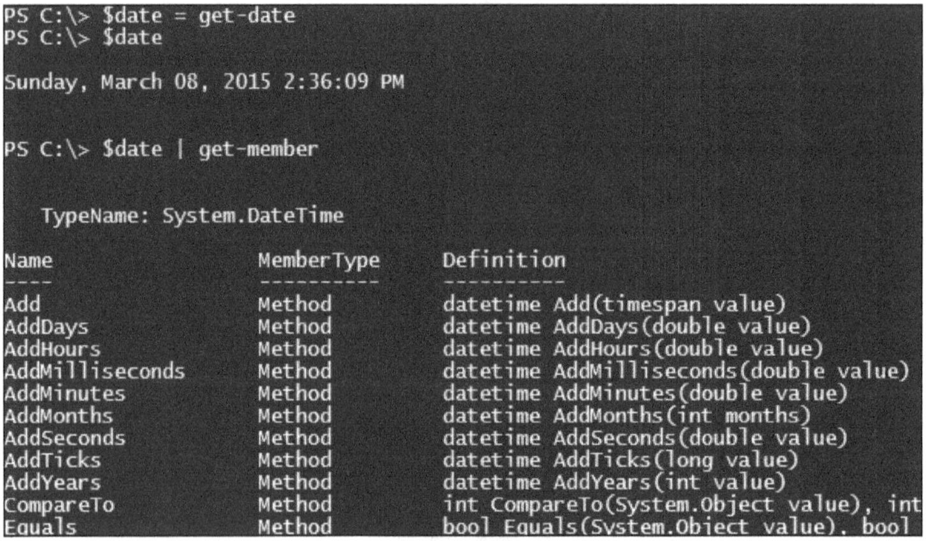

```
PS C:\> $date = get-date
PS C:\> $date

Sunday, March 08, 2015 2:36:09 PM


PS C:\> $date | get-member


   TypeName: System.DateTime

Name                 MemberType     Definition
----                 ----------     ----------
Add                  Method         datetime Add(timespan value)
AddDays              Method         datetime AddDays(double value)
AddHours             Method         datetime AddHours(double value)
AddMilliseconds      Method         datetime AddMilliseconds(double value)
AddMinutes           Method         datetime AddMinutes(double value)
AddMonths            Method         datetime AddMonths(int months)
AddSeconds           Method         datetime AddSeconds(double value)
AddTicks             Method         datetime AddTicks(long value)
AddYears             Method         datetime AddYears(int value)
CompareTo            Method         int CompareTo(System.Object value), int
Equals               Method         bool Equals(System.Object value), bool
```

In this example, you will learn how to place an object into a variable. You first start by declaring the `$date` variable and setting it equal to the output from the `get-date` cmdlet. When you execute this, the `get-date` cmdlet references the `System.Date` class, and the `$date` variable inherits all of that object's attributes. You then call the `$date` variable and you see that the output is the date and time from when that command was run. In this instance, it is displaying the `DateTime ScriptProperty` attribute on the screen. To view all of the attributes of the `System.Date` object in the `$date` variable, you pipe those results to the `get-member` cmdlet. You will see all of the attributes of that object displayed on the screen.

If you want to use the properties and method attributes of that object, you can simply call them using dot notation. This is done by calling the variable, followed by a period, and referencing the property or method.

To reference an object's properties and method attributes, you need to do this:

```
$date = get-date
$date.Year
$date.addyears("5")
```

The output of this is shown in the following screenshot:

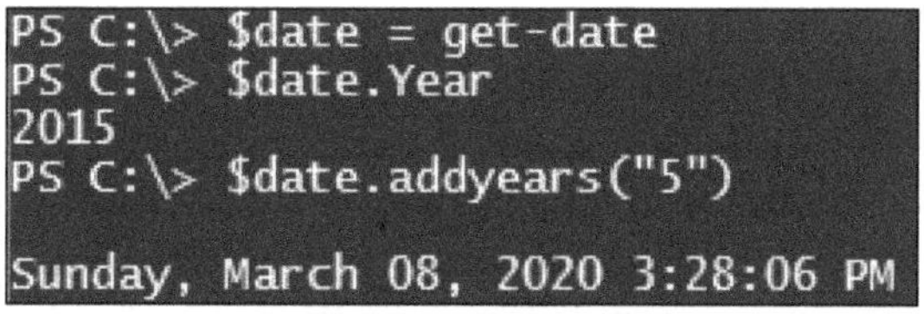
PS C:\> $date = get-date
PS C:\> $date.Year
2015
PS C:\> $date.addyears("5")
Sunday, March 08, 2020 3:28:06 PM

This example shows you how to reference an object's properties and method attributes using dot notation. You first start by declaring the `$date` variable and setting it equal to the output from the `get-date` cmdlet. When you execute this, the `get-date` cmdlet references the `System.Date` class, and the `$date` variable inherits all of that object's attributes. You then leverage dot notation to reference the `Year` property attribute by calling `$date.Year`. The attribute will return `2015` as the `Year` property. You then leverage dot notation to use the `AddYears()` method to increase the years by `5`. After entering the `$date.addyears("5")` command, you will see an output on the screen of the same month, day, and time; however, the year is incremented by `5` years.

Arrays

Arrays are the second most used containers in PowerShell. An array, in simple terms, is a multi-dimensional variable or a variable containing more than one value. The two core components to an array are the index number and the position value. When you use an array, you reference an index number and it will return the position value.

Single-dimension arrays

The following table represents an array with a single dimension:

Index number	Position value
0	Example 1
1	Example 2
2	Example 3
3	Example 4
4	Example 5

When you are storing, manipulating, or reading the data in an array, you have to reference the position in the array the data is residing. The numbers populated in the table's **Index number** column are representative of the location within the array. You will see that array's numbering starts at the number `0`, and so the first data would be in cell `0`. If you call the array at position `0`, the result would be the position value of `Example 1`. When building the array, you will see that each value in the array values is separated by a comma. This tells the PowerShell interpreter to set a new array value.

First, you can start by building the array in the preceding table by entering the following command:

```
$myArray = "Example 1", "Example 2", "Example 3", "Example 4",
"Example 5"
$myArray
```

The output of this is shown in the following screenshot:

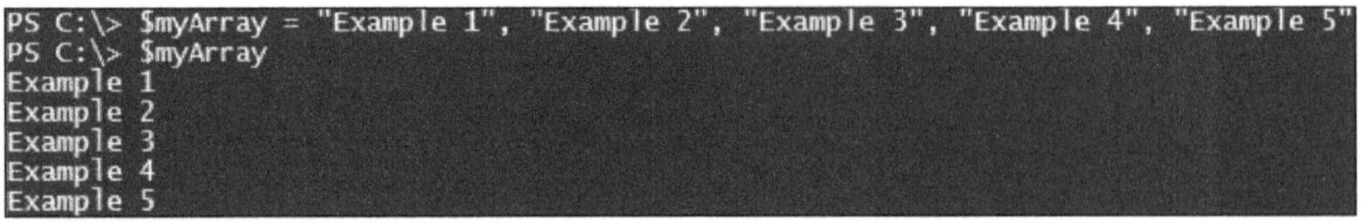
PS C:\> $myArray = "Example 1", "Example 2", "Example 3", "Example 4", "Example 5"
PS C:\> $myArray
Example 1
Example 2
Example 3
Example 4
Example 5

The preceding example displays how to create an array of strings. You first start by declaring a variable named `$myArray`. You then place multiple strings of text separated by commas to build the array. After declaring the array, you call the `$myArray` array to print the values to the console. It will return `Example 1`, `Example 2`, `Example 3`, `Example 4`, and `Example 5`.

Retrieving data at a specific position in an array is done through the use of brackets. To retrieve the value of `0` from the array, you would do the following:

```
$myArray = "Example 1", "Example 2", "Example 3", "Example 4",
"Example 5"
$myArray[0]
```

The output of this is shown in the following screenshot:

PS C:\> $myArray = "Example 1", "Example 2", "Example 3", "Example 4", "Example 5"
PS C:\> $myArray[0]
Example 1

The preceding example displays how you can obtain array data at a specific position. You first start by declaring a variable named `$myArray`. You then place multiple strings of text separated by commas to build the array. After declaring the array, you call `$myArray[0]` to access the position value of index number `0` from the array. The preceding example returns the value of `Example 1` for the index number `0`.

Jagged arrays

Arrays can become more complex as you start adding dimensions. The following table represents a jagged array or an array of arrays:

Index number	**Position value 0**	**Position value 1**
0	Example 1	Red
1	Example 2	Orange
2	Example 3	Yellow
3	Example 4	Green
4	Example 5	Blue

While accessing data in a jagged array, you will need to read the cell values counting at `0` for both dimensions. When you are accessing the data, you start reading from the index number first and then the position value. For example, the `Example 1` data is in the index number of `0` and the position value of `0`. This would be referenced as position `[0][0]`. Subsequently, the data `Blue` is in the index number of `4` and position value of `1`. This would be referenced as position `[4][1]`.

To do this for yourself, you can build the preceding table by entering the following command:

```
$myArray = ("Example 1","Red"), ("Example 2","Orange"), ("Example 3",
"Yellow"), ("Example 4", "Green"), ("Example 5", "Blue")
$myArray[0][0]
$myArray[4][1]
```

The output is shown in the following screenshot:

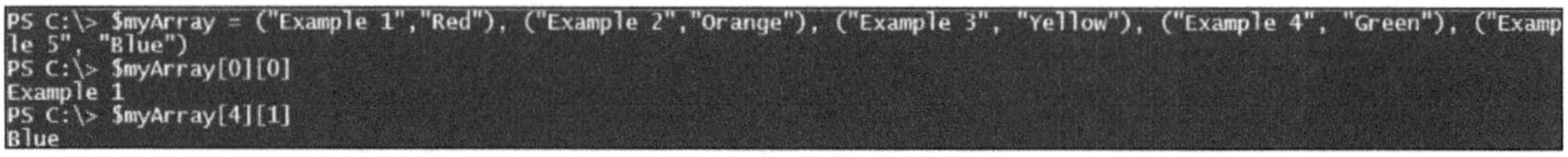

This example displays how to create a jagged array and accessing values in the array. You first start building the jagged array by declaring the first array of `"Example 1" "Red"`, second array of `"Example 2" "Orange"`, third array of `"Example 3" "Yellow"`, fourth array of `"Example 4" "Green"`, and fifth array of `"Example 5" "Blue"`. After building the array, you access the word `Example 1` by referencing `$myArray[0][0]`. You then access the word `Blue` by referencing `$myArray[4][1]`.

Updating array values

After you create an array, you may need to update the values inside the array itself. The process for updating values in an array is similar to retrieving data from the array. First you need to find the cell location that you want to update, and then you need to set that array location as equal to the new value:

Index number	Position value 0	Position value 1
0	John	Doe
1	Jane	Smith

Given the preceding table, if Jane's last name needed to be updated to display `Doe` instead of `Smith`, you would first need to locate that data record. That incorrect last name is located at index number `1` and position value `1`, or `[1][1]`. You will then need to set that data location equal (=) to `Doe`.

To do this, you need to enter the following command:

```
$myArray = ("John","Doe"), ("Jane","Smith")
$myArray
$myArray[1][1] = "Doe"
$myArray
```

The output of this is shown in the following screenshot:

```
PS C:\> $myArray = ("John","Doe"), ("Jane","Smith")
PS C:\> $myArray
John
Doe
Jane
Smith
PS C:\> $myArray[1][1] = "Doe"
PS C:\> $myArray
John
Doe
Jane
Doe
```

This example displays how you can create an array and update a value in the array. You first start by defining `$myArray` and use `"John"`, `"Doe"`, `"Jane"`, and `"Smith"` as the array values. After calling the variable to print the array to the screen, you update the value in index number `1`, position value `1`, or `$myArray[1][1]`. By setting this position equal to `Doe`, you change the value from `Smith` to `Doe`:

Index number	Position value 0	Position value 1
0	John	Doe
1	Jane	Smith
2	Sam	Smith

In instances where you want to append additional values to the array, you can call the array variable with the `+=` command and the data you want to add to the array. This looks like `$array += "New Array Values"`. The `+=` command is a more efficient method of performing the commands `$array = $array + "New Array Values"`.

To add data into an array and make the preceding table, you can do the following operation:

```
# Create the Array
$myArray = ("John","Doe"), ("Jane","Smith")
$myArray
# Append Data to the Array
$myArray += ("Sam","Smith")
$myArray
```

The output of this is shown in the following screenshot:

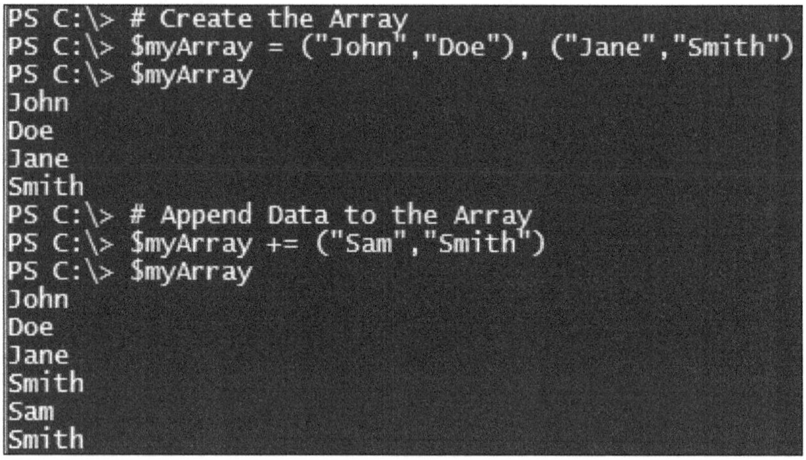
PS C:\> # Create the Array
PS C:\> $myArray = ("John","Doe"), ("Jane","Smith")
PS C:\> $myArray
John
Doe
Jane
Smith
PS C:\> # Append Data to the Array
PS C:\> $myArray += ("Sam","Smith")
PS C:\> $myArray
John
Doe
Jane
Smith
Sam
Smith

In this example, you add values to an existing array. You first start by defining an array of `$myArray`. You then print the existing contents of the array to the screen. You then add additional content by setting the array `+=` to the new array data of `("Sam","Smith")`. After reprinting the contents of the array to the screen, you see the values `Sam` and `Smith` added to the array.

> To search and remove items from an array, you will need to create a `ForEach` loop to cycle through all of the index numbers and position values. *Chapter 4, Functions, Switches, and Loop Structures*, explores the `ForEach` looping structure.

Hashes

Hashes are used like arrays. The main difference is that they use the values as indexes versus sequentially numbered indexes. This provides easy functionality to add, remove, modify, and find data contained in the hash table. Hash tables are useful for static information that needs a direct correlation to other data:

Name	**Value**
`John.Doe`	`Jdoe`
`Jane.Doe`	`jdoe1`

A good example of a hash table would be in the instance of an Active Directory migration. In most Active Directory migrations, you would need to correlate old usernames to new usernames. The preceding table represents a username mapping table for these types of migrations. While a traditional array would work, a hash table makes this much easier to do.

To create the preceding hash table, enter the following command:

```
$users = @{"john.doe" = "jdoe"; "jane.doe" = "jdoe1"}
$users
```

The output of this is shown in the following screenshot:

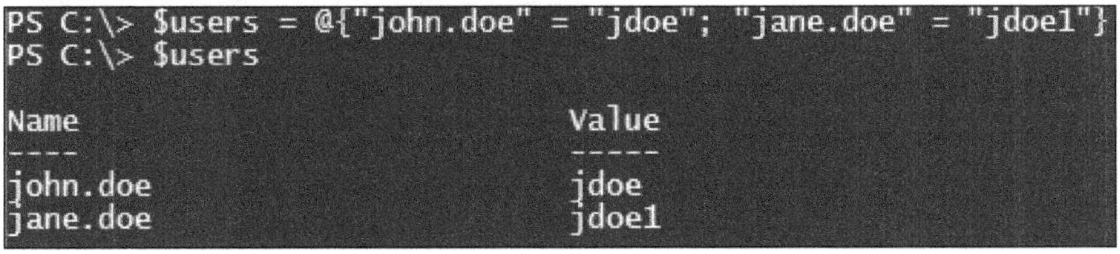

After you create the table, you may want to find a specific user. You can search a hash table by using the hash's indexing function. This is done by calling `$hashName["value"]`. An example of this would look like the following command:

```
$users = @{"john.doe" = "jdoe"; "jane.doe" = "jdoe1"}
$users["john.doe"]
```

The output of this is shown in the following screenshot:

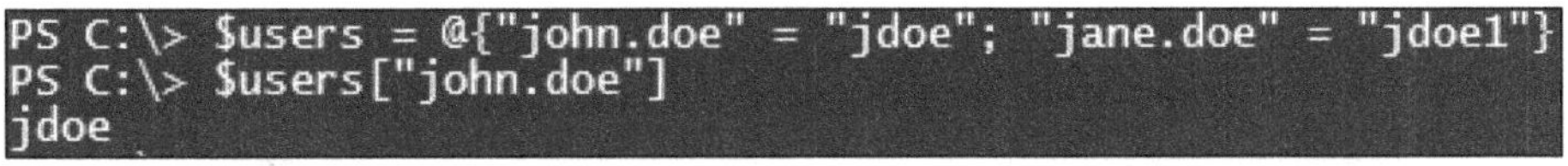

PS C:\> $users = @{"john.doe" = "jdoe"; "jane.doe" = "jdoe1"}
PS C:\> $users["john.doe"]
jdoe

After entering the command, you will see that `$users["john.doe"]` returns `jdoe` as the correlating value in the hash.

One of the most popular methods to use with hash tables is the `add` method. The `add` method allows you to enter new values within the hash table. You can use this while building the hash table, as most hash tables are built within a script. If you want to add another user to the hash table, use the `add` method as shown here:

```
$users = @{"john.doe" = "jdoe"; " jane.doe" = "jdoe1"}
$users
$users.add("John.Smith", "jsmith")
$users
```

The output of this is shown in the following screenshot:

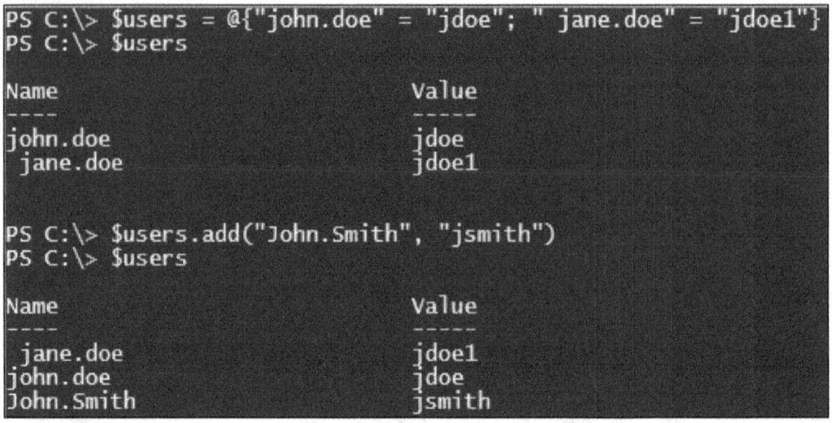
PS C:\> $users = @{"john.doe" = "jdoe"; " jane.doe" = "jdoe1"}
PS C:\> $users
Name
Value
john.doe
jdoe
jane.doe
jdoe1
PS C:\> $users.add("John.Smith", "jsmith")
PS C:\> $users
Name
Value
jane.doe
jdoe1
john.doe
jdoe
John.Smith
jsmith

You will see that `John.Smith` with the value of `jsmith` is now added to the hash table.

You can also update values in a hash by leveraging the hash's index. This is done by searching for a value and then setting its correlating hash value equal to a new value. This looks like `$arrayName["HashIndex"] = "New value"`. An example of this is given here:

```
$users = @{"john.doe" = "jdoe"; "jane.doe" = "jdoe1"}
$users
$users["jane.doe"] = "jadoe"
$users
```

The output of this is shown in the following screenshot:

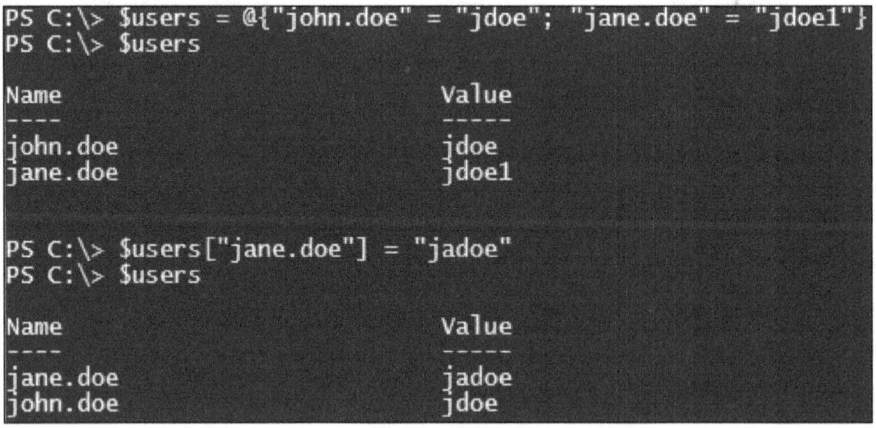
PS C:\> $users = @{"john.doe" = "jdoe"; "jane.doe" = "jdoe1"}
PS C:\> $users
Name
Value
john.doe
jdoe
jane.doe
jdoe1
PS C:\> $users["jane.doe"] = "jadoe"
PS C:\> $users
Name
Value
jane.doe
jadoe
john.doe
jdoe

You will see that the mapped value for `Jane.Doe` now reads `jadoe`. This is vastly different from an array, where you would have to search for a specific value location to replace the value.

If you want to remove a user from the hash table, use the `remove` method, as shown here:

```
$users = @{"john.doe" = "jdoe"; "jane.doe" = "jdoe1"}
$users
$users.remove("Jane.Doe")
$users
```

The output of this is shown in the following screenshot:

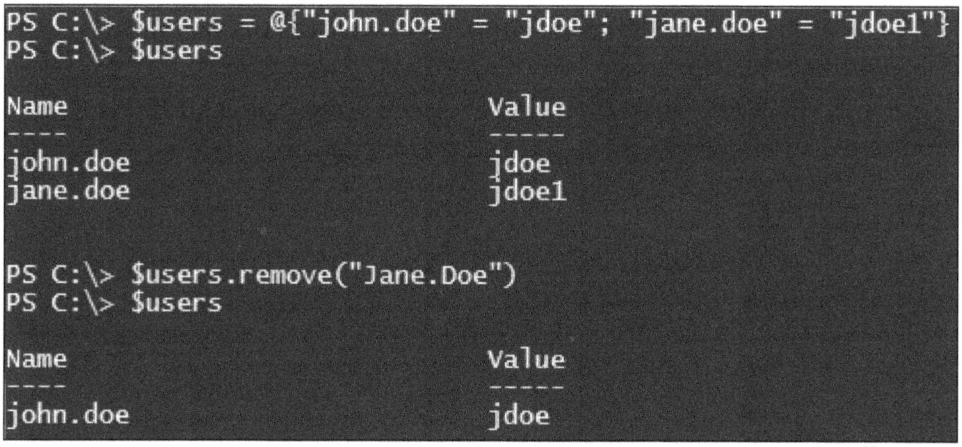
PS C:\> $users = @{"john.doe" = "jdoe"; "jane.doe" = "jdoe1"}
PS C:\> $users
Name Value
---- -----
john.doe jdoe
jane.doe jdoe1
PS C:\> $users.remove("Jane.Doe")
PS C:\> $users
Name Value
---- -----
john.doe jdoe

You will see that `Jane.Doe` is now removed from the hash table. This method is helpful when you need to remove specific values, which meet certain criteria, from the hash table.

Deciding the best container for your scripts

When you are scripting, it is important to put consideration into what kind of container you will be using. Sometimes the simplicity of creating a singular variable and updating that variable is less complex than creating an array or hash table to search through. At other times, it may be more efficient to pull the whole dataset and use individual pieces of that data within your script.

Single-line variables can be used for:

- Math operations that require calculations of single or multiple values
- Catching single-line output from executing a non-PowerShell command
- Tracking current position in a loop like "percent complete"

Arrays are best used for:

- Storing a list of items for individual processing within a script
- Dumping error information from a PowerShell cmdlet

Hashes are best used for:

- Mapping data from one value to another value
- Data that requires frequent searching, updating, or building during script execution
- Storing multiple values of correlated data like user object attributes

Summary

This chapter explores the use of a variety of containers. You learned that variables, arrays, and hashes have the commonality of being able to store data, but they do it in different ways. You learned that different types of data can be stored in these containers. These types of data include numbers, strings, and objects.

This chapter explored that variables are best used for the storage of single-dimensional datasets. These datasets can contain strings but also include mathematical equations that PowerShell has the ability to inherently calculate. You also now know that arrays are primarily used in situations where you want to store more than one set of data. You are able to navigate, add, and remove values in the array based off of a starting value of 0. Last, you learned that hashes are best used while correlating data from one value to another. You are able to add, remove, and search data contained in the hash tables with the use of simple commands. In the next chapter, you will learn techniques to perform data parsing and manipulation by leveraging variables and arrays.

2

Data Parsing and Manipulation

One of the most powerful features of PowerShell is its ability to retrieve and manipulate data. Many a times when you retrieve data from a PowerShell session, the format in which it is available is different from what you would want to display in the PowerShell window or in a log file. For this purpose, PowerShell provides powerful cmdlets and methods to perform data manipulation to best suit your needs as a PowerShell scripter.

While reading this chapter, you'll learn the following concepts:

- String manipulation
- Number manipulation and parsing
- Date/time manipulation
- Forcing data types
- PowerShell pipeline

String manipulation

String manipulation is something that you'll need to do in almost every script you create. While some of the string methods will be used more often than others, they all serve different purposes for your script. It is ultimately up to your creativity on how you want data to look when it is displayed on the screen.

To change the text to uppercase, execute the following command:

```
$a = "Error: This is an example error"
$a.toUpper()
```

The output of this is shown in the following screenshot:

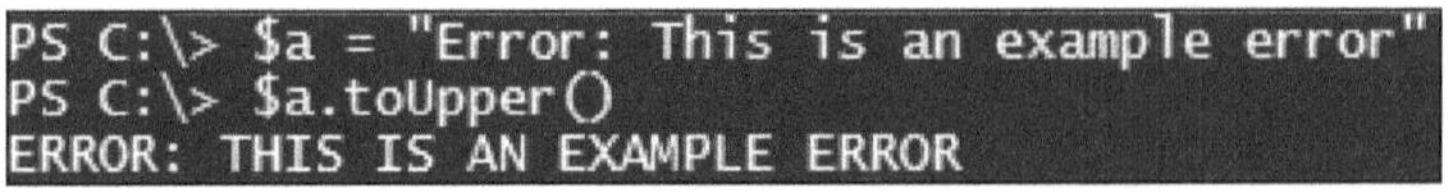

PS C:\> $a = "Error: This is an example error"
PS C:\> $a.toUpper()
ERROR: THIS IS AN EXAMPLE ERROR

The `toUpper()` method is used to format the text to uppercase. This is helpful in situations where messages need to be emphasized or should stand out. The result of this command will change the case.

To change the string to lowercase, execute the following command:

```
$string = "The MAC Address is "

$mac = "00:A0:AA:BB:CC:DD"

$message = $string + $mac.toLower()

$message
```

The output of this is shown in the following screenshot:

PS C:\> $string = "The MAC Address is "
PS C:\> $mac = "00:A0:AA:BB:CC:DD"
PS C:\> $message = $string + $mac.toLower()
PS C:\> $message
The MAC Address is 00:a0:aa:bb:cc:dd

The inverse of `toUpper()` is the use of `toLower()`. This command will convert the entire string to lowercase in the instance when you do not want to emphasize a string. `toLower()` is typically used in situations where a single word or a variable is uppercase, and you want to transition it to lowercase. This command shows taking two separate strings, formatting the `$MAC` string to the lowercase, and outputting both variables together.

Replacing and splitting strings

PowerShell also provides the ability to replace characters in strings using the `Replace()` method. This is useful within your scripts when you have to replace characters from the output of another method. For instance, if you pull a list of common usernames from Active Directory, they are prefixed with `cn=`. If you wanted to replace `CN=` with nothing `("")`, you can easily accomplish this with the `Replace()` method.

To replace items in a string, execute the following command:

```
$usernames = "CN=juser,CN=jdoe,CN=jsmith,CN=bwhite,CN=sjones"
$usernames = $usernames.replace("CN=","")
$usernames
```

The output of this is shown in the following screenshot:

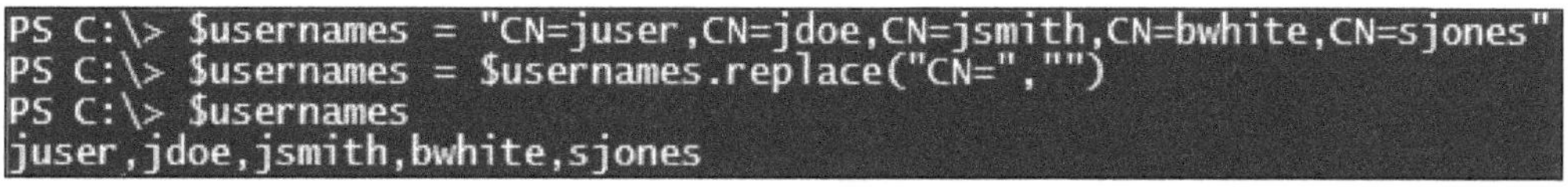

This script will replace the characters `CN=` with nothing as designated by `""`. The output of this script is a list of usernames with comma separators. As you can see, this is very helpful in the manipulation of the data being output from Active Directory. Building on the prior example, if you wanted to process the usernames individually, you can leverage the `split()` method. The `split()` method will separate values in a string, by declaring a specific character to split.

To split items in a string, execute the following command:

```
$usernames = "juser,jdoe,jsmith,bwhite,sjones"
$userarray = $usernames.split(",")
$userarray
```

The output of this is shown in the following screenshot:

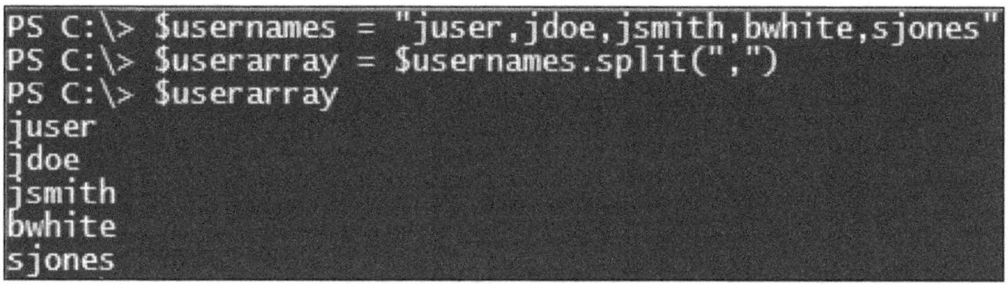

PS C:\> $usernames = "juser,jdoe,jsmith,bwhite,sjones"
PS C:\> $userarray = $usernames.split(",")
PS C:\> $userarray
juser
jdoe
jsmith
bwhite
sjones

When you leverage the `split()` method, as shown in this example, the script uses the comma as designation that the next item needs to be a new value within the array. The output from this script allows you to interact with these usernames individually. You will frequently use the `split()` method while working with **comma separated values** (**CSV**) files or XML files. It's common for these types of files to contain multiple objects per line, which makes sense to leverage the `split()` method.

Counting and trimming strings

PowerShell has two methods to count objects within variables and arrays. The first is done by using the `Count` method. The `Count` method is used to count the number of objects that are contained within an array. This is useful when you are attempting to determine the quantity of items you'll be processing within your script.

To count items in an array, execute the following command:

```
$services = get-service
$services.count
```

The output of this is shown in the following screenshot:

A good example of determining how many objects are present in an array is obtaining the number of services running on a system. The previous command displays a query of the services on a box and uses the `Count` method to obtain the quantity of services. The system in this example has `210` services.

The second method to count objects is used for instances in your scripts where you need to determine the length or the number of characters in a string. This is completed by using the `Length` method. The `Length` method will count the number of characters in a string, including spaces, and output the quantity of characters.

A common scenario where you would use the `Length` method is with Windows file and folder paths. Since the Windows operating systems are well known for having a file path limitation of `255` characters, we can leverage the `Length` method to qualify in cases where the path is over that limitation.

To get the length of a string, execute the following command:

```
$path = "c:\windows\system32\drivers\1394bus.sys"
$path.length
```

The output of this is shown in the following screenshot:

PS C:\> $path = "c:\windows\system32\drivers\1394bus.sys"
PS C:\> $path.length
39

In this example, you are counting the number of characters in a file and folder path to ensure that you do not exceed the maximum number of characters. This command counted the length of `$path` to be `39` characters. Through this command, you've determined that it is not over the limitations of the Windows operating system.

The Trim method

As you script, you'll run into situations where the output from a command or the input from a file may not be in a format that can be easily parsed. For example, if you import values from a CSV file and those values have extra spaces, it can cause your script to fail. PowerShell provides the ability to trim strings of spaces and other characters with the `Trim()` method. The `Trim()` method comes in three different variations, which are `Trim()`, `TrimStart()`, and `TrimEnd()`.

To trim the spaces out of a string, use the following command:

```
$csvValue = "    servername.mydomain.com    "
$csvValue.trim()
```

The output of this is shown in the following screenshot:

PS C:\> $csvValue = "   servername.mydomain.com   "
PS C:\> $csvValue.trim()
servername.mydomain.com

By default, when you use the `Trim()` method without declaring any characters to trim, it will automatically remove the spaces that surround the text values in a string. This example displays a computer name that is surrounded by spaces. After running the `Trim()` method, you'll see that the spaces are successfully trimmed from the string.

To trim values out of a string, execute the following command:

```
$csvValue = "servername.mydomain.com"
$csvValue = $csvValue.trim(".mydomain.com")
$csvValue
```

The output of this is shown in the following screenshot:

PS C:\> $csvValue = "servername.mydomain.com"
PS C:\> $csvValue = $csvValue.trim(".mydomain.com")
PS C:\> $csvValue
servername

If you want to trim a specific value from a string, you can declare it within the `Trim()` method. By executing the preceding script, you'll see that declaring a text value of `.mydomain.com` within the `Trim()` method will remove those characters from the entire string.

The `TrimStart()` method provides the same functionality of the `Trim()` method; however, it only removes characters from the beginning of the string. Likewise, the `TrimEnd()` method will only remove characters from the ending of the string. These are helpful in situations where you need to parse the data into values that can be read easily.

To trim the beginning and end of a string, execute the following command:

```
$csvValue = "FQDN: servername.mydomain.com"
$csvValue = $csvValue.trimStart("FQDN: ")
$csvValue = $csvValue.trimEnd(".mydomain.com")
$csvValue
```

The output of this is shown in the following screenshot:

PS C:\> $csvValue = "FQDN: servername.mydomain.com"
PS C:\> $csvValue = $csvValue.trimStart("FQDN: ")
PS C:\> $csvValue = $csvValue.trimEnd(".mydomain.com")
PS C:\> $csvValue
servername

The preceding example displays the use of both `TrimStart()` and `TrimEnd()` methods. In this example, you trim the `"FQDN: "` characters from the start of the string and `.mydomain.com` from the end of the string. The final output of this is `servername`.

When you use the `Trim()` method, you'll want to remember that it will remove all instances of the words found at the beginning and ending of the string. If you used `computername` instead of `servername`, you would have noticed that the output from the method would have `putername`. The `Trim()` method would have matched the words `com` and removed it from the string. It is best to use the `Trim()` method to remove spaces and unneeded characters in strings. Use the `Replace()` method to remove series of strings such as `.mydomain.com`.

This would look like this:

```
$csvValue = "computername.mydomain.com"
$csvValue.Trim("com")
```

The output of this is shown in the following screenshot:

The preceding example displays how the `Trim()` method will remove strings from the front and the end of a string. You first need to start by declaring the `$csvValue` variable as equal to `computername.mydomain.com`. You then need to leverage the `Trim()` method on the variable searching for the word `com`. You'll see that the method trims both the beginning `com` and end `com` on the string itself. The end result is `putername.mydomain`.

The Substring method

The `Substring()` method is another string manipulator within the PowerShell toolset. It is based on the requirement that you may want to remove characters present at a fixed position within a string. The following table displays the string positions for the string `TESTING123`. Like an array, the string position starts counting at `0`, as shown here:

String position	0	1	2	3	4	5	6	7	8	9
String value	T	E	S	T	I	N	G	1	2	3

To obtain a substring from a string, execute the following command:

```
$string = "TESTING123"
$string = $string.substring("7")
$string
```

The output of this is shown in the following screenshot:

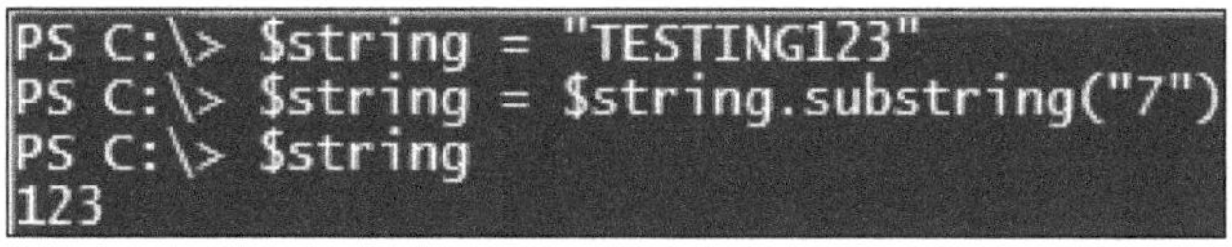

PS C:\> $string = "TESTING123"
PS C:\> $string = $string.substring("7")
PS C:\> $string
123

The `Substring()` method is designed to extract data present at specific locations in a string. If you wanted to extract the numbers `123` from the preceding table, you can use the `Substring()` method referencing the start position of `7`. All of the remaining characters after position `7` will be displayed and the output of the method is `123`.

To obtain a substring range from a string, execute the following command:

```
$string = "TESTING123"
$string = $string.substring("0","4")
$string
```

The output of this is shown in the following screenshot:

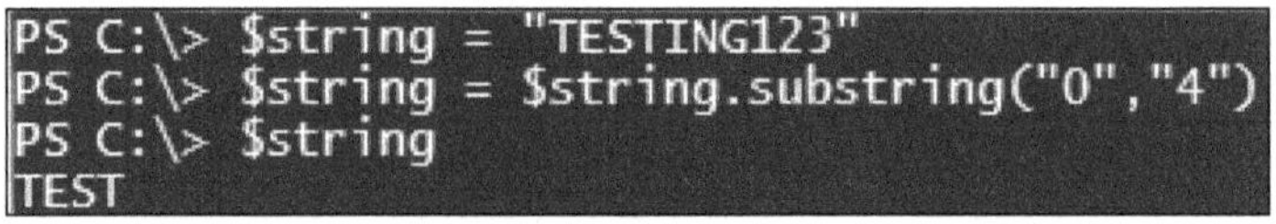
PS C:\> $string = "TESTING123"
PS C:\> $string = $string.substring("0","4")
PS C:\> $string
TEST

The `Substring()` method allows you to enter a second value within the method. While the first value designates the start position, the second value designates how many characters after the start position you want to include. In the previous script example, the script starts at position `0` and counts `4` spaces after the position of `0`. The result of this command is `TEST`.

The string true and false methods

PowerShell has built-in string searching capabilities that provide you with the ability to quickly determine whether a string contains a specific value. The three methods that can perform the searching in a string are `Contains()`, `Startswith()`, and `Endswith()`. All of these methods are based on the same principle, that is, finding a specific value and reporting `True` or `False`.

To see whether a string contains a value, do this:

```
$ping = ping ThisDoesNotExistTesting.com -r 1
$ping
$deadlink = $ping.contains("Ping request could not find host")
$deadlink
```

The output of this is shown in the following screenshot:

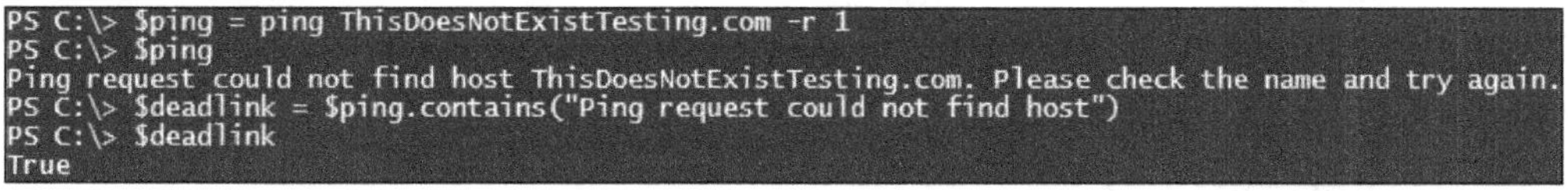
PS C:\> $ping = ping ThisDoesNotExistTesting.com -r 1
PS C:\> $ping
Ping request could not find host ThisDoesNotExistTesting.com. Please check the name and try again.
PS C:\> $deadlink = $ping.contains("Ping request could not find host")
PS C:\> $deadlink
True

This example leverages the ping command to determine whether a specific website or host is alive. In our example, you capture the ping command in the `$ping` variable. You then search that variable for text that matches `Ping request could not find host`. As the output from the ping command returns the value you are looking for, the `Contains()` method will return `True` and the `$deadlink` variable is set to `True`.

To see whether a string starts with a value, execute the following command:

```
$ping = ping ThisDoesNotExistTesting.com -r 1
$ping
$deadlink = $ping.StartsWith("Ping request could not find host")
$deadlink
```

The output of this is shown in the following screenshot:

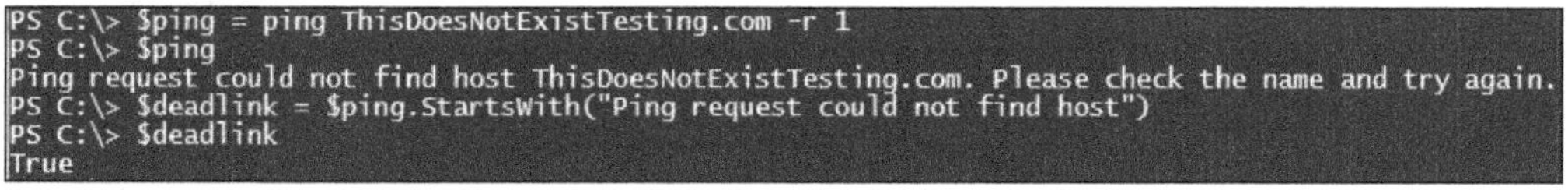
PS C:\> $ping = ping ThisDoesNotExistTesting.com -r 1
PS C:\> $ping
Ping request could not find host ThisDoesNotExistTesting.com. Please check the name and try again.
PS C:\> $deadlink = $ping.StartsWith("Ping request could not find host")
PS C:\> $deadlink
True

When you run the same script with the `Startswith()` method, it will return the same result of `True`. That is because the value that you are searching for starts with `Ping request could not find host`.

To see whether a string ends with a specific value, execute the following command:

```
$ping = ping ThisDoesNotExistTesting.com -r 1
$ping
$deadlink = $ping.EndsWith("Please check the name and try again.")
$deadlink
```

The output of this is shown in the following screenshot:

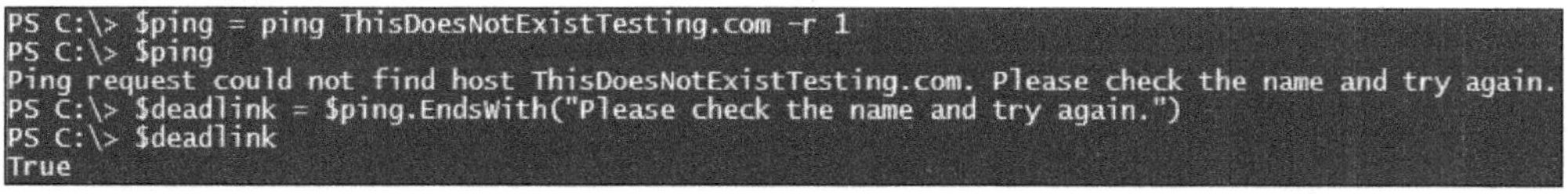
PS C:\> $ping = ping ThisDoesNotExistTesting.com -r 1
PS C:\> $ping
Ping request could not find host ThisDoesNotExistTesting.com. Please check the name and try again.
PS C:\> $deadlink = $ping.EndsWith("Please check the name and try again.")
PS C:\> $deadlink
True

When you run a similar script with the `Endswith()` method, it will return the result of `True`. That is because the value that you are searching for ends with `Please check the name and try again.`

Number manipulation and parsing

PowerShell is a powerful mathematics calculator. In fact, PowerShell has an entire Windows class dedicated to mathematics calculations that can be called by using the `[System.Math]` .NET class. When you are working with the `[System.Math]` classes, it is common to call *static fields* within a class. Static fields are static properties, methods, and objects that can be called to display data or do actions. To call a static field, you call the `[Math]` (shortened version of `[System.Math]`) class, followed by two colons `::` and the static field name.

To use the math operation to calculate pi, execute the following command:

```
[math]::pi
```

The output of this is shown in the following screenshot:

This simple command will provide *PI* if you ever need it for a calculation by using the `pi` method of the math class. The result of this command returns `3.14159265358979`.

To use the math operation to calculate Euler's number, execute the following command:

```
[math]::e
```

The output of this is shown in the following screenshot:

Likewise, if you ever need to reference Euler's Number (`e`), you can achieve this by leveraging the e method of the math class. The result of this command returns `2.71828182845905`.

To calculate the square root of a number, execute the following command:

```
[math]::sqrt("996004")
```

The output of this is shown in the following screenshot:

If you need to calculate the square root of a large number, you can use the `sqrt` method of the math class. The result of this command returns `998`.

To round a number, execute the following command:

```
$number = "214.123857123495731234948327312341657"
[math]::Round($number,"5")
```

The output of this is shown in the following screenshot:

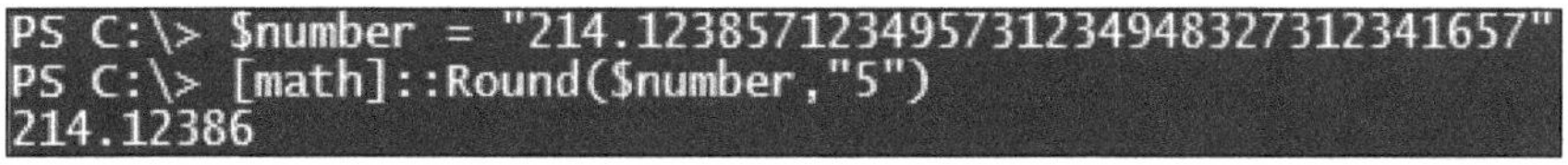

PS C:\> $number = "214.123857123495731234948327312341657"
PS C:\> [math]::Round($number,"5")
214.12386

Rounding is very common for integers in your scripts. When you want to use the `Round()` method, you'll have to specify a number and the number of digits you want to round it to. In this command, you take the number of `214.123857123495731234948327312341657` and round it to the fifth digit. The result of this command returns `214.12386`.

Formatting numbers

While PowerShell can perform mathematics very well, it does not have any native commands for the formatting of numbers. In order to format numbers, you'll need to leverage PowerShell's ability to use the .NET Framework's formatting methods. The construct for the .NET Framework format methods is called by specifying `"{StartingCharacter:FormatTypePrecision}" -f  $variable`. The start character is the position where you want to start formatting the number. The most common format types are currency (`C`), decimal (`D`), numeric (`N`), percentage (`P`), and hexadecimal (`X`). The precision field is the number of decimal places you want the number to be accurate to.

To format your number in a numeric formatting, execute the following command:

```
$number =12375134.132412
"{0:N4}" -f $number
```

The output of this is shown in the following screenshot:

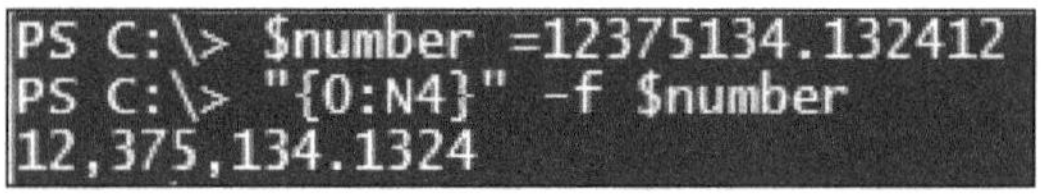
PS C:\> $number =12375134.132412
PS C:\> "{0:N4}" -f $number
12,375,134.1324

In this example, you are taking the `12375134.132412` number and formatting it in numeric format starting at the first character. This command also rounds the number to the fourth digit.

To format a number to make it hexadecimal, execute the following command:

```
$number =12375134
$number = "{0:X0}" -f $number
$number
```

The output of this is shown in the following screenshot:

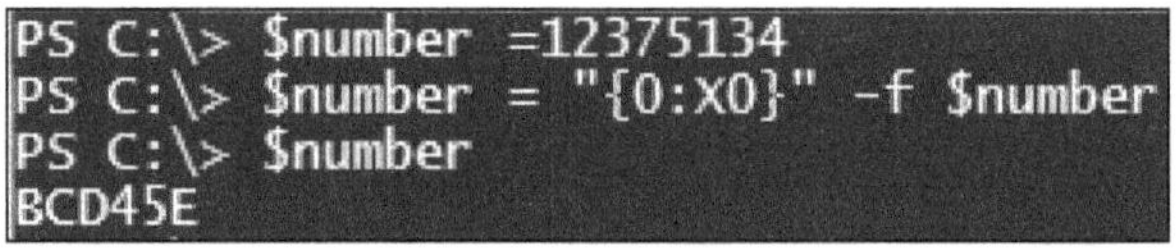
PS C:\> $number =12375134
PS C:\> $number = "{0:X0}" -f $number
PS C:\> $number
BCD45E

If you want to convert an integer to hexadecimal, you can format the integer to hexadecimal by specifying `"{0:X0}" -f $number`. The output of this command is `BCD45E`. It is important to remember that hexadecimal only supports formatting from whole numbers. If you do not use whole numbers, the script will fail due to it being in an invalid format.

Formatting bytes

PowerShell has the ability to directly convert numbers to kilobytes (`KB`), megabytes (`MB`), gigabits (`GB`), and terabytes (`TB`) through predefined aliases for conversions. This is helpful when you are pulling data values, which by default, are formatted in bytes. Some of these may include disk space and memory on a system. The use of the alias is number in bytes divided by one unit of measure.

To format bytes to KB, MB, GB, and TB, use the following operations:

```
# 16 GB of Memory in Bytes
$ComputerMemory = 16849174528
$ComputerMemory / 1TB
$ComputerMemory / 1GB
```

```
$ComputerMemory / 1MB
$ComputerMemory / 1KB
```

The output of this is shown in the following screenshot:

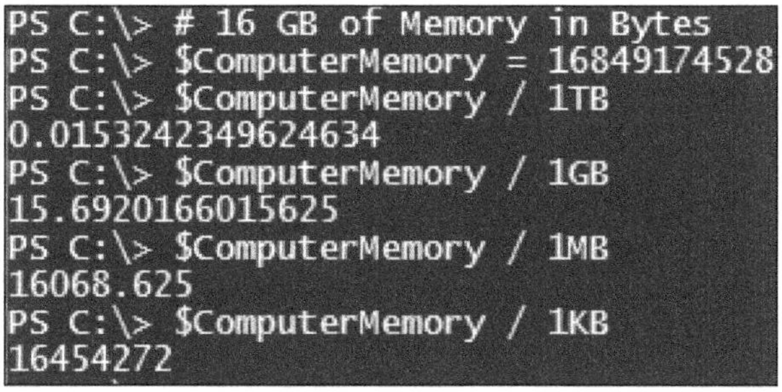
PS C:\> # 16 GB of Memory in Bytes
PS C:\> $ComputerMemory = 16849174528
PS C:\> $ComputerMemory / 1TB
0.0153242349624634
PS C:\> $ComputerMemory / 1GB
15.6920166015625
PS C:\> $ComputerMemory / 1MB
16068.625
PS C:\> $ComputerMemory / 1KB
16454272

When you execute the preceding script, PowerShell will take the memory size of a computer in bytes and convert it to terabytes, gigabytes, megabytes, and kilobytes. As you can see, PowerShell provides a quick ability to determine data calculations using the predefined aliases.

Date and time manipulation

When you are scripting, there are times where you may need to get the date and time of a system. PowerShell offers the `get-date` cmdlet, which provides the date and time in many different formats of your choice.

To obtain the date object, execute the following command:

```
$time = get-date
$time
```

The output of this is shown in the following screenshot:

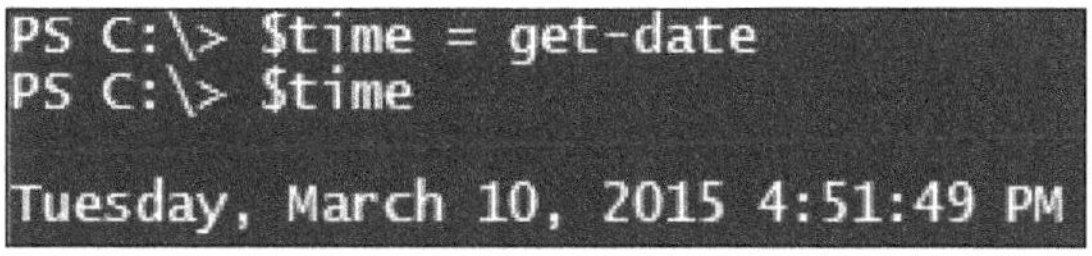
PS C:\> $time = get-date
PS C:\> $time
Tuesday, March 10, 2015 4:51:49 PM

The standard `get-date` cmdlet, without any triggers, will generate the long date and time format. When you store the `date` object in a variable, it is important to remember that the data captured from the cmdlet is a snapshot in time. You'll have to call the `get-date` cmdlet again to get new values for the updated date and time.

The following table displays all of the date time formatting codes:

Format code	Result	Example
MM	Month in numeric format	04
DD	Day in numeric format	15
YYYY	Year in numeric format	2014
HH	Hour in numeric format (24hrs)	14
hh	Hour in numeric format (12hrs)	02
mm	Minutes in numeric format	15
ss	Seconds in numeric format	12
tt	AM/PM (12hr)	PM

When you call the `get-date` command, you also have the ability to format it in multiple ways using the `-format` property. The preceding table displays different formatting options you can use to create your own date time format. These values are case- sensitive.

To format the date object to specific values, execute the following command:

```
$date = get-date -format "MM/dd/yyyy HH:MM:ss tt"
$date
```

The output of this is shown in the following screenshot:

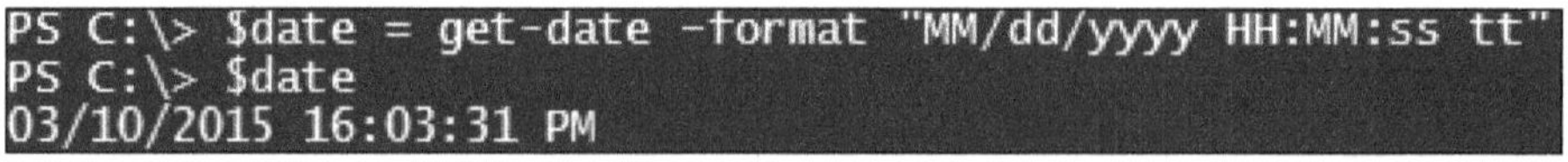

PS C:\> $date = get-date -format "MM/dd/yyyy HH:MM:ss tt"
PS C:\> $date
03/10/2015 16:03:31 PM

The previous command displays how you leverage the `get-date` cmdlet with the `-format` trigger. When you execute the command, it returns the values for the month, day, year, hours, minutes, seconds, and the AM/PM indicator. As you can see, you can leverage the date time formatting in conjunction with strings and other characters to create the time format you desire.

To format the date object and insert it between strings, you can execute the following command:

```
$date = get-date -format "MMddyyyyHHMMss"
$logfile = "Script" + $date + ".log"
$logfile
```

The output of this is shown in the following screenshot:

PS C:\> $date = get-date -format "MMddyyyyHHMMss"
PS C:\> $logfile = "Script" + $date + ".log"
PS C:\> $logfile
Script03102015160327.log

The preceding example displays how you can leverage the `get-date` cmdlet, with the `-format` trigger to generate a name for a log file. This is helpful in situations where you may have to run a command in PowerShell frequently, and you have to label the execution time. The preceding script will generate the date and time, append the word `Script` in front, and `.log` at the end of the string. The resulting filename from this is unique.

To add days using the date object, execute the following command:

```
$date = (get-date).AddDays(30).ToString("MM/dd/yyyy")
$date
```

The output of this is shown in the following screenshot:

The `get-date` cmdlet is also robust enough to be able to perform math operations with dates. The preceding example will take the current date, add 30 days to it, and set it to the `$date` variable. You can also use `AddYears()`, `AddMonths()`, `AddHours()`, `AddSeconds()`, `AddMilliseconds()`, and `AddTicks()` to increase the time. If you want to use subtraction, you can enter a negative value in the method and it will subtract that value from the methods. This would look like `AddDays(-30)` to subtract `30` days.

> For more information on date time formatting values, you can go to `http://technet.microsoft.com/en-us/library/ee692801.aspx`.

The last formatting technique important for scripting is converting system time/ticks to legible time formats. This is achieved by calling the `[DateTime]` class and leveraging the `FromFileTime` method. The preceding example displays formatting the tick number of `130752344000000000`, leveraging the `[DateTime]` class, and formatting it to `Monday, May 04, 2015 1:33:20 PM`. This is useful for system attributes that are only displayed in tick format such as `LastLogonTimestamp` or `LastBootUpTime`.

To convert file time to a different format, execute the following command:

```
$date = [datetime]::FromFileTime("130752344000000000")
$date
```

The output of this is shown in the following screenshot:

PS C:\> $date = [datetime]::FromFileTime("130752344000000000")
PS C:\> $date
Monday, May 04, 2015 12:33:20 PM

The preceding example displays how to take system ticks and convert them into a legible date time format. You first start by declaring a `$date` variable. You then call the `[datetime]` class and reference the `FromFileTime` static filed. You feed the tick time of `130752344000000000` into the static filed. This formats the tick time to the default date time format and stores the value in the `$date` variable. You then call the `$date` variable, and you see the converted value of `Monday, May 04, 2015 1:33:20 PM`.

Forcing data types

While developing scripts, you may run into instances where you may want to force a specific data type. This is helpful in cases where PowerShell automatically interprets the output from a command incorrectly. You can force data types by the use of brackets specifying a data type and a variable.

To force a string data type, execute the following command:

```
[string]$myString = "Forcing a String Container"
$myString
```

The output of this is shown in the following screenshot:

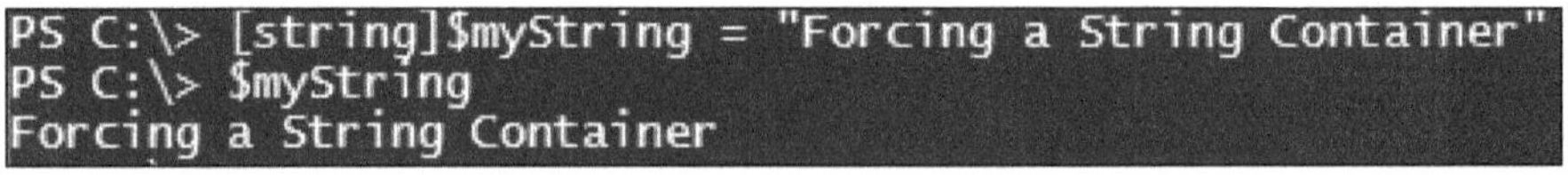

The preceding command forces the string data type to the `$myString` variable. The result is that the `$myString` variable will always remain a string. It is important to know that if the object or item that you are trying to force to a data type doesn't have a direct conversion to that data type, it will throw an error or exception. This would be the case if you try to insert a string into an integer data type.

To force a string data type and generate a data exception, execute the following command:

```
[int]$myInt = "Trying to Place a String in an Int Container"
```

The output of this is shown in the following screenshot:

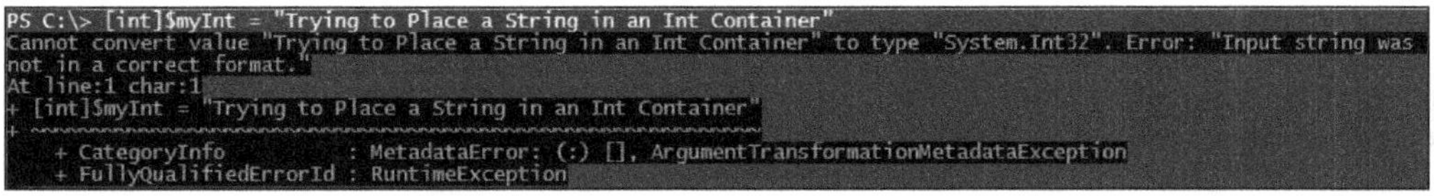

PS C:\> [int]$myInt = "Trying to Place a String in an Int Container"
Cannot convert value "Trying to Place a String in an Int Container" to type "System.Int32". Error: "Input string was
not in a correct format."
At line:1 char:1
+ [int]$myInt = "Trying to Place a String in an Int Container"
+ CategoryInfo : MetadataError: (:) [], ArgumentTransformationMetadataException
+ FullyQualifiedErrorId : RuntimeException

The preceding example displays trying to insert a string into an `[int]` data type. You first start by forcing the `$myInt` variable to be a `[int]` data type. You then try to set that equal to a string value of `"Trying to Place a String in an Int Container"`. After entering the command, you immediately receive an exception of `Cannot convert value "Trying to Place a String in an Int Container" to type System.Int32`. This example shows that you cannot mix and match data types that do not have direct conversions to each other.

There are a variety of data types that you can force within PowerShell. The following table represents the common data types for use with PowerShell and an explanation and an example of its use:

Data type	**Explanation**	**Example**	**$a value**
[string]	String of Unicode characters	`[string]$a = "Hello"`	`Hello`
[char]	A Unicode 16-bit character	`[char]$a = 0xA9`	©
[byte]	An 8-bit character	`[byte]$a = 0x0001D`	`29`
[int]	32-bit integer	`[int]$a = 12345`	`12345`
[long]	64-bit integer	`[long]$a = 1234.243`	`1234`
[bool]	Boolean True/False value	`[bool]$a = 1`	`True`
[decimal]	A 128-bit decimal	`[decimal]$a = 1234.243`	`1234.243`
[single]	A single-precision 32-bit number	`[single]$a = 1234.243`	`1234.243`
[double]	A double-precision 64-bit number	`[double]$a = 1234.243`	`1234.243`

Data type	Explanation	Example	$a value
[datetime]	A data time value	[datetime]$a = "01-APR-2014"	Tuesday, April 1, 2014 12:00:00 AM
[xml]	A XML-styled value	[xml]$a = "<test><a>Testing</a></test>" $a.test.a	Testing
[array]	An array-styled value	[array]$a = 1,2,3	1 2 3
[hashtable]	A hashtable-styled value	[hashtable]$a = @{"Old" = "New"}	Name Value ---- ----- Old New

Piping variables

The concept of piping isn't anything new to the scripting world. Piping, by definition, is directing the output of an object to another object. When you use piping in PowerShell, you are taking the output of one command and sending the data for use with another section of code. The manipulation can be either to a more legible format, or can be by selecting a specific object and digging deeper into those attributes. A pipe is designated by the '|' symbol and is used after you enter a command. The construct of a pipe looks like this: `command | ResultManipulation | SortingObjects`. If you need to access the individual items in the pipeline, you can leverage the pipeline output `$_` command. This tells the pipeline to evaluate the results from the pipeline and their attributes.

The pipeline offers a wide variety of uses; you can leverage commands such as `sort-object` to sort by a specific attribute, `format-list` to format the objects into a list, and even the `select-object` where you can select specific attributes to form the pipeline for additional processing. `Select-object` also allows you to leverage the `-first` and `-last` parameters with a number to select a record set from the beginning or ending of the pipeline. Another popular command is the `where` command, which allows you to write an expression to select items in the pipeline that meet certain criteria.

To pipe values from a cmdlet, execute the following command:

```
$services = get-service | where{$_.name -like "*Event*"} | Sort-object
name
$services
```

The output of this is shown in the following screenshot:

```
PS C:\> $services = get-service | where{$_.name -like "*Event*"} | Sort-object name
PS C:\> $services

Status   Name               DisplayName
------   ----               -----------
Running  eventlog           Windows Event Log
Running  EventSystem        COM+ Event System
```

This example displays the use of piping the `get-services` cmdlet. It starts by getting all the services on a system, the user then *pipes* those results to the selection criteria where the object's name is like the word `event`, which then *pipes* those results to the sorting of objects in alphabetical order by their name property. The output is only the services with the names that contain `Event` in alphabetical order.

To obtain all files that are larger than a specific size, execute the following command:

```
$largeFiles = get-childitem "c:\windows\system32\" | where{$_.length -gt
20MB}
$count = $largeFiles.count
Write-host "There are $count Files over 20MB"
write-host "Files Over 20MB in c:\Windows\System32\ :"
$largefiles | select-object name,length,lastwritetime | format-list
```

The output of this is shown in the following screenshot:

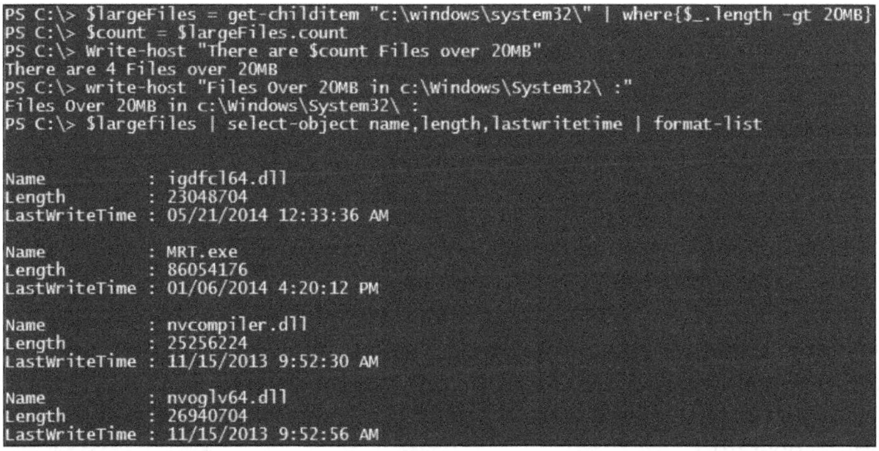

```
PS C:\> $largeFiles = get-childitem "c:\windows\system32\" | where{$_.length -gt 20MB}
PS C:\> $count = $largeFiles.count
PS C:\> Write-host "There are $count Files over 20MB"
There are 4 Files over 20MB
PS C:\> write-host "Files Over 20MB in c:\Windows\System32\ :"
Files Over 20MB in c:\Windows\System32\ :
PS C:\> $largefiles | select-object name,length,lastwritetime | format-list


Name          : igdfcl64.dll
Length        : 23048704
LastWriteTime : 05/21/2014 12:33:36 AM

Name          : MRT.exe
Length        : 86054176
LastWriteTime : 01/06/2014 4:20:12 PM

Name          : nvcompiler.dll
Length        : 25256224
LastWriteTime : 11/15/2013 9:52:30 AM

Name          : nvoglv64.dll
Length        : 26940704
LastWriteTime : 11/15/2013 9:52:56 AM
```

When you leverage the pipe command, you have the ability to find specific data pertaining to an object. In this example, you search all of the files in `c:\windows\system32` to determine whether there are any files that have a size greater than `20 MB`. You were able to pipe the `get-childitem` cmdlet to the `where` operator with the selection criteria `$_.length` is greater than `20MB`. These results were placed in the `$largeFiles` variable. From there, you use the `count()` method to count the number of files that are larger than `20MB`. You then print to screen the text `There are $count files over 20MB`. You also print to the screen `Files over 20MB in c:\Windows\System32\ :` to provide text for the following piped command. You then need to take the results in the `$largeFiles` variable and pipe the results to the `select-object` command to select the `name`, `length`, and `lastwritetime`. Finally, you pipe those results to the `format-list` command, which provides a formatted list of results.

Summary

This chapter explores the many methods you can use to manipulate and parse data with PowerShell. You learned techniques that will help you better work with data and provide a richer experience for individuals using your scripts.

The string manipulation section taught you many different methods to work with strings. This included changing the case, splitting and replacing strings, counting and trimming strings, searching strings, and viewing substrings. The number manipulation section taught you how to use mathematical operations within PowerShell. This section displayed different ways to format numbers, round numbers, and calculating complex mathematical operations. The date time section of this chapter provided you with tools to use when you need to gather date and time information from a system. You learned how to format the `get-date` cmdlet, manipulate the results, and add or subtract from date values.

This chapter also explored the forcing of data types while working with variables. This section provided examples of different data types that are available to use, and provided an example on how to force a specific data type. You then wrapped up with an explanation on piping and how to construct proper piping clauses. It explored how to leverage piping to sort data after a result is returned and provided examples of piping with and without a data sort.

Data parsing and manipulation is essential to successful scripting with PowerShell. Without using these manipulation techniques in this chapter, you may be overly complicating your scripts. While it may take time to fully learn these techniques, it's essential to become a good PowerShell scripter. In the next chapter, you'll learn how the manipulated data you generate can be correlated to see whether it matches certain criteria. You'll learn that the comparisons are done with the use of comparison operators.

3

Comparison Operators

PowerShell comparison operators are used to validate data present within your scripts. These operators enable you to compare data and execute code based on the data. This makes PowerShell an extremely effective tool to use for processing complicated data with the available comparison operators.

In this chapter, you will learn the following concepts:

- Comparison operator basics
- Equal and not equal comparison operators
- Greater than and less than comparison operators
- Contains, like, and match comparison operators
- -AND / -OR comparison operators
- Best practices for comparison operators

Comparison operator basics

When you are using comparison operators, you are creating expressions that evaluate to either `True` or `False`. In programming, this is known as Boolean. In the simplest form, you are asking PowerShell to evaluate similarities or dissimilarities between two items. Based on the findings from that expression, it will return `True` or `False`. When the whole expression returns `False`, PowerShell doesn't continue to process items in the statement. When the whole expression returns `True`, PowerShell will proceed forward into the statement and execute the code within the statement.

Of the many built-in variables that PowerShell has, there are two built-in Boolean variables. These two variables are `$True` and `$False`. When you call `$True`, it implies that the value is Boolean and is set to `True`. When you call `$False`, it implies that the value is Boolean and is set to `False`.

A script that shows how to use basic comparison operators would look like this:

```
$TrueVariable = $True
$FalseVariable = $False
if ($TrueVariable) { Write-Host "Statement is True." }
if ($FalseVariable) { Write-Host "Statement is False." }
```

The output of this command is shown in the following screenshot:

PS C:\> $TrueVariable = $True
PS C:\> $FalseVariable = $False
PS C:\> if ($TrueVariable) { Write-Host "Statement is True." }
Statement is True.
PS C:\> if ($FalseVariable) { Write-Host "Statement is False." }
PS C:\>

This example displays how to do a basic Boolean comparison. You first start by declaring `$TrueVariable` and setting it equal to `True`. You then declare `$FalseVariable` and set it to `False`. You then create an `if` statement to evaluate the expression `$TrueVariable` to see whether it evaluates to `True`. Since the variable is set to `True`, it will evaluate to `True` and continue to process the remaining items in the statement. PowerShell will print to the screen the message `Statement is True`. You then create another `if` statement to evaluate the expression `$FalseVariable` to see whether it evaluates to `True`. As the variable is set to `False`, the expression will evaluate to `False` and stop processing the statement.

Equal and not equal comparison

The most basic and most used comparison operator is *equal to* (`-eq`). This operator is flexible in nature as it can be used for strings, integers, and objects. The `-eq` operator is used by calling `value1` *is equal to* `value2`. When the `-eq` operator evaluates the statement, it will return a Boolean value of either `True` or `False`. If the expression evaluates to be `True`, PowerShell will continue to proceed to execute the code.

A script that shows how to use equal comparison operators would look like this:

```
$value1 = "PowerShell"
$value2 = "PowerShell"
if ($value1 -eq $value2) { Write-Host "It's Equal!" }
```

The output of this is shown in the following screenshot:

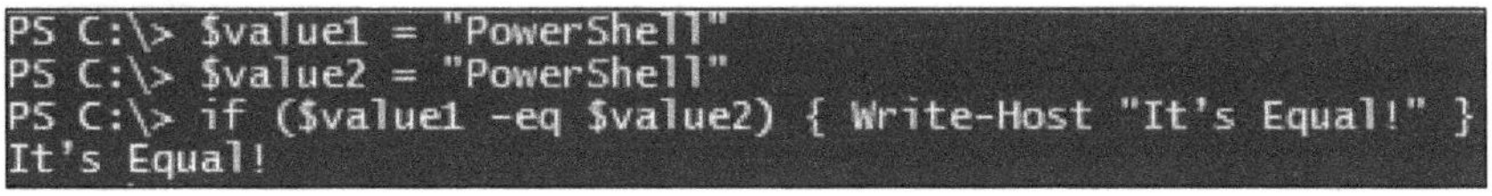

PS C:\> $value1 = "PowerShell"
PS C:\> $value2 = "PowerShell"
PS C:\> if ($value1 -eq $value2) { Write-Host "It's Equal!" }
It's Equal!

From the preceding example, you will see that the equal comparison operator determines that `$value1` is equal to `$value2` and it writes to the screen `It's Equal!`. In the instance that you want to determine whether two values are not equal, you can use the `-ne` operator. This does the inverse of the `-eq` operator.

A script that shows how to use not equal comparison operators would look like this:

```
$value1 = "PowerShell"
$value2 = "POSH"
if ($value1 -ne $value2) { Write-Host "Values Are Not Equal" }
```

The output of this command is shown in the following screenshot:

PS C:\> $value1 = "PowerShell"
PS C:\> $value2 = "POSH"
PS C:\> if ($value1 -ne $value2) { Write-Host "Values Are Not Equal" }
Values Are Not Equal

When you run the preceding script, PowerShell will determine that `$value1` and `$value2` are not equal. The script will write to the screen the message `Values Are Not Equal`. While scripting, it is important to minimize the use of the *not equal* -`ne` operator. When you start layering *is equal to* and *not equal to* in your scripts, the logical complexity of the script significantly increases. This is why it is recommended that beginners should typically only use the `-ne` operator in instances where a value cannot equal a specific value and every other value is acceptable.

A script that shows how to use "not equal" comparison operators would look like this:

```
$value = "This is a value."
$length = $value.length
If ($length -ne 0) { Write-Host "The variable has data in it. Do this action" }
```

The output of this command is shown in the following screenshot:

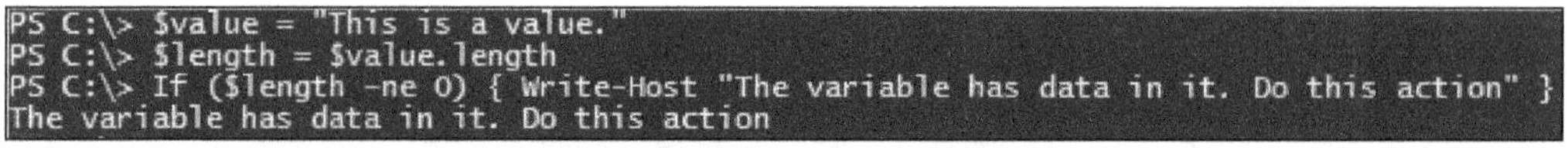
PS C:\> $value = "This is a value."
PS C:\> $length = $value.length
PS C:\> If ($length -ne 0) { Write-Host "The variable has data in it. Do this action" }
The variable has data in it. Do this action

The preceding example displays the proper use of the `-ne` operator for best practices. This script counts the characters in `$value`, and if the length of the variable is not equal to `0`, the script will write to the console `The variable has data in it. Do this action`. In your scripting, you will want to follow suit where you use `-ne` for verification that the data is *not valid* before continuing with your script.

Greater than and less than comparison

PowerShell has two operators to compare two values to determine whether they are greater than (`-gt`) or less than (`-lt`) each other. This is not just limited to numbers, but also has the ability to compare dates and times as well. These are helpful in instances where you need to compare file sizes or modification dates on files.

A script that shows how to use the "less than" comparison operator would look like this:

```
$number1 = 10
$number2 = 20
If ($number1 -lt $number2) { Write-Host "Value $number1 is less than
$number2" }
```

The output of this command is shown in the following screenshot:

PS C:\> $number1 = 10
PS C:\> $number2 = 20
PS C:\> If ($number1 -lt $number2) { Write-Host "Value $number1 is less than $number2" }
Value 10 is less than 20

In the preceding example, you set the `$number1` variable to `10` and the `$number2` variable to `20`. You then use the "less than" `(-lt)` operator to determine whether the `$number1` variable is less than `$number2`. Since this a true statement, the console outputs the message `Value $number1 is less than $number2`.

A script that shows how to use the "greater than" comparison operator would look like this:

```
$olddate = Get-Date
Start-Sleep -seconds 2
$newdate= Get-Date
```

```
If ($newdate -gt $olddate) { Write-Host "Value $newdate is greater than
$olddate" }
```

The output of this command is shown in the following screenshot:

PS C:\> $olddate = Get-Date
PS C:\> Start-Sleep -seconds 2
PS C:\> $newdate= Get-Date
PS C:\> If ($newdate -gt $olddate) { Write-Host "Value $newdate is greater than $olddate" }
Value 02/17/2015 12:51:46 is greater than 02/17/2015 12:51:44

In this script, you start by setting the `$olddate` variable to the current date and time. The `start-sleep` cmdlet is then used to pause the script for `2` seconds. When the script continues, you set `$newdate` and time variable to `2` seconds later. By using the greater than (`-gt`) operator, you determine that the values are different and that the `$newdate` value is greater than the `$olddate` value.

> In addition to "greater than" and "less than" operators, you also have the option to compare "greater" or "equal" (`-ge`) and "less" or "equal" (`-le`). These comparison operators can be handy when creating counters or loops that require you to increment a number until it equals or is greater than a specific value.

Contains, like, and match operators

The `-contains`, `-like`, and `-match` operators are very similar in function. While they all compare data, they all have their own purpose in your scripts. Each of these operators are case-insensitive. This means that when you are searching for items using these operators, they will match all instances of the value in the expression. In instances where you need the search to be case-specific, you can append `c` in front of the operator to force case sensitivity. These would look like `-ccontains`, `-clike`, and `-cmatch`. To force case insensitivity, you can also append `i` in front of the operator. These would look like `-icontains`, `-ilike`, and `-imatch`.

Each of these operators also has an inverse operator that is formed by appending the word "not" in front of the operator. Examples of these operators include `-notcontains`, `-notlike`, and `-notmatch`. You may also append case sensitivity and case insensitivity to these operators.

The `-contains` operator looks for an exact match to a value in an expression. It will then return a `True` and `False` result. The `-contains` operator is flexible as it can evaluate the individual values in an array with a single expression. This allows you to create efficiency in your code by evaluating more than one item per line of code.

A script that shows how to use the `-Contains` comparison operator would look like this:

```
$myarray = "this", "is", "my", "array"
If ($myarray -contains "this") { Write-Host "The array contains the word: this" }
If ($myarray -notcontains "that") { Write-Host "The array does not contain the word: that" }
```

The output of this command is shown in the following screenshot:

PS C:\> $myarray = "this", "is", "my", "array"
PS C:\> If ($myarray -contains "this") { Write-Host "The array contains the word: this" }
The array contains the word: this
PS C:\> If ($myarray -notcontains "that") { Write-Host "The array does not contain the word: that" }
The array does not contain the word: that

In the preceding example, you create an array with four values in it. You then use the `-contains` operator to determine whether the array has the `this` value. As the array does have this value, it then evaluates the statement to be `True`, and proceeds to write to the console the message `The array contains the word: this`. The second part of this evaluation is to check to see whether `$myarray` does not contain the word `that` by using the `-notcontains` operator. Since `$myarray` does not have the word `that`, it proceeds to write to the console `The array does not contain the word: that`.

The `-like` comparison operator is different than the `-contains` operator. The `-like` operator requires that both sides of the expression should be evaluated to match the full string. You can quickly determine whether there are values that are close to a value you are looking for, which will then return `True` or `False`. This is why the `-like` comparison operator typically uses wildcard characters designated by an asterisk (`*`) or question mark (`?`). It provides the flexibility to quickly search a variety of values using a single expression. The asterisk wildcard designates that the expression can match any values before or after the stated word, depending on where the asterisk is placed. The question mark allows you to match any values present between two strings. For example, you can use `-like "myfile?.txt"`, which will match any value that starts with `myfile` and ends with the extension `.txt`. Any values between those characters will be returned as `True`.

A script that shows how to use the `-like` comparison operator would look like this:

```
$myexample = "This is a PowerShell example."
If ($myexample -like "*shell*") { Write-Host "The variable has a word that is like shell" }
If ($myexample -notlike "*that*") { Write-Host "The variable doesn't have a word that is like that" }
```

The output of this command is shown in the following screenshot:

PS C:\> $myexample = "This is a PowerShell example."
PS C:\> If ($myexample -like "*shell*") { Write-Host "The variable has a word that is like shell" }
The variable has a word that is like shell
PS C:\> If ($myexample -notlike "*that*") { Write-Host "The variable doesn't have a word that is like that" }
The variable doesn't have a word that is like that

The preceding script displays the string `$myexample`, for which you search for the value of `shell`. As the value is part of another word, you need to append the wildcard character on both sides of the word "shell". When you search for the word `*shell*`, including the wildcard characters, the result returns true. The console then outputs the message `The variable has a word that is like shell`. When you execute the second comparison using the `-notlike` operator, you are able to search the string for words that are not like `that`. Since you use the wildcards on each side of the word, it does a secondary comparison to make sure that there aren't partial values in the variable that reflect `that`. Since there are no values in the variable that evaluate to be like `that`, it outputs to the screen the message `The variable doesn't have a word that is like shell.`

> You have to use an asterisk (`*`) on both sides of the search evaluation criteria as PowerShell interprets every character in the sentence as a value. While inherently you may break apart each word in the variable as separate values, PowerShell sees it as one contiguous group of characters. To find a substring of a variable and have it evaluate to "True" using the `-like` operator, you will need to use an asterisk (`*`) on both sides.

The match comparison operator uses regular expressions to match information between two variables. The `-match` operator is unique in the fact that it autopopulates a variable named `$matches` with the word that matches your search. This is helpful in the instance where you need to only retrieve objects that match a certain criteria. With "match", you can also leverage the use of regular expressions to match criteria to a variable.

A script that shows how to use the `-match` and `-notmatch` comparison operators would look like this:

```
$myexample = "The network went down."
If ($myexample -match "[o]") { Write-Host "The variable matched the letter o. (Contains two o's)" }
$matches
If ($myexample -notmatch "[U]") { Write-Host "The variable does not match U. (Doesn't have a U)" }
```

The output of this command is shown in the following screenshot:

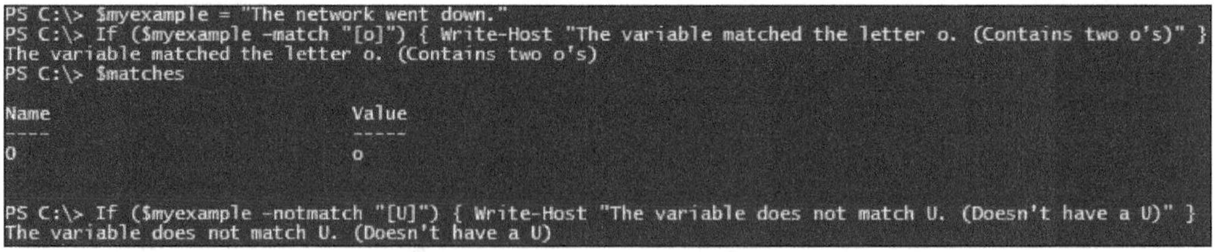
PS C:\> $myexample = "The network went down."
PS C:\> If ($myexample -match "[o]") { Write-Host "The variable matched the letter o. (Contains two o's)" }
The variable matched the letter o. (Contains two o's)
PS C:\> $matches
Name
Value

0
o
PS C:\> If ($myexample -notmatch "[U]") { Write-Host "The variable does not match U. (Doesn't have a U)" }
The variable does not match U. (Doesn't have a U)

The preceding example creates a new variable named `$myexample` with the string value of `The network went down.`. You then compare the `$myexample` variable to the regular expression `[o]` or one that contains an instance of `o` to see that it's a match. Since `o` exists at least once contained in `$myexample`, the expression returns `True` and the console outputs the message `The variable matched the letter o. (Contains two o's)`. After you make that comparison, you then display the contents of the `$matches` variable. You will see that the `$match` variable autopopulates with the value of an index of `0` and name of `o`. The last part of the script is an evaluation to see whether `$myexample` does not match the regular expression of `[U]` or does not contain an instance of `U`. Since the variable does not contain an instance of the letter `U`, it evaluates to be `True` and writes to the console the message `The variable does not match U. (Doesn't have a U)`.

And / OR comparison operators

The `-and` and `-or` comparison operators are used to evaluate multiple expressions present within a single line of code. These are used to see whether two or more expressions evaluate to be `True`. The `-and` comparison operator mandates that both evaluations must evaluate to be `True` to proceed in the statement. This means that `expression1` and `expression2` must be `True` to continue. The `-or` comparison operator only requires one of the two expressions to be `True`. This means that `expression1` or `expression2` can be `True` to continue. As you are learning PowerShell, you will want to use caution while using the `-and` and `-or` comparison operators as they can quickly complicate the logic of your scripts.

A script that shows how to use `-and` and `-or` comparison operators would look like this:

```
$myvar = $True
$myothervar = $False
If ($myvar -eq $True -AND $myothervar -eq $False) { Write-Host "Both
statements evaluate to be True" }
```

```
If ($myvar -eq $True -OR $myothervar -eq $True) { Write-Host "At least
one statement evaluates to be True" }
```

The output of this is shown in the following screenshot:

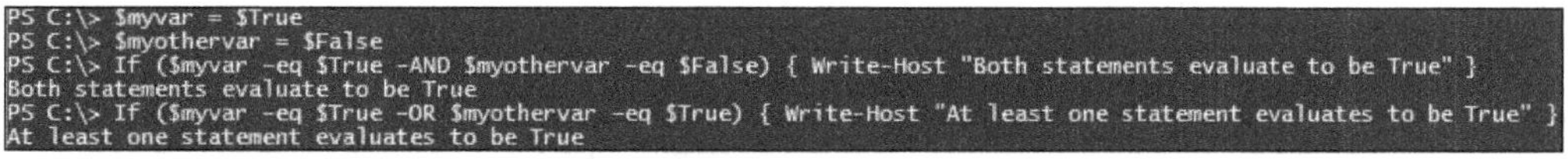
PS C:\> $myvar = $True
PS C:\> $myothervar = $False
PS C:\> If ($myvar -eq $True -AND $myothervar -eq $False) { Write-Host "Both statements evaluate to be True" }
Both statements evaluate to be True
PS C:\> If ($myvar -eq $True -OR $myothervar -eq $True) { Write-Host "At least one statement evaluates to be True" }
At least one statement evaluates to be True

The preceding example briefly displays how to use the `-and` operator and the `-or` operator. In this example, you create two different variables. You then check to see whether `$myvar` equals `True`, which evaluates to be `True`. You evaluate whether `$myothervar` is equal to `False`, which evaluates to be `True`. In order for the `-and` operator to be successful, both statements have to evaluate to be `True` in the evaluation criteria. Since both the statements evaluate to be `True`, the console outputs the message `Both statements evaluate to be True`. Even though the `$myothervar` variable is set to `False`, the evaluation to see whether that variable is set to `False` makes that statement `True`.

The second statement you evaluate is when either `$myvar` or `$myothervar` equals `True` by using the `-OR` operator. Like the first evaluation, the first variable evaluates to be `True`. However, the second variable evaluates to be `False`. Since the `-or` operator only requires one of the two statements to be `True`, the entire statement evaluates to be `True`. The console will output the message `At least one statement evaluates to be True`.

Best practices for comparison operators

PowerShell offers many different comparison operators for use within your scripts. It is easy to start building overly complex scripts by overusing comparison operators or by evaluating items that you may not have to use in PowerShell functioning. Refer to the following guidelines to stick to when you are developing your scripts. These will help you avoid overuse of comparison operators:

- **Assume the script is designed to proceed**: When you assume your script is designed to proceed to the next step, you can reduce the number of comparison operators you use. If you expect a value to be `True`, only make a statement to catch whether the statement is `False`. Don't check to see whether the statement is `True`, as PowerShell is designed to sequentially proceed anyway to the next step.

- **Avoid double negative statements**: When you are developing your code, avoid the use of double negative statements. Avoid checking to see whether a value *does not equal False*. What you're really trying to do is check to see whether a statement evaluates to be `True`. Double negatives can be confusing to you and other developers reading your code.
- **Stay positive (True) while you're coding**: Always attempt to avoid the use of *not* and negative evaluation statements. While there can be a place for the *not* based operators, try to create code that evaluates when statements are `True`. The *not* based operators grow significantly in complexity when used with regular expressions and can be confusing to you and other developers reading your code.

Summary

This chapter explored the many methods with which you can use PowerShell operators. You started by learning the comparison operator basics. You then learned about the *equal* and *not equal* and *greater than* and *less than* comparison operators. You learned that you can use these operators to compare numbers, strings, dates, and times. You then proceeded to explore the `-contains`, `-like`, and `-match` operators. You learned that you can add *not* to these operators to create the inverse of the operator. You also understood that you can add *c* for case sensitivity and *i* for case insensitivity to the comparison operators. You also saw how to join multiple operators using the `-and` / `-or` operators.

The chapter ends by providing the best practices for the implementation of comparison operators. By the end of this chapter, you should be proficient in using comparison operators, know what to avoid, and be well on your way to evaluating variables and arrays. In the next chapter, you will explore how you can create code that can be called multiple times and leverage comparison operators with functions, loops, switches, and methods.

4

Functions, Switches, and Loops Structures

When you are scripting in PowerShell, you will find that a lot of your coding efforts will require the code to be repeated multiple times in the same script. While repeating the same code may help you accomplish the task, there are many other options for coding more efficient scripts. This chapter explores different techniques for which you can reuse code instead of repeating the same code segments within the same script.

In this chapter, you will learn about the following concepts:

- Creation of functions
- Creation of loops
- Creation of switches
- Combining the use of functions, switches, and loops
- Best practices for functions, switches, and loops

Functions

When you need to query or execute code more than once, the general rule is that you should create a function to perform the action. Functions are blocks of reusable code, which you can execute multiple times by calling the function's name. You must place a function near the beginning or top of the script. This allows PowerShell to interpret the whole function before you use it later in the code. All other code, including invoking the functions, should follow the functions section. If you call a function that has not yet been parsed by PowerShell, it will throw an exception stating that no such cmdlet or function exists.

Function names can be any word or set of words; however, it is recommended to name the function similar to the `verb-noun` cmdlet naming syntax. To create a function, you need to use the word `Function` and declare a function name like `display-text`. You then need to enclose the repeatable commands in curly brackets after the function name.

The proper syntax of a function looks like this:

```
Function Display-Text { Write-Host "Showing Text" }
Display-Text
```

The output of this command is shown in the following screenshot:

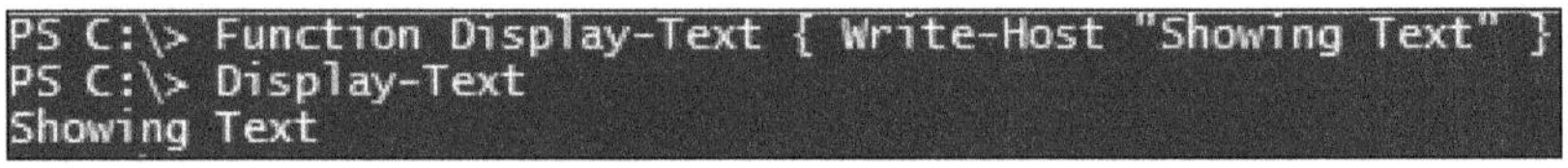

PS C:\> Function Display-Text { Write-Host "Showing Text" }
PS C:\> Display-Text
Showing Text

This example displays how to properly declare a function. You first call the `Function` command with the `Display-Text` function name. You then place `Write-Host "Show Text"` in the curly brackets after declaring the function name. You then call the function by typing `Display-Text`. After executing the script, the console will print to the screen the message `Showing Text`.

Functions also allow you to *pass in data* for processing. One of the methods to *pass in data* into a function is to declare variables after the function name in parentheses. This function will then be able to use those variables and the data in those variables within itself. If you want to pass in multiple arguments into a function, you can separate each variable with a comma.

The format to declare a function with parameters in parentheses looks like this:

```
Function Display-Text($variable1,$variable2) {
Write-Host "First Function Argument: $variable1"
Write-Host "Second Function Argument: $variable2"
}
Display-Text "Hello" "Readers"
```

The output of this is shown in the following screenshot:

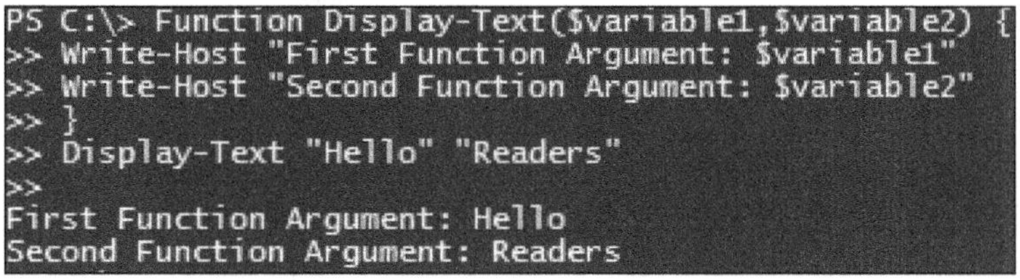
PS C:\> Function Display-Text($variable1,$variable2) {
>> Write-Host "First Function Argument: $variable1"
>> Write-Host "Second Function Argument: $variable2"
>> }
>> Display-Text "Hello" "Readers"
>>
First Function Argument: Hello
Second Function Argument: Readers

This example displays how to properly declare a function with the parameter in parentheses. You first call the `Function` command with the `Display-Text` function name. You then place the variables, `$variable1` with a comma and `$variable2` in parentheses, before the curly brackets. Inside the curly brackets, you declare `Write-Host "First Function Argument: $variable1"` and `Write-Host "Second Function Argument: $variable2"`. You then call the function by typing `Display-Text` with the arguments of `Hello` and `Readers`. After executing the script, the console will print to the screen `First Function Argument: Hello` and `Second Function Argument: Readers`.

Another method to *pass in data* to a function is through the use of a parameter block of `Param`. `Param` takes in whatever data you pass into the function and stores that data in declared variables. If you want to pass in multiple arguments into a function, you can separate each variable with a comma. When you are declaring parameters using this method, `Param` needs to be the first item declared after the open curly bracket in a function.

The format to declare a function with `param` looks like this:

```
Function Display-Text { Param($variable1, $variable2)
Write-Host "First Function Argument: $variable1"
Write-Host "Second Function Argument: $variable2"
}
Display-Text "Hello" "Readers"
```

The output of this command is shown in the following screenshot:

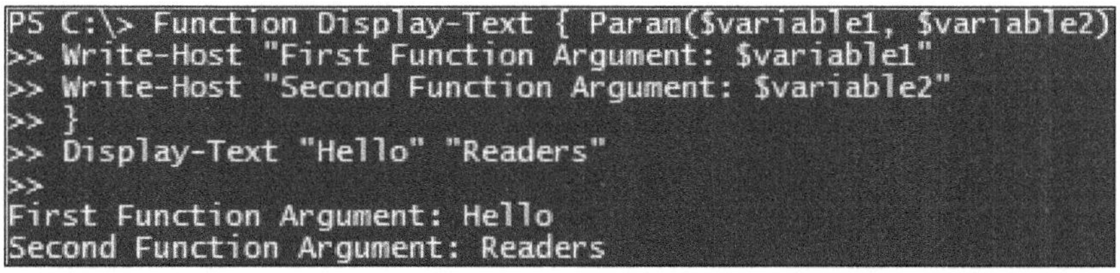
PS C:\> Function Display-Text { Param($variable1, $variable2)
>> Write-Host "First Function Argument: $variable1"
>> Write-Host "Second Function Argument: $variable2"
>> }
>> Display-Text "Hello" "Readers"
>>
First Function Argument: Hello
Second Function Argument: Readers

This example displays how to properly declare a function with parameters in a `Param` block. You first call the `Function` command with the `Display-Text` function name. You then call the `Param` block as the first command inside the curly brackets. Inside the `Param` block, you declare the variables `$variable1` with a comma and `$variable2`. After the `Param` block, you declare `Write-Host "First Function Argument: $variable1"` and `Write-Host "Second Function Argument: $variable2"`. You then call the function by typing `Display-Text` with the arguments `Hello` and `Readers`. After executing the script, the console will print to the screen `First Function Argument: Hello` and `Second Function Argument: Readers`.

The `Param` block is special as it can also accept additional decorators when declaring the variables. The `[Parameter()]` decorator allows you to include additional arguments that enable you to validate variables and even provide help information for variables in functions. When you declare the `Mandatory` argument and set it equal to `$True`, it will require that the variable is used in the function to continue. If you set the `Mandatory` argument to `$False`, it will not be required when using the function. You can also call the `Position` argument, which declares what position the variable will be declared. This means that if you set the `Position` argument to `1`, it must be the first argument passed into the function. If you don't use the `Position` argument, you will only be able to pass in the variables using parameter that references the variable name. Another popular argument is the `HelpMessage` argument, which enables you to declare a help message for the individual arguments being passed in. This message is what is displayed in the console when mandatory arguments are missing when a function is being executed. To add multiple parameter arguments in a decorator, you can separate the arguments with commas.

The format to declare a function with `Param` looks with the `[Parameter()]` decorator and parameter arguments looks like this:

```
Function Display-Text {
  #Declare the Parameter Block
Param(
#Set The First Parameter as Mandatory with a Help Message
[Parameter(Mandatory=$True,HelpMessage="Error: Please Enter A Computer
Name")]$computername,
#Set the Second Parameter as Not Mandatory
[Parameter(Mandatory=$False)]$Message
)
Write-Host "First Mandatory Function Argument: $computername"
Write-Host "Second Function Argument: $Message"
```

```
}
Display-Text -computername "MyComputerName" "MyMessage"
Display-Text
```

The output of this command is shown in the following screenshot:

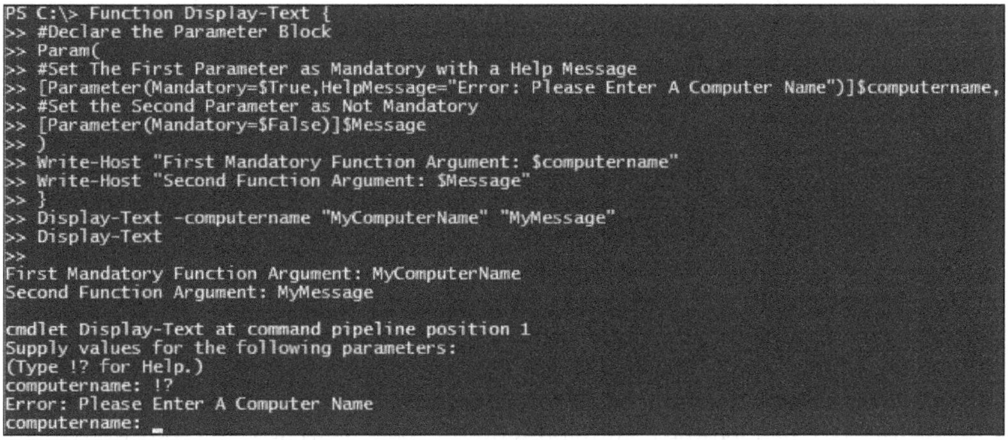
PS C:\> Function Display-Text {
>> #Declare the Parameter Block
>> Param(
>> #Set The First Parameter as Mandatory with a Help Message
>> [Parameter(Mandatory=$True,HelpMessage="Error: Please Enter A Computer Name")]$computername,
>> #Set the Second Parameter as Not Mandatory
>> [Parameter(Mandatory=$False)]$Message
>>)
>> Write-Host "First Mandatory Function Argument: $computername"
>> Write-Host "Second Function Argument: $Message"
>> }
>> Display-Text -computername "MyComputerName" "MyMessage"
>> Display-Text
>>
First Mandatory Function Argument: MyComputerName
Second Function Argument: MyMessage
cmdlet Display-Text at command pipeline position 1
Supply values for the following parameters:
(Type !? for Help.)
computername: !?
Error: Please Enter A Computer Name
computername:

This example displays how to create a function using `param` with the `[Parameter()]` decorator and parameter arguments. You first call the `Function` command with the `Display-Text` function name. You then call the `Param` block as the first command inside the curly brackets. Inside the `Param` block, you declare the several parameter arguments for the variables. The first argument you call is the `[Parameter]` decorator, and the `Mandatory=$True` attribute. You then include a comma to accept the second attribute of `HelpMessage="Error: Please Enter A Computer Name"`. You then close the parameter decorator and complete the first `Param` item by defining the `$computername` variable.

You include a comma to create a second `Param` item. This `Param` item uses the `[Parameter]` decorator and the `Mandatory=$False` attribute. You close the parameter decorator and complete the second `Param` item by defining the `$message` variable. You then close the `Param` block.

After the `Param` block, you declare `Write-Host "First Mandatory Function Argument: $computername"` and `Write-Host "Second Function Argument: $Message"`. You then call the function by typing `Display-Text` with the arguments `-computername "MyComputerName"` and `"MyMessage"`. You also call `Display-Text` without any arguments.

After executing the script, the console will first print to the screen `First Mandatory Function Argument: MyComputerName` and `Second Function Argument: MyMessage`. When the script executes the second `Display-Text`, however, it will print on the screen cmdlet `Display-Text at command pipeline position 1 Supply values for the following parameters: Type !? for help..` It will then prompt for the `computername` argument. If you type `!?` and press `Enter`, you will see the `HelpMessage` attribute displayed in the console with the message `Error: Please Enter A Computer Name`. It will then prompt for the `computername` argument again until you enter a value.

> Additional detailed information on advanced parameters for functions can be found on TechNet at `https://technet.microsoft.com/en-us/library/dd347600.aspx`.

Functions allow you to *pass back data* to the section of the script that called the function in the first place. One of the methods with which you can achieve this is with the use of the `return` command. For example, if after execution of a function you want to pass back the value of `$True`, you can state `return $True`. The section of the script that executed the command will then be able to use the value of `$True` to execute on. You may also use the `write-output` cmdlet, which acts like the return command and *passes back* the values to the script. You could also choose the piping method to *pass back data*. To use the piping method, you take the output from the function and pipe it to a cmdlet or another section of code.

The format to declare functions that return values to the script looks like this:

```
Function Create-WarningMessage {
  $MyError = "This is my Warning Message!"
  $MyError
}
Function Create-Message { Return "My Return message." }
Function Create-Message2 { Write-Output "My Write-Output message." }
Create-WarningMessage | Write-Warning
Create-Message
Create-Message2
```

The output of this command is shown in the following screenshot:

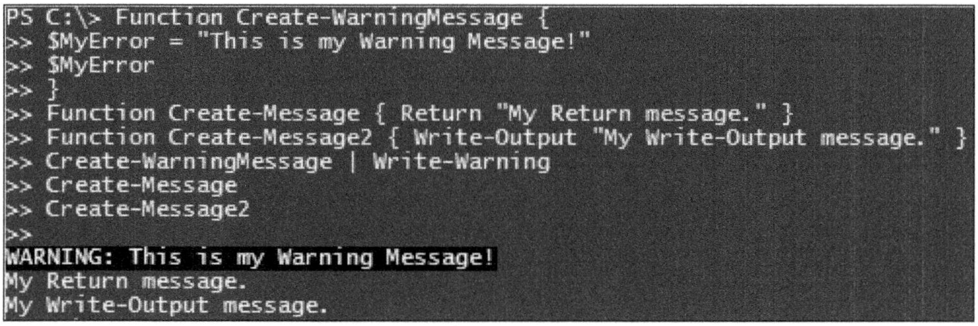
PS C:\> Function Create-WarningMessage {
>> $MyError = "This is my Warning Message!"
>> $MyError
>> }
>> Function Create-Message { Return "My Return message." }
>> Function Create-Message2 { Write-Output "My Write-Output message." }
>> Create-WarningMessage | Write-Warning
>> Create-Message
>> Create-Message2
>>
WARNING: This is my Warning Message!
My Return message.
My Write-Output message.

This example displays how to declare functions that return values to the script. You first call the `Function` command with the `Create-WarningMessage` function name. Inside the curly brackets, you create a variable named `$MyError` and set it equal to `This is my Warning Message`. You then call the `$MyError` variable and close the function. You create a second function by using the `Function` command with the `Create-Message` function name. Inside the curly brackets, you use the `Return` command with the message `My Return message`. Finally, you create a third function by using the `Function` command with the `Create-Message2` function name. Inside the curly brackets, you use the `write-output` cmdlet with the text `My Write-Output message`.

When you run the script, you first call the `Create-WarningMessage` function and pipe it to `Write-Warning`. When you do this, the output from `Create-WarningMessage` of `This is my Warning Message!` is passed to the `Write-Warning` via the pipeline, and a warning message of `WARNING: This is my Warning Message!` is printed to the console. You then call the `Create-Message` function, which returns from the function and prints to the screen `My Return message`. Finally, you call the `Create-Message2` function, which passes back the `write-output` cmdlet message and prints to the screen `My Write-Output message`.

> If you need to exit a function, you can simply use the `return` command, which gracefully exits the function. This avoids having to stop the whole script by using the `EXIT` or `BREAK` commands.

Looping structures

PowerShell provides a variety of looping structures for evaluating and executing objects. Loops are helpful in situations where you need to take in an array of objects and process the individual values in the array. Subsequently, loops are also helpful in situations where you need to wait for a specific value within an array before proceeding in the script.

There are four main looping structures in PowerShell. These looping structures include `Do/While`, `Do/Until`, `ForEach`, and `For`. The `Do/While` looping structure is used to execute a task when a value doesn't equal a specific value. The inverse of this looping structure is `Do/Until`, where it will keep looping the structure until a value equals a specific value. `ForEach` is a looping structure that allows you to process each individual object in an array or set of objects. The `For` loop is typically used to execute a task a set number of times.

To create a new `Do/While` looping structure, you first start by declaring the `Do` command. You then place the PowerShell commands that you want to repeat in curly brackets. After closing the curly brackets, you declare the `While` command with a conditional statement. The condition typically leverages a comparison operator and you tell the loop to repeat when the statement equals a specific condition. Once the evaluation of the condition no longer returns `True`, the loop will stop.

The format of a `Do/While` looping structure looks like this:

```
$x = 1
$myVar = $False
Do {
  If ($x -ne "4") {
    Write-Host "This Task Has Looped $x Times"
  }
  If ($x -eq "4") {
    $myVar = $True
    Write-Host "Successfully executed the script $x times"
  }
  $x++
  }
While ($myVar -eq $False)
```

The output of this is shown in the following screenshot:

```
PS C:\> $x = 1
PS C:\> $myVar = $False
PS C:\> Do {
>>     If ($x -ne "4") {
>>     Write-Host "This Task Has Looped $x Times"
>>     }
>>     If ($x -eq "4") {
>>     $myVar = $True
>>     Write-Host "Successfully executed the script $x times"
>>     }
>>     $x++
>> }
>> While ($myVar -eq $False)
>>
This Task Has Looped 1 Times
This Task Has Looped 2 Times
This Task Has Looped 3 Times
Successfully executed the script 4 times
```

The preceding script displays the proper usage of the `Do/While` loop structure. The script starts by declaring a variable `$x` equal to `1`. The `$x` variable designates that it is the first time you are executing the script. You will then declare the `$myVar` equal to `False` to allow the script to execute while the variable is `False`. The `Do` clause will then execute while `$myVar` equals `False`. With each iteration of the loop, the script will evaluate whether the `$x` variable equals `4`. If it doesn't equal `4`, it will write to the console `This task has Looped $x Times`. It will increment `$x` by one value designated by the `$x++` command and restart from the beginning of the loop. When `$x` equals `4`, the script will set `$myVar` value to `True` and write to the console the message `Successfully executed the script $x times`. The loop will evaluate `$myVar` and determine that it no longer equals `False` and exit the loop.

To create a new `Do/Until` looping structure, you first start by declaring the `Do` command. You then place the PowerShell commands that you want to repeat in curly brackets. After closing the curly brackets, you declare the `Until` command with a conditional statement. The condition typically leverages a comparison operator and you tell the loop to repeat until the statement equals a specific condition. Once the evaluation of the condition no longer returns `False`, the loop will stop.

> When you are creating looping structures, it's inevitable that you will accidently create an infinite looping structure. When you do, you may be flooding your console with text or create a large amount of data. To pause a loop, press *Pause* on your keyboard. If you want to continue, you can hit *Enter* on the keyboard. To completely exit a loop, you can press the key combination of *Ctrl* + C in the console window. This will break the looping structure.

The format of a `Do/Until` looping structure looks like this:

```
$x = 1
$myVar = $False
Do {
  If ($x -ne "4") {
      Write-Host "This Task Has Looped $x Times"
  }
  If ($x -eq "4") {
      $myVar = $True
      Write-Host "Successfully executed the script $x times"
  }
  $x++
  }
Until ($myVar -eq $True)
```

The output of this is shown in the following screenshot:

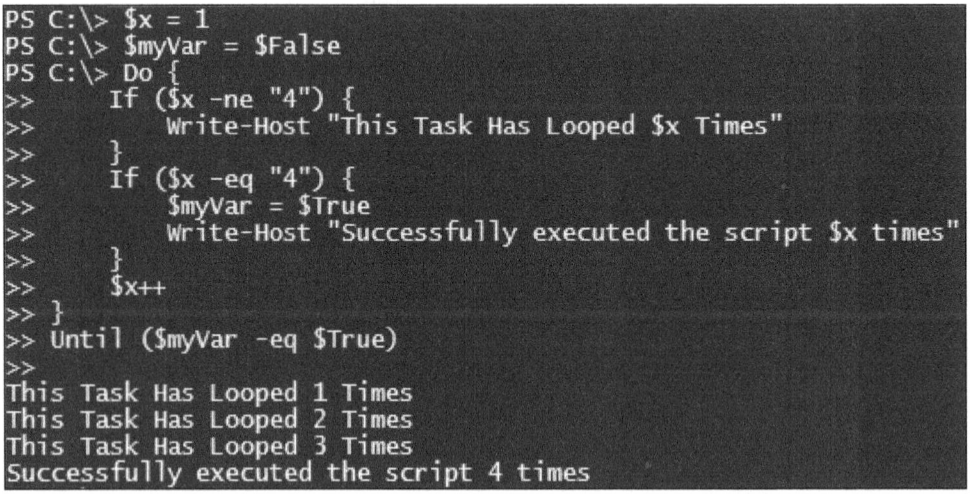
PS C:\> $x = 1
PS C:\> $myVar = $False
PS C:\> Do {
>>   If ($x -ne "4") {
>>   Write-Host "This Task Has Looped $x Times"
>>   }
>>   If ($x -eq "4") {
>> $myVar = $True
>>   Write-Host "Successfully executed the script $x times"
>>   }
>> $x++
>> }
>> Until ($myVar -eq $True)
>>
This Task Has Looped 1 Times
This Task Has Looped 2 Times
This Task Has Looped 3 Times
Successfully executed the script 4 times

The preceding script displays the proper usage of the `Do/Until` loop structure. The script starts by declaring a variable `$x` equal to `1`. The `$x` variable designates that it is the first time you are executing the script. You will then declare `$myVar` equal to `False` to allow the script to execute while the variable is `False`. The `Do` clause will then execute until `$myVar` equals `True`. With each iteration of the loop, the script will evaluate whether the `$x` variable equals `4`. If it doesn't equal `4`, it will write to the console `This task as Looped $x Times`. It will increment `$x` by one value designated by the `$x++` command and restart from the beginning of the loop. When `$x` equals `4`, the script will set the `$myVar` value to `True` and write to the console `Successfully executed the script $x times`. The loop will evaluate `$myVar` and determine that it no longer equals `True` and exit the loop. You will see that the `Do/Until` loop structure is declared exactly as the previous script; however, PowerShell interprets the `Until` statement as a conditional statement to continue *until something equals a value*.

The `ForEach` loop structure has a very simple construct. The `ForEach` looping structure is declared by calling `ForEach`. You then specify parentheses containing a variable, the word `in`, and typically a second variable that contains an array of data. This may look like `($object in $array)`. While the `$array` variable typically contains a set of objects, the `$object` variable is considered the *processing variable*. This variable enables you to access each object in the array and its properties. After you declare the variables in the parentheses, you place the PowerShell code you want to repeat in curly brackets. In the instance that you want to interact with the individual objects in the array, you can leverage the processing variable in your PowerShell code.

While creating the `ForEach` loop for processing variables and arrays, it's important to name the variables reflective of what you are processing. If you had a list of account numbers, you could create variables that reflected `ForEach ($account in $accountNumbers)`. This will reduce confusion while reading your scripts.

The format of a `ForEach` looping structure looks like this:

```
$users = "Mitch", "Ted", "Tom", "Bill"
ForEach ($user in $users) {
    Write-host "Hello $user!"
}
```

The output of this is shown in the following screenshot:

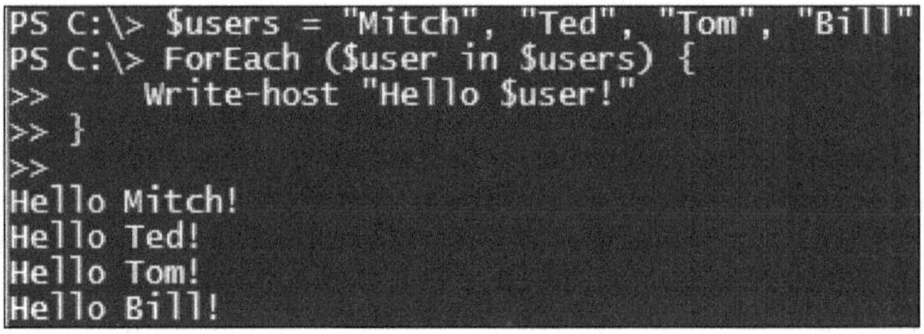

PS C:\> $users = "Mitch", "Ted", "Tom", "Bill"
PS C:\> ForEach ($user in $users) {
>> Write-host "Hello $user!"
>> }
>>
Hello Mitch!
Hello Ted!
Hello Tom!
Hello Bill!

In this example, you define an array named `$users` with the individual values of `Mitch`, `Ted`, `Tom`, and `Bill`. You then declare the `ForEach` loop with a processing variable of `$user`. This loop will then process each `$user` in the array `$users` and write to the console the message `Hello $user!`. The `$user` variable will be reflecting the current value of the current object that the loop is processing.

The `For` looping structure has a slightly more complex construct. You first start by declaring the `For` command. You then declare three required sections of code separated by semicolons and enclose these sections in parentheses. The first section of code is declaring a variable that will interact with the looping structure. This typically is a number that is incremented or decreased as the looping structures proceeds through the loops. This variable must contain a value, otherwise the looping structure will not proceed. This value can be either defined before you enter the looping structure, or when you are declaring the looping structure itself.

The second section of code is the conditional statement, which tells the loop to continue while this statement is `True`. Once the statement is `False`, the loop terminates. The last section of code tells the loop to either increment or decrease the first variable and by how many. You can use shorthand to increase a variable by entering `$variable++` to increase the value `1`, or you can decrease the value by performing a math operation like `$variable - 1`. After enclosing the required sections of the `For` loop structure, you enclose the code you want to repeat in curly brackets.

The format of a `For` looping structure may look like this:

```
For ($x = 1; $x -lt "5"; $x++) {
  write-host "Hello World! Loop Attempt Number: $x"
}
```

The output is shown in the following screenshot:

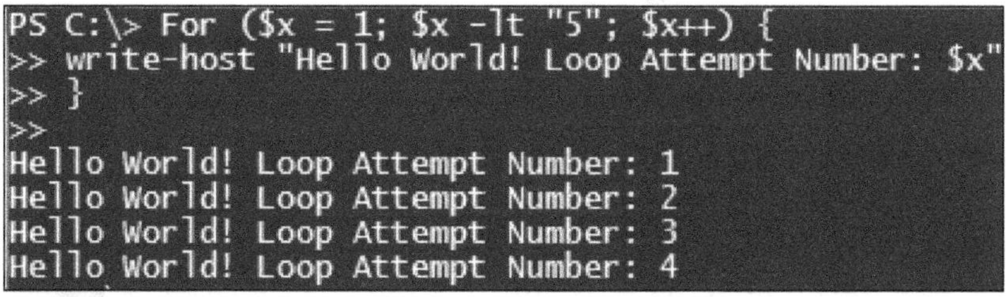
PS C:\> For ($x = 1; $x -lt "5"; $x++) {
>> write-host "Hello World! Loop Attempt Number: $x"
>> }
>>
Hello World! Loop Attempt Number: 1
Hello World! Loop Attempt Number: 2
Hello World! Loop Attempt Number: 3
Hello World! Loop Attempt Number: 4

This example displays how to properly use a `For` looping structure. You first start by declaring the `For` command. You then declare the required sections for the structure; you start by defining `$x` equal to the value `1`, which starts the first loop at the value of `1`. You then declare the conditional statement of loop while `$x` is less than `5`. In the last required section, you declare `$x++`, which increments the `$x` variable by `1` in every loop throughout the structure. You then declare the PowerShell command `Write-host "Hello World! Loop Attempt Number: $x"` in curly brackets. When you run this script, the `For` looping structure will loop `4` times writing to the console the message `Hello World! Loop Attempt Number: $x`, where `$x` equals the iteration of the script's loop.

> Also, it is important to remember that the `Do/While`, `Do/Until`, and `For` loop structures do not increment the `$x` variable until it processes once. This is why you set the `$x` variable to `1` when you build the construct as it's implied that the first run through the loop has already executed.

Switches

Switches enable you to quickly test multiple scripting scenarios without actually writing `if` statements with comparison operators. Switches are the most efficient flow control commands as they can quickly funnel data into different code sections based on an item. The `Switch` command allows you to evaluate the contents of a single variable and execute subsequent tasks based on the value of the variable. Switches also have a `default` value that is used by the switch when none of the values equal any of the suggested values in the switch statement. To invoke the `Switch` command, you declare `Switch ($variableToEvaluate)`. The second part of the `Switch` command is to declare potential values that the `$variableToEvaluate` could be, as shown here:

```
$x = "that"
Switch ($x) {
```

```
  this { write-host "Value $x equals this." }
  that { write-host "Value $x equals that." }
  Default { write-host "Value Doesn't Match Any Other Value" }
}
```

The output of this is shown in the following screenshot:

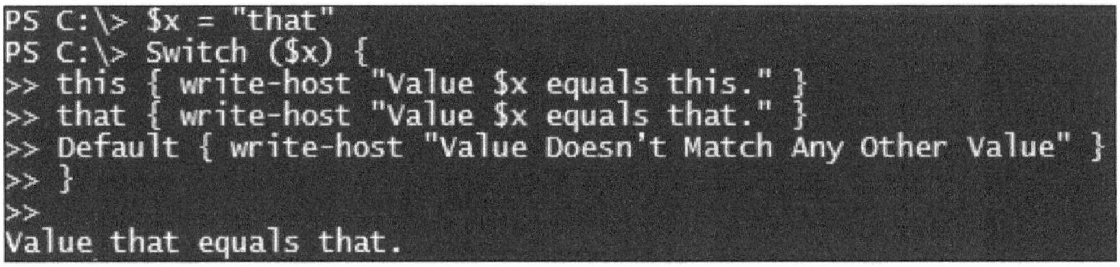
PS C:\> $x = "that"
PS C:\> Switch ($x) {
>> this { write-host "Value $x equals this." }
>> that { write-host "Value $x equals that." }
>> Default { write-host "Value Doesn't Match Any Other Value" }
>> }
>>
Value that equals that.

The preceding script displays the proper construct of a `Switch` command. This example starts by setting the `$x` variable to `that`. It then enters the `Switch` construct that compares the `$x` variable to the suggested values. In this example, the `$x` variable equals `that`, after which the `Switch` will then write to the console the message `Value that equals that`. If the value of `$x` was set to `this`, it would write to the console the message `Value this equals this`. Last, if the value of `$x` is set to anything other than `this` or `that`, it would write to the console `Value Doesn't Match Any Other Value`.

Combining the use of functions, switches, and loops

There may be instances where you will want to combine the use of the different structures explained in this chapter. The example that you will create is a simple menu system that can be modified for use within your scripts. This script will prompt for your interaction and perform actions based on your response, as shown here:

```
# A Menu System for Use With This Example
Function menu-system {
    Write-host "**********************************************"
    Write-Host "* Please Make A Selection Below:"
    Write-Host "*"
    Write-Host "* [1] Backup User Permissions."
    Write-host "*"
    Write-Host "* [2] Delete User Permissions."
```

```
    Write-host "*"
    Write-Host "* [3] Restore User Permissions."
    Write-host "*"
    Write-host "**********************************************"
    Write-host ""
    Write-host "Please Make A Selection:"
    # Prompt for a User Input.
    $x = $host.UI.RawUI.ReadKey("NoEcho,IncludeKeyDown")
    # A Switch to Evaluate User Input.
    Switch ($x.character) {
      1 { write-host "Option 1: User Permissions Backed Up." }
      2 { write-host "Option 2: User Permissions Deleted." }
      3 { write-host "Option 3: User Permissions Restored." }
      Default {
        return $True
      }
  }
}
# A Loop Structure That will Loop Until $Restart doesn't equal true.
Do {
    $restart = Menu-system
    If ($restart -eq $True) {
      cls
      write-host "!! Invalid Selection: Please Try Again"
      write-host ""
    }
}
Until ($restart -ne $True)
```

The output of this is shown in the following screenshot:

```
PS C:\> Function menu-system {
>>     Write-host "*********************************************"
>>     Write-Host "* Please Make A Selection Below:"
>>     Write-Host "*"
>>     Write-Host "* [1] Backup User Permissions."
>>     Write-host "*"
>>     Write-Host "* [2] Delete User Permissions."
>>     Write-host "*"
>>     Write-Host "* [3] Restore User Permisssions."
>>     Write-host "*"
>>     Write-host "*********************************************"
>>     Write-host ""
>>     Write-host "Please Make A Selection:"
>>     # Prompt for a User Input.
>>     $x = $host.UI.RawUI.ReadKey("NoEcho,IncludeKeyDown")
>>     # A Switch to Evaluate User Input.
>>     Switch ($x.character) {
>>         1 { write-host "Option 1: User Permissions Backed Up." }
>>         2 { write-host "Option 2: User Permissions Deleted." }
>>         3 { write-host "Option 3: User Permissions Restored." }
>>         Default {
>>             return $True
>>         }
>> }
>> }
>> # A Loop Structure That will Loop Until $Restart doesn't equal true.
>> Do {
>>     $restart = Menu-system
>>     If ($restart -eq $True) {
>>         cls
>>         write-host "!! Invalid Selection: Please Try Again"
>>         write-host ""
>>     }
>> }
>> Until ($restart -ne $True)
>>
*********************************************
* Please Make A Selection Below:
*
* [1] Backup User Permissions.
*
* [2] Delete User Permissions.
*
* [3] Restore User Permisssions.
*
*********************************************

Please Make A Selection:
```

This script displays the proper syntax to create a menu system within PowerShell. It first starts by declaring a function named `menu-system`. The `menu-system` function prints to the console instructions on how to use the `menu-system`. It then pauses and waits for user interaction by declaring `$x = $host.UI.RawUI.ReadKey("NoEcho,IncludeKeyDown")`. When you press a key on the keyboard, the input is set to the `$x` variable and the script continues. The script then enters the `Switch` command and evaluates the input character `($x.character)` against the options that you set up. If you press `1`, the console will write `Option 1: User Permissions Backed Up.` and exit the `Switch`. If you press `2`, the console will write `Option 2: User Permissions Deleted.` and exit the `Switch`. If you press `3`, the console will write `Option 3: User Permissions Restored.` and exit the `Switch`. If you press any other keys than `1`, `2`, or `3`, the script will return `$True`.

This script also leverages a `Do/Until` loop to restart the `menu-system` method each time the user presses an invalid key. The `Do` loop is entered and will execute the `menu-system` method and catches any `returns` from the method into the `$restart` variable. Upon successful key entry from the method, the method will write to the console and exit the method. When the method exits, it doesn't return any data to the `$restart` variable and the `$restart` variable will be blank. Since this does not equal `$True`, the `Do/Until` loop will successfully exit the script. Inversely, if the user doesn't enter a correct value, the `Method` will `return $True` and set the `$restart` variable to `$True`. The `if` statement will evaluate to be `$True`, clear the screen using the `cls` command, write to the console `!! Invalid Selection: Please Try Again`, write to the console a line spacer `""`, and restart at the top of the `Do/Until` loop structure.

Best practices for functions, switches, and loops

When you are scripting, you will find that you frequently need to utilize functions, loops, switches, and methods. Each of these code structures enable you to produce code faster so that you don't have to repeat code within your script. As you work with each of these structures, there are several best practices that you can follow.

Best practices for functions

There are a few recommended steps that can be followed to obtain optimum performance from functions. They are listed as follows:

- If you need to execute a sequence of code more than once, you should create a function. This will allow you to quickly repeat the same action without significantly increasing the size of the script.
- If you need to pass information into a function for processing, you should leverage arguments. Arguments will need to be declared in the order by which the function will use them.
- If you need to pass information back from a function, you should utilize the `return` command. When used with arguments, it allows you to input data, manipulate data, and return it to a variable for use in other areas of the script.
- Functions need to be declared in the script before you use them. When you are stacking multiple functions in a script, place the functions that will be used first near the top of the file, and the others can follow based on the execution order.
- When you are creating new functions, they should be named as `"verb-noun"`. This will allow for other people to quickly read your scripts and determine what action is being performed. The most common verbs are `get-`, `set-`, `write-`, `delete-`, `read-`, `new-`, `replace-`, `insert-`, `add-`, `show-`, and `remove-`.

Best practices for looping structures and switches

As you are working with looping structures and switches, there are several recommended best practices that will ensure scripting success, as shown here:

- It is recommended to keep the looping structures positive in nature. Use `Do/While` and `Do/Until` with the `-eq` conditional operator. This will promote performing actions `until` a variable equals a value or performing an action `while` a variable equals a value. Positive conditional operators make reading the script much easier and avoid double negative statements.
- While the `For` looping structure works well for iterative processing of multiple values, it is recommended to leverage the `ForEach` looping structure. While both looping structures will achieve the same output, `ForEach` has a much easier format to read.

- When you are declaring variables for use with the `ForEach` looping structure, it is one of the best practices to use words as variables. For example, you can declare `ForEach($user in $list)`. This makes it clear that you want to process each `$user` in the `$list`. This is much better than stating `ForEach($x in $y)` from a legibility standpoint.
- When you need to create multiple `if` statements in your script to evaluate a variable, you should leverage the use of switches.
- When you declare the multiple switch options, it is important to create only the necessary values that require action, and set the `default` value for all other values. This will reduce the complexity of your switch statements.

Summary

This chapter explored some of the fundamental components that are required for creating PowerShell scripts. These components include functions, loops, and switches. Each of these structures has a purpose within your scripts and can reduce the amount of effort in creating your scripts.

During this chapter, you explored how to create the structure of functions. You also learned how to feed arguments into these scripts and return values from a function.

The chapter also explained how you can create different types of looping structures. These looping structures include `Do/Until`, `Do/While`, `ForEach`, and `For`. The `Do/Until` loop was designed to execute until a variable equals a value. The `Do/While` loop will execute while a variable equals a value. The `ForEach` loop will execute for each object in an array. The final looping structure is `For`, which will execute for a set number of times as defined in the initial structure of the loop.

You went through the process of creating a `Switch`. You learned that switches are used in place of multiple "if" statements to evaluate what the contents of a variable are. You also learned that switches have a *default* value; if a switch doesn't match any of the criteria, it will execute the default section of code.

After learning about the core fundamentals of these components, we pulled the chapter together with an example on how to leverage functions, looping structures, and switches together for creating a simple menu system. This chapter ends by explaining multiple best practices that can be leveraged for the use of functions, loops, and switches.

The next chapter explores regular expressions. Regular expressions enable you to validate data syntax and structure. Regular expressions are frequently used with comparison operators, functions, loops, and switches to do advanced validation of data. You will learn how to leverage regular expressions within your PowerShell scripts.

5
Regular Expressions

When you are scripting, you will run into situations where you need to validate strings to see if they meet certain criteria. While you have the ability to use comparison operators to view if a string matches a certain value, you don't have the ability to validate parts of a string. A good example is of *IP addresses*. The comparison operators don't have the ability to validate the syntax of an IP address. If you were to use the normal comparison operators to validate an IP address syntax, you would have to build a script that would split the numerical values, verify that it has 4 octets, validate the individual numerical values, and pass a `True` or `False` value. Regular expressions solve this problem by providing deep comparison operations in a single string to verify that strings meet certain criteria.

In this chapter, you will learn about:

- Common metacharacters
- Grouping constructs and ranges
- Regular expression quantifiers
- Regular expression anchors
- Regular expression examples

Regular expressions are mostly language neutral. This means expressions created in a different programming language have the versatility to be used in your PowerShell scripts. While there are some minor differences between the implementations in programming languages, the base syntax is the same. With this being stated, regular expressions are not for every developer. Since there is a fairly large learning curve to using regular expressions, sometimes writing out longer evaluation scripts using comparison operators may be simpler than leveraging regular expressions. If you choose to use regular expressions in your scripts, it is recommended that you thoroughly comment the code to help any other developers quickly decipher the regular expression you are using.

Getting started with regular expressions

In the most basic form, regular expressions are used to match a specific set of characters contained in a string. To use regular expressions in PowerShell, you need to leverage the `-match`, `-notmatch`, and `-replace` operators in conjunction with an expression. The proper syntax for the comparison operators is referencing a variable or string, followed by the `-match`, `-notmatch`, or `-replace` operator and then the expression you want to evaluate. If the comparison operator is `-match` or `-notmatch`, the expression will return either `True` or `False`. If you use the `-replace` operator, the expression will return the string or variable with the replaced values.

> By default, PowerShell's `-match` operator is case-insensitive. This means it will return `$True` if the letter exists. To fully leverage the regular expression's case sensitivity, use `-cmatch`. The `-cmatch` operator is for case match and will make the matching case-sensitive.

Regular expressions have characters that are reserved for use in evaluation. Each of these metacharacters have a specific meaning for the interpretation of regular expressions. Some of these common characters include:

- \: This character indicates an escape character. This is used to perform a literal interpretation of symbol characters. So, if you don't want the regular expression to evaluate the symbol metacharacter, place \ in front of the character and it will use the literal character. For all other word and number characters, if you want to use the special meaning, you need to leverage the \ symbol, and the expression will use the special meaning as seen in the following common characters.
- `\d`: This character matches a single digit. It will return `True` if the string contains a number. It will return `False` if the string contains no numbers.
- `\D`: This is a negative character class of `\d`. It will return `True` if the string doesn't contain any character other than just numbers. It will return `False` if the string contains just numbers.
- `\s`: This character matches any white space character such as a space or a tab. It will return `True` if the string contains white space characters. It will return `False` if the string contains no white space characters.
- `\S`: This is a negative character class of `\s`. It will return `True` if the string doesn't contain white space characters. It will return `False` if the string contains white space characters.
- `\w`: This character matches any character that can be used in a word. It will return `True` if the string contains letters and numbers. It will return `False` if the string only contains symbols.

- `\W`: This is a negative character class of `\w`. It will return `True` if the string contains symbols. It will return `False` if the string only contains letters and numbers.
- `.`: This metacharacter is a wildcard character which indicates that it can be matched to a character. This character is commonly used inside a word to designate a wildcard character in the matching process. You can use the regular expression `Jo.`, which would match the words `Joe` and `Jon` in a string and return `True`.

To match single items in a string, do the following action:

```
# Match any character in string
"This Matches Any Character" -cmatch "."
# Match any character in string that is $null
"" -cmatch "."
# Match the Period in string
"This Matches Just The Period." -cmatch "\."
# Match the period - no periods exist.
"This Matches Nothing" -cmatch "\."
```

The output of this is shown in the following screenshot:

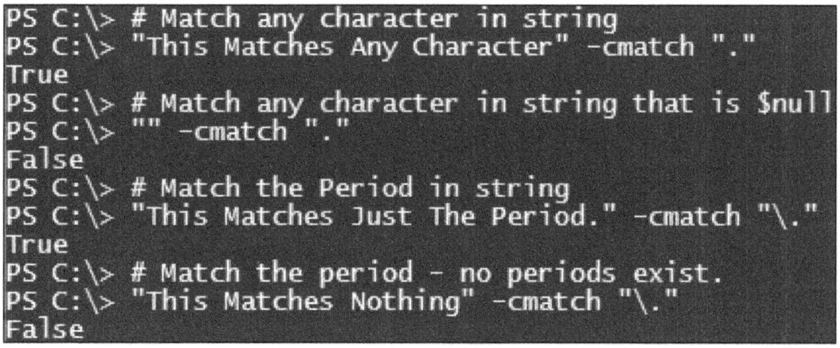

PS C:\> # Match any character in string
PS C:\> "This Matches Any Character" -cmatch "."
True
PS C:\> # Match any character in string that is $null
PS C:\> "" -cmatch "."
False
PS C:\> # Match the Period in string
PS C:\> "This Matches Just The Period." -cmatch "\."
True
PS C:\> # Match the period - no periods exist.
PS C:\> "This Matches Nothing" -cmatch "\."
False

This example displays how to use a regular expression to detect characters in a string. It also shows you how to properly use the escape character `\` to evaluate the literal character meaning of `.`. You first start by declaring the string `This Matches Any Character`, calling the `-cmatch` comparison operator and the value you want to search for which is `.`. When PowerShell evaluates this regular expression, it will return `True` because the string `This Matches Any Character` contains a character.

The second part of this script is the evaluation of a string that contains no characters. You first declare `""` followed by the `-cmatch` comparison operator and `.`. When PowerShell evaluates this regular expression, it determines that there are no characters in the string and will return `False`.

The third part of this script leverages the escape character. In this example, you examine the string `This Matches Just The Period.` by using the `-cmatch` comparison operator and the regular expression `\.`. When PowerShell evaluates this string, it searches for the character period. Since the string contains a period, the regular expression will return `True`.

The last part of this script also leverages the escape character. In this example, you examine the string `This Matches Nothing` with the `-cmatch` comparison operator and the regular expression of `\.`. Since there are no periods in the string, the regular expression returns `False`.

To use the `-replace` operator with regular expressions, do the following action:

```
"This is PowerShell." -replace "Power","a Turtle"
```

The output of this is shown in the following screenshot:

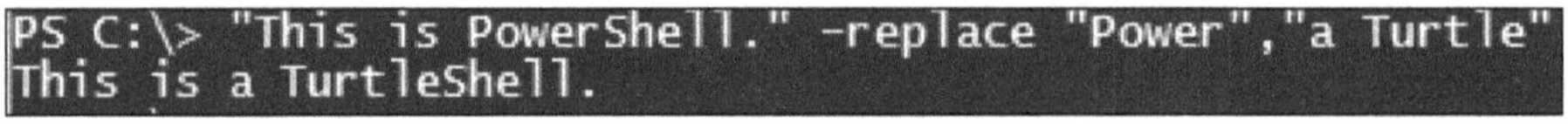

PS C:\> "This is PowerShell." -replace "Power","a Turtle"
This is a TurtleShell.

The preceding example displays how to use a regular expression to replace characters in a string. You first start by declaring the string `This is PowerShell.` calling the `-replace` comparison operator, the value you want to replace, which is `Power` followed by a comma and then the value you want to replace it with, which is `a Turtle`. When the PowerShell evaluates this regular expression, it will return `This is a TurtleShell.` because the string `This is PowerShell.` contains `Power` and replaces that value with `a Turtle`. The `-replace` operator will return `This is a TurtleShell.`.

To match specific numbers, words, and nonword characters, perform the following actions:

```
# Match to Digit Characters
"0132465789" -cmatch "\d"
# Match to Non-Digit Characters
"This String Contains Word Characters" -cmatch "\D"
# Match to Word Characters
"This String Contains Words" -cmatch "\w"
# Match to Non-word Characters
```

```
"!!@#@##$" -cmatch "\W"
# Match to Space Characters
"This String Contains A Space" -cmatch "\s"
# Match to Non Space Characters
"ThisCannotContainSpaces" -cmatch "\S"
```

The output of this is shown in the following screenshot:

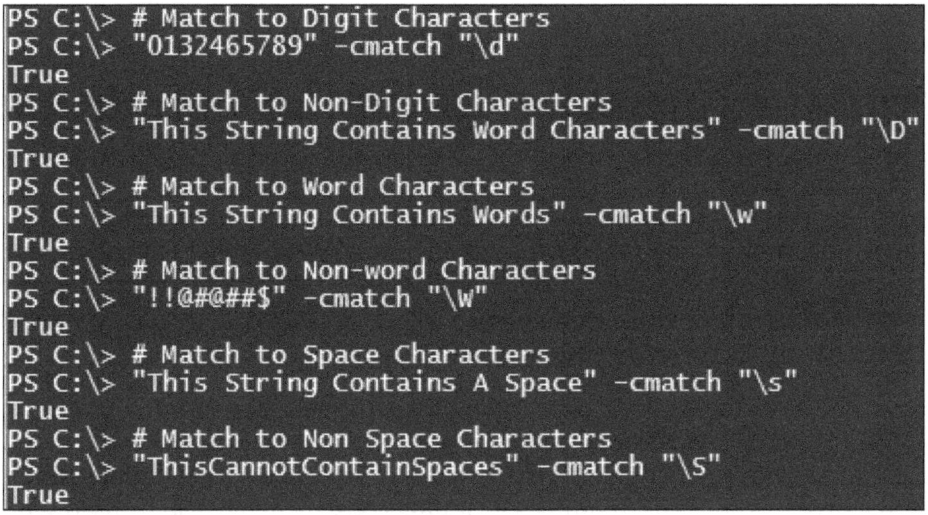

PS C:\> # Match to Digit Characters
PS C:\> "0132465789" -cmatch "\d"
True
PS C:\> # Match to Non-Digit Characters
PS C:\> "This String Contains Word Characters" -cmatch "\D"
True
PS C:\> # Match to Word Characters
PS C:\> "This String Contains Words" -cmatch "\w"
True
PS C:\> # Match to Non-word Characters
PS C:\> "!!@#@##$" -cmatch "\W"
True
PS C:\> # Match to Space Characters
PS C:\> "This String Contains A Space" -cmatch "\s"
True
PS C:\> # Match to Non Space Characters
PS C:\> "ThisCannotContainSpaces" -cmatch "\S"
True

This example displays how to match a variety of data types in strings using regular expressions. The first evaluation uses the `-cmatch` comparison operator on the string `0132465789` to see if it matches the regular expression of `\d` or contains digits. As the string contains numerical characters, the regular expression returns `True`.

The second evaluation uses the `-cmatch` comparison operator on the string `This String Contains Word Characters` to see if it matches the regular expression of `\D` or contains non digits. As the string contains all word characters, the regular expression returns `True`.

The third evaluation uses the `-cmatch` comparison operator on the string `This String Contains Words` to see if it matches the regular expression of `\w` or contains word characters. As the string contains word characters, the regular expression returns `True`.

The fourth evaluation uses the `-cmatch` comparison operator on the string `!!@#@##$` to see if it matches the regular expression of `\W` or contains non-word characters. As the string contains symbols, the regular expression returns `True`.

The fifth evaluation uses the `-cmatch` comparison operator on the string `This String Contains A Space` to see if it matches the regular expression of `\s.` or contains space characters. As the string contains space characters, the regular expression returns `True`.

The last evaluation uses the `-cmatch` comparison operator on the string `ThisCannotContainSpaces` to see if it matches the regular expression of `\S` or contain only whitespace characters. As the string doesn't contain only whitespace characters, the regular expression returns `True`.

Regular expression grouping constructs and ranges

A regular expression grouping construct is similar to what a parenthetical statement is to math operations. Group constructs bind expressions together to evaluate specific information in a specific order. The bracket `[ ]` grouping construct groups evaluation criteria together for evaluation. The regular expression will consider all data in the group `[ ]` for matching to remain `True`.

The parentheses grouping constructs in regular expressions are used to group commands together to determine the order of processing. Similar to other programming languages, equations in the parentheses are evaluated first before the rest of the expression. The parentheses grouping constructs can also be used with the OR alternation construct. The content will be evaluated as this OR that. The `( )` operator is used with the pipe | to designates multiple OR operations. The proper syntax would be `(this|that)` to designate `this` OR `that`.

Regular expression ranges are a way to designate evaluations between two word or number characters. Ranges are used with the grouping constructs to evaluate as the expressions are more than one. To declare a range, you first start with a letter or number followed by the use of a hyphen and then end with a letter or number. When you are declaring a range, it is important to know that you need to group all lowercase, all uppercase, and all numbers separate from each other. These ranges would look like `[a-z]`, `[A-Z]`, or `[0-9]`. You don't have to use the full alphabet or number range while declaring the range. It can be a partial range.

Some examples of how grouping constructs can be used are shown here:

- `[a-z]` or `[A-Z]`: This indicates a character range from one character to another character. This will return `True` if any of the characters in the string contain the characters within the range. This will return `False` if all of the characters are out of the range of characters provided.
- `[0-9]`: This indicates a number range from one number to another number. This will return `True` if any of the numbers in the string contain the numbers in the range. This will return `False` if all of the numbers are out of the range of numbers provided.
- `[abcd1234]`: This indicates specific characters `abcd123` that are to be matched in a string. This will return `True` if any of the `abcd1234` characters in the string contain the characters specified in the regular expression group. This will return `False` if the complete string doesn't contain the `abcd1234` characters provided in the regular expression group.
- `|`: This metacharacter indicates the alternation operator of OR. When you use this metacharacter, it will match one set of characters or another set of characters in a string. If any of the characters exist, the regular expression will return `True`.

When you are creating regular expressions, there are often times when you want to provide flexibility in your ranges. With regular expressions, you have the ability to evaluate multiple ranges such as searching for both upper and lower case word characters. Regular expressions allow you to combine the ranges together by specifying one range after another. The syntax for this would look like `[a-zA-Z1-9]`. If any of those word characters are found in upper or lower case, the evaluation would return `True`. When the expression doesn't match any of those ranges, the expression would return `False`.

To match using the OR operator and ranges, do the following action:

```
# Match Uppercase O OR Lowercase u
"Domain\User23" -cmatch "(O|u)"
# Match Uppercase O OR Uppercase U
"Domain\User23" -cmatch "(O|U)"
# Match Lowercase a-u or Uppercase A-U
"Domain\User23" -cmatch "[a-uA-U]"
# Match Lowercase a-u or Uppercase A-U or numbers 2-3
"Domain\User23" -cmatch "[a-uA-U2-3]"
```

The output of this is shown in the following screenshot:

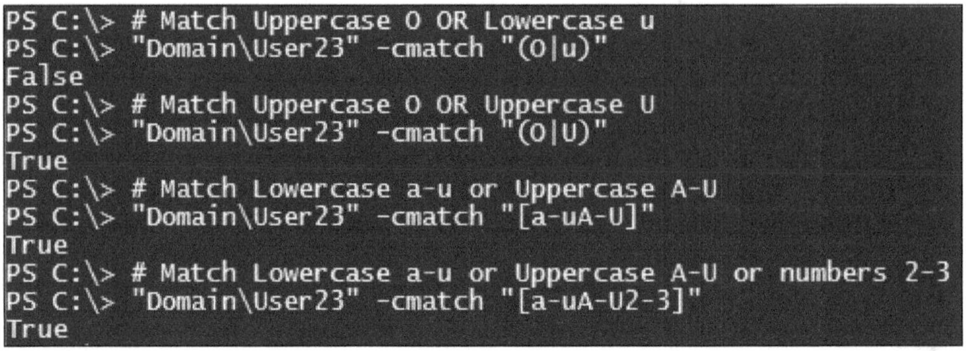

```
PS C:\> # Match Uppercase O OR Lowercase u
PS C:\> "Domain\User23" -cmatch "(O|u)"
False
PS C:\> # Match Uppercase O OR Uppercase U
PS C:\> "Domain\User23" -cmatch "(O|U)"
True
PS C:\> # Match Lowercase a-u or Uppercase A-U
PS C:\> "Domain\User23" -cmatch "[a-uA-U]"
True
PS C:\> # Match Lowercase a-u or Uppercase A-U or numbers 2-3
PS C:\> "Domain\User23" -cmatch "[a-uA-U2-3]"
True
```

This example displays how to use ranges and the OR alternation construct to evaluate a string. Your first expression evaluates `Domain\User23` string with the `-cmatch` comparison operator and the regular expression of `(O|u)`. As the string doesn't contain an uppercase `O` or a lowercase `u`, the expression evaluates to be `False`.

The second expression evaluates `Domain\User23` string with the `-cmatch` comparison operator and the regular expression of `(O|U)`. Even though the expression doesn't contain an uppercase `O`, it contains an uppercase `U`. As one of the two evaluations are `True`, the whole expression evaluates to be `True`.

The third expression evaluates `Domain\User23` string with the `-cmatch` comparison operator and the regular expression range of `[a-uA-U]`. As regular expressions only require one character to be matched for the expression to be `True`, the first character evaluated in the ranges makes the whole expression to be evaluated as `True`.

The fourth expression evaluates `Domain\User23` string with the `-cmatch` comparison operator and the regular expression range of `[a-uA-U2-3]`. As regular expressions only require one character to be matched for the expression to be `True`, the first character evaluated in the ranges makes the whole expression to be evaluated as `True`.

Regular expression quantifiers

When you are writing regular expressions, there are instances where you need to validate if one or more characters exist in the string being evaluated. Regular expression quantifiers evaluate a string to determine if it has a certain number of characters. In the instance of the string `ABC`, you can write a quantifier expression to evaluate that the string has at least one `A`, one `B`, one `C`, and no `D`. If the expression has the designated number of characters, it will evaluate as `True`. If the expression contains less or more than the designated amount, it will return as `False`.

The regular expression quantifiers include the following characters:

- `*`: This character requires zero or more matches of the preceding character to be `True`. This means that if you specify `abc*d`, it will match `a`, `b` and then zero or more of `c` followed by the letter `d`. In the instance of `aaabbbbccccd`, the string will evaluate to be `True` because the letters `a`, `b`, and `c` are in the exact order before the letter `d`. If the string doesn't contain `a`, `b`, then zero or more of `c` in order followed by the letter `d` somewhere in the string, it will evaluate as `False`.
- `+`: This character designates one or more matches of the referenced character. For example, if you specify the expression of `c+`, it will evaluate the string `abc` and determine that there are one or more `c` characters in the string. If the string contains one or more `c` characters, the expression would be `True`. If you evaluate `c+` against the string of `abd`, it will evaluate to be `False` as the letter `c` is not contained with in that string.
- `?`: This character designates zero or one character match. Consider this as an optional character for evaluation. This means that if you specify the expression `abc?d`, the `c` doesn't have to exist for the `abd` string to be `True`. However, if the string which is being evaluated is `cba`, it will return `False` because the prerequisite of `a` and `b` followed by `d` in order are not matched.
- `{ }`: This bracket grouping specifies a specific number or a specific range of consecutive matches that must occur in an expression for it to be `True`. The proper syntax of a specific number of evaluated characters looks like `character{number}`. In the example of `a{4}`, it designates that a string must contain `4` `a` characters to evaluate to be `True`. The proper syntax for a range of required characters looks like `character{min,max}`. In the example of `a{3,4}`, it designates that a string must contain a minimum of `3` consecutive `a` characters and a maximum of `4` consecutive `a` characters to evaluate to be `True`. If the string doesn't have a minimum of `3` consecutive `a` characters and a maximum of `4` consecutive `a` characters, the expression will evaluate as `False`.

When you are grouping multiple expressions together, you may need to use the `.*` regular expression. This designates that any `.` character may or may not exist before or after where that expression is declared. Essentially, you are creating a *wildcard* to construct the string you are looking to evaluate. So if you were to use `.*abc.*` as the expression, it would allow any characters before and after `abc` as long as `abc` exists with in the string.

To match specific items in a string, do the following action:

```
# Match the Word "Domain" and a backslash
"Domain\User23" -cmatch "Domain.*\\.*"
# Match the Word "Domain" and a backslash
"Domain.com\User23" -cmatch "Domain.*\\.*"
# Match the Word "Domain" and a backslash

"User23.Domain.com" -cmatch "Domain.*\\.*"
```

The output of this is shown in the following screenshot:

```
PS C:\> # Match the Word "Domain" and a backslash
PS C:\> "Domain\User23" -cmatch "Domain.*\\.*"
True
PS C:\> # Match the Word "Domain" and a backslash
PS C:\> "Domain.com\User23" -cmatch "Domain.*\\.*"
True
PS C:\> # Match the Word "Domain" and a backslash
PS C:\> "User23.Domain.com" -cmatch "Domain.*\\.*"
False
```

This example displays how to properly use the `*` metacharacter in an expression to evaluate the syntax of a username. The first expression leverages the `-cmatch` comparison operator to evaluate if `Domain\User23` matches the expression of `Domain.\*\\.*`. When you break down the expression, it evaluates if the string starts with `Domain` followed by `any set of characters` and then the mandatory escaped character of \ which is again ending with `any set of characters`. When the expression evaluates the string as `Domain \ User23`, it will return `True` as it follows the expression pattern.

The second expression leverages the `-cmatch` comparison operator to evaluate if `Domain.com\User23` matches the expression of `Domain.\*\\.*`. When you break down the expression, it evaluates whether the string starts with `Domain` followed by `any set of characters` and then the mandatory escaped character of \ which again ends with `any set of characters`. When the expression evaluates the string as `Domain .com \ User23`, it will return `True` because it follows the expression pattern.

The last expression leverages the `-cmatch` comparison operator to evaluate whether `User23.Domain.com` matches the expression of `Domain.\*\\.*`. When you break down the expression, it evaluates whether the string starts with `Domain` followed by `any set of characters` and then the mandatory escaped character of \ which again ends with `any set of characters`. When the expression evaluates the string as `User23.Domain.com`, it will return `False` because it doesn't contain the right order of the evaluation criteria.

To match at least one sequence in a string, do the following action:

```
# Match the Word "Domain" at least once.
"Domain\User23" -cmatch "Domain+"
# Match the Word ".com" at least once.
"Domain\User23" -cmatch "\.com+"
# Match the Word "Domain.com" at least once and a backslash
"Domain.com\User23" -cmatch "Domain\.com+.*\\"
```

The output of this is shown in the following screenshot:

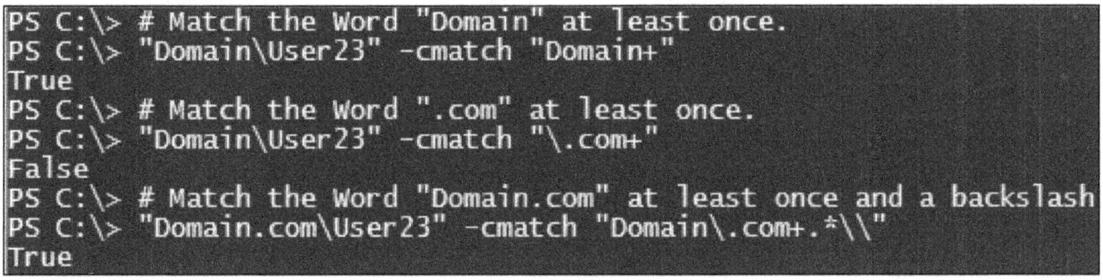
PS C:\> # Match the Word "Domain" at least once.
PS C:\> "Domain\User23" -cmatch "Domain+"
True
PS C:\> # Match the Word ".com" at least once.
PS C:\> "Domain\User23" -cmatch "\.com+"
False
PS C:\> # Match the Word "Domain.com" at least once and a backslash
PS C:\> "Domain.com\User23" -cmatch "Domain\.com+.*\\"
True

This example displays how to use the + metacharacter to evaluate the syntax of a username. The first expression leverages the `-cmatch` comparison operator to evaluate if `Domain\User23` matches the expression of `Domain+`. When you break down the expression, it evaluates whether the string contains one or more `Domain` strings. When the expression evaluates the string as `Domain\User23`, it will return `True` as the string contains one or more instances of the string `Domain`.

The second expression leverages the `-cmatch` comparison operator to evaluate if `Domain\User23` matches the expression of `.\com+`. When you break down the expression, it evaluates whether the string contains one or more `.com` strings. When the expression evaluates the string as `Domain\User23`, it will return `False` because the string doesn't contain `.com`.

The last expression leverages the `-cmatch` comparison operator to evaluate whether `Domain.com\User23` matches the expression of `Domain\.com+.*\\`. When you break down the expression, it evaluates whether the string contains one or more `Domain.com` strings and at least one backslash in the evaluated string. When the expression evaluates the string as `Domain.com\User23`, it will return `True` as the string contains one or more instances of the string `Domain.com and one backslash`.

To evaluate optional characters exist, do the following action:

```
# Match "Domain", optional "com", and a backslash
"Domain.com\User23" -cmatch "Domain.*(com)?\\"
# Match "Domain", optional "com", and a backslash
"Domain\User23" -cmatch "Domain.*(com)?\\"
# Match "Domain", optional "com", and a backslash
"Domain.comUser23" -cmatch "Domain.*(com)?\\"
```

The output of this is shown in the following screenshot:

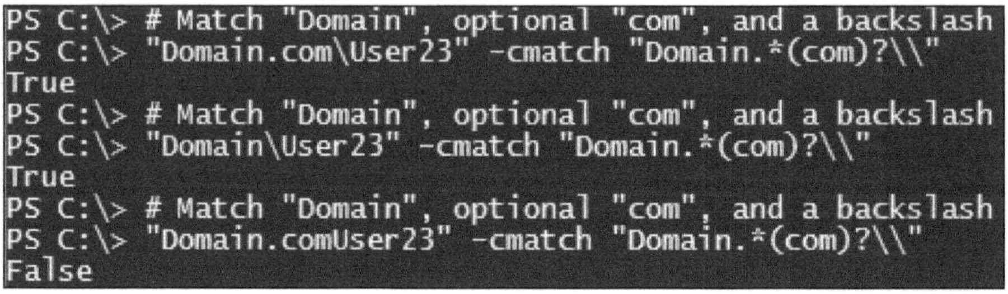
PS C:\> # Match "Domain", optional "com", and a backslash
PS C:\> "Domain.com\User23" -cmatch "Domain.*(com)?\\"
True
PS C:\> # Match "Domain", optional "com", and a backslash
PS C:\> "Domain\User23" -cmatch "Domain.*(com)?\\"
True
PS C:\> # Match "Domain", optional "com", and a backslash
PS C:\> "Domain.comUser23" -cmatch "Domain.*(com)?\\"
False

This example displays how to use the `?` metacharacter to evaluate the syntax of a username. The first expression leverages the `-cmatch` comparison operator to evaluate if `Domain.com\User23` matches the expression of `Domain.*(com)?\\`. When you break down the expression, it evaluates whether the string contains the `Domain` string followed by `any characters`, the optional word of `com`, and the `\` character. When the expression evaluates the string as `Domain.com\User23`, it will return `True`. This is a result of the string containing the `Domain` string, the optional word of `com`, and the `\` character.

The second expression leverages the `-cmatch` comparison operator to evaluate whether `Domain\User23` matches the expression of `Domain.*(com)?\\`. When you break down the expression, it evaluates whether the string contains the `Domain` string, followed by `any characters`, the optional word of `com`, and the `\` character. When the expression evaluates the string as `Domain\User23`, it will return `True`. This is a result of the string containing the `Domain` string and the `\` character. As `com` is an optional requirement, this will not cause the expression to return `False`.

The last expression leverages the `-cmatch` comparison operator to evaluate if `Domain.comUser23` matches the expression of `Domain.*(com)?\\`. When you break down the expression, it evaluates whether the string contains the `Domain` string followed by `any characters`, the optional word of `com`, and the \ character. When the expression evaluates the string as `Domain.comUser23`, it will return `False`. This is a result of the string missing one of the required characters of the \ character. Despite the other components existing, all conditions must return true for the expression to be `True`.

To verify that a string has one or more instances of something, do the following action:

```
# Match exactly one "Domain" and exactly one backslash
"Domain\User23" -cmatch "Domain{1}.*\\{1}"
# Match exactly one "Domain" and exactly two backslashes
"Domain\User23" -cmatch "Domain{1}.*\\{2}"
# Match exactly one "Domain" and exactly one backslash
"User32.Domain.com" -cmatch "Domain{1}.*\\{1}"
```

The output of this is shown in the following screenshot:

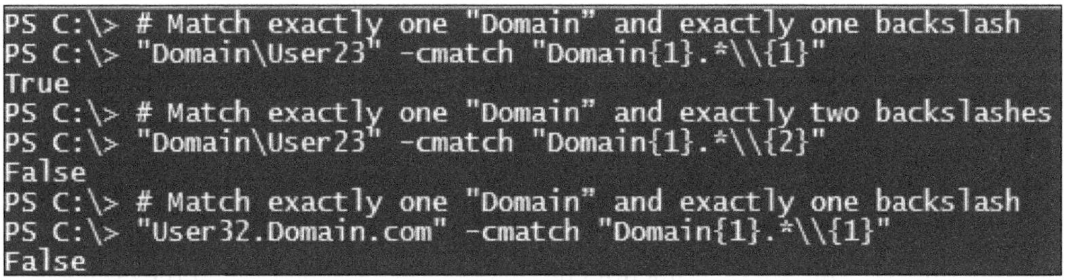
PS C:\> # Match exactly one "Domain" and exactly one backslash
PS C:\> "Domain\User23" -cmatch "Domain{1}.*\\{1}"
True
PS C:\> # Match exactly one "Domain" and exactly two backslashes
PS C:\> "Domain\User23" -cmatch "Domain{1}.*\\{2}"
False
PS C:\> # Match exactly one "Domain" and exactly one backslash
PS C:\> "User32.Domain.com" -cmatch "Domain{1}.*\\{1}"
False

This example displays how to leverage the { } quantifier to verify the syntax of a username. The first expression leverages the `-cmatch` comparison operator to evaluate if `Domain\User23` matches the expression of `Domain{1}.*\\{1}`. When you break down the expression, it evaluates whether the string contains only one instance of `Domain` string, followed by `any characters`, and only one instance of the \ character. When the expression evaluates the string as `Domain\User23`, it will return `True`. This is a result of the string containing only one `Domain` string and only one \ character.

The second expression leverages the `-cmatch` comparison operator to evaluate whether `Domain\User23` matches the expression of `Domain{1}.*\\{2}`. When you break down the expression, it evaluates whether the string contains only one instance of `Domain` string, followed by `any characters`, and only two instances of the \ character. When the expression evaluates the string as `Domain\User23`, it will return `False`. This is a result of the string containing only one `Domain` string and only one \ character.

The last expression leverages the `-cmatch` comparison operator to evaluate whether `User23.domain.com` matches the expression of `Domain{1}.*\\{1}`. When you break down the expression, it evaluates whether the string contains only one instance of `Domain` string, followed by `any characters`, and only one instance of the \ character. When the expression evaluates the string as `User23.domain.com`, it will return `False`. This is a result of the string containing only one `Domain` string and not the \ character.

Regular expression anchors

Anchors are used to tell the regular expression where to start and end the evaluation of a string. The most common anchors evaluate the characters at the beginning or the end of a string. This allows you to validate that the string starts and/or ends with a digit, symbol, or letter character. The most common anchors are:

- ^ and `\A`: The ^ and `\A` anchor characters indicates matching at the start of a string for evaluation. If you want to ensure that a certain pattern is matched at the beginning, you will use ^ or `\A`. The `\A` syntax is symbolic of the first character in the alphabet which is `a`. This is why regular expressions use this character to designate the evaluation from the *start* of a string.
- `$` and `\Z`: The `$` and `\Z` anchor characters indicate matching at the end of a string for evaluation. If you want to ensure that a certain pattern is matched at the end, you will use `$` or `\Z`. The `\Z` syntax is symbolic of the last character in the alphabet which is `z`. This is why regular expressions use this character to designate the evaluation from the *end* of a string.
- `\b`: The `\b` anchor characters indicate a whole word boundary. The `\b` character matches a whole word in a string rather than just an individual character or character type. If the whole word exists, the expression will return `True`. If the whole word doesn't exist, the expression will return `False`.
- The placement of this anchor is important. In the example of `\btest`, `\b` is placed in front of the word, which means it will match all words that begin with `test` like `testing`. If you choose the expression `test\b`, `\b` is placed at the end of the word, which means it will match all words that end with `test`, such as `contest`.

- `\B`: The `\B` anchor is a negative character class indicating a "not whole word" boundary. `\B` matches a whole word in a string rather than just an individual character or character type. If the whole word doesn't exist, the expression will return `True`. If the word partially makes up another word, the expression will also return `True`. If the whole word exists, the expression will return `False`. If the word partially doesn't make up another word, it will also return `False`.

To evaluate strings using anchors, do the following action:

```
# Match at the beginning, if the string contains a word.
"Successfully connected to Active Directory." -cmatch "^\w"
# Match at the end, if the string contains a word. (does not)
"Successfully connected to Active Directory." -cmatch "\w$"
# Match at the end, if the string doesn't contain a word.
"Successfully connected to Active Directory." -cmatch "\W$"
# Match at the beginning, it contains a word, match any characters in
between, and match at the end, it doesn't contain a word.
"Successfully connected to Active Directory." -cmatch "^\w.*\W$"
```

The output of this is shown in the following screenshot:

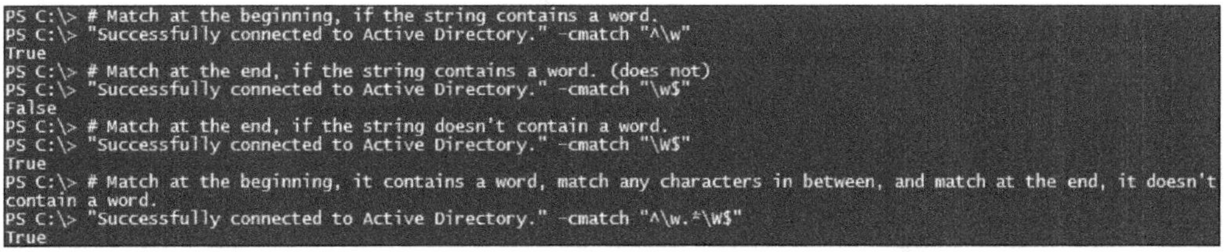

This example displays how to successfully use the ^ and `$` metacharacters to validate the syntax at the beginning and the end of a string. The first expression leverages the `-cmatch` comparison operator to evaluate if `Successfully connected to Active Directory.` matches the expression of `^\w`. When you break down the expression, it evaluates whether the start of the string contains a word character. When the expression evaluates the string as `Successfully connected to Active Directory.`, it will return `True`. This is a result of the first character in the string being the word character of `S`.

The second expression leverages the `-cmatch` comparison operator to evaluate whether `Successfully connected to Active Directory.` matches the expression of `\w$`. When you break down the expression, it evaluates whether the end of the string contains a word character. When the expression evaluates the string as `Successfully connected to Active Directory.`, it will return `False`. This is a result of the last character in the string being the non word character of `.`.

The third expression leverages the `-cmatch` comparison operator to evaluate whether `Successfully connected to Active Directory.` matches the expression of `\W$`. When you break down the expression, it evaluates whether the end of the string contains a non word character. When the expression evaluates the string as `Successfully connected to Active Directory.`, it will return `True`. This is a result of the last character in the string being the non-word character of `.`.

The last expression leverages the `-cmatch` comparison operator to evaluate whether `Successfully connected to Active Directory.` matches the expression of `^\w.*\W$`. When you break down the expression, it evaluates whether the beginning of the string contains a word character, followed by `any set of characters`, and that the end of the string contains a non-word character. When the expression evaluates the string as `Successfully connected to Active Directory.`, it will return `True`. This is a result of the first character in the string being a word character of `S` and the last character in the string being the nonword character of `.`.

To evaluate whole words in strings, do the following action:

```
# Matches the whole word "to".
"Error communicating to Active Directory." -cmatch "\bto\b"
# Matches the whole word "to".
"Error communicating with Active Directory." -cmatch "\bto\b"
# Matches where the whole word "to" does not exist.
"Error communicating with Active Directory." -cmatch "\Bto\B"
# Matches where the whole word "to" does not exist.
"Error communicating with AD." -cmatch "\Bto\B"
```

The output of this is shown in the following screenshot:

```
PS C:\> # Matches the whole word "to".
PS C:\> "Error communicating to Active Directory." -cmatch "\bto\b"
True
PS C:\> # Matches the whole word "to".
PS C:\> "Error communicating with Active Directory." -cmatch "\bto\b"
False
PS C:\> # Matches where the whole word "to" does not exist.
PS C:\> "Error communicating with Active Directory." -cmatch "\Bto\B"
True
PS C:\> # Matches where the whole word "to" does not exist.
PS C:\> "Error communicating with AD." -cmatch "\Bto\B"
False
```

This example displays how to properly use the regular expressions of `\b` and `\B` to evaluate whole words in a string. The first expression leverages the `-cmatch` comparison operator to evaluate if `Error communicating to Active Directory.` matches the expression of `\bto\b`. When you break down the expression, it evaluates whether the string contains the whole word of `to`. When the expression evaluates the string as `Error communicating to Active Directory.`, it will return `True`. This is a result of the expression matching the whole word of `to` between `communicating` and `Active`.

The second expression leverages the `-cmatch` comparison operator to evaluate whether `Error communicating with Active Directory.` matches the expression of `\bto\b`. When you break down the expression, it evaluates whether the string contains the whole word of `to`. When the expression evaluates the string as `Error communicating with Active Directory.`, it will return `False`. This is a result of the expression not being able to match the whole word of `to`. While the word `Directory` contains the letters `to`, it is part of the whole word of `Directory` and is skipped by the expression.

The third expression leverages the `-cmatch` comparison operator to evaluate whether `Error communicating with Active Directory.` matches the expression of `\Bto\B`. When you break down the expression, it evaluates whether the string doesn't contain the whole word of `to`. When the expression evaluates the string as `Error communicating with Active Directory.`, it will return `True`. This is a result of the expression being able to match the non whole word of `to` in the word `Directory`.

The last expression leverages the `-cmatch` comparison operator to evaluate whether `Error communicating with AD.` matches the expression of `\Bto\B`. When you break down the expression, it evaluates whether the string doesn't contain the whole word of `to`. When the expression evaluates the string as `Error communicating with AD.`, it will return `False`. This is a result of the expression not being able to match any part of the word `to` in another word.

Regular expressions examples

When you are developing scripts, there will be many instances where you may want to use regular expressions. This section will explore regular expressions that you may run into in your environment. Since there are many methods to creating regular expressions, these are to be used as suggested starting points for your scripts.

The following diagram shows how to evaluate a MAC Address:

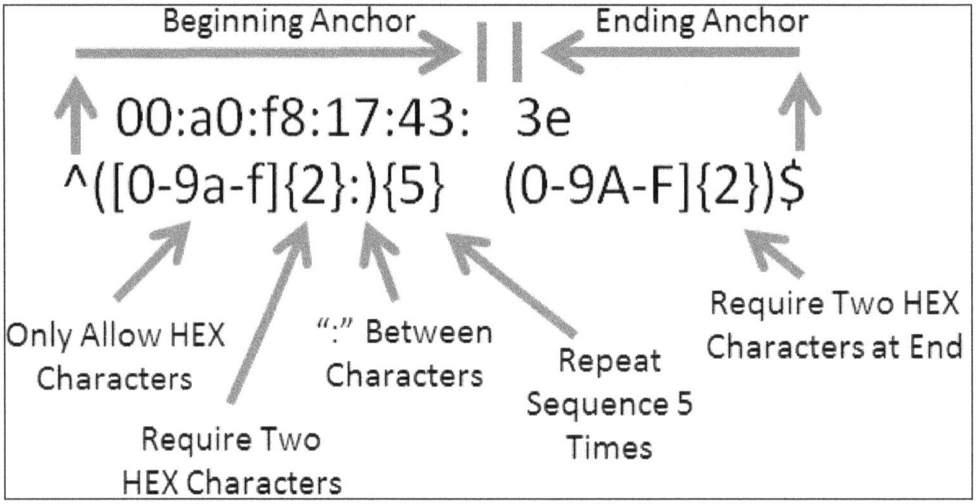

To test a MAC address against a regular expression, use this syntax:

```
"00:a0:f8:12:34:56" -match "^([0-9a-f]{2}:){5}[0-9a-f]{2}$"
```

The output of this is shown in the following screenshot:

PS C:\> "00:a0:f8:12:34:56" -match "^([0-9a-f]{2}:){5}[0-9a-f]{2}$"
True

The preceding example shows how to create a regular expression to validate a MAC address. This expression leverages the `-match` comparison operator to evaluate whether `00:a0:f8:12:34:56` matches the expression of `^([0-9a-f]{2}:){5}[0-9a-f]{2}$`. You may choose to use the `-cmatch` operator over the `-match` operator as some applications require MAC addresses to be in uppercase. When you break down the expression, it starts by using the anchor of ^ to start evaluating from the beginning. It then uses the grouping construct of `( )` to group the expression of `[0-9a-f]{2}:`.

This expression validates to see whether each character is a valid hexadecimal `[0-9a-f]` value and uses a quantifier to specify only 2 characters per sequence. The expression ends with `:`, which is the separator between each set of values. Proceeding forward, you then use another quantifier of `{5}` to repeat the two hexadecimal characters with a colon at the end 5 times. The final part of the expression is matched from the ending anchor of `$`. The ending anchor validates to see whether each character is a valid hexadecimal `[0-9a-f]` value and uses a quantifier to specify only 2 characters as the ending of the string. When the expression evaluates the string as `00:a0:f8:12:34:56`, it will return `True`. This is a result of the expression seeing 5 sets of two hexadecimal characters, individually followed by colons, and ending with two hexadecimal characters.

The following diagram shows how to validate a UNC path:

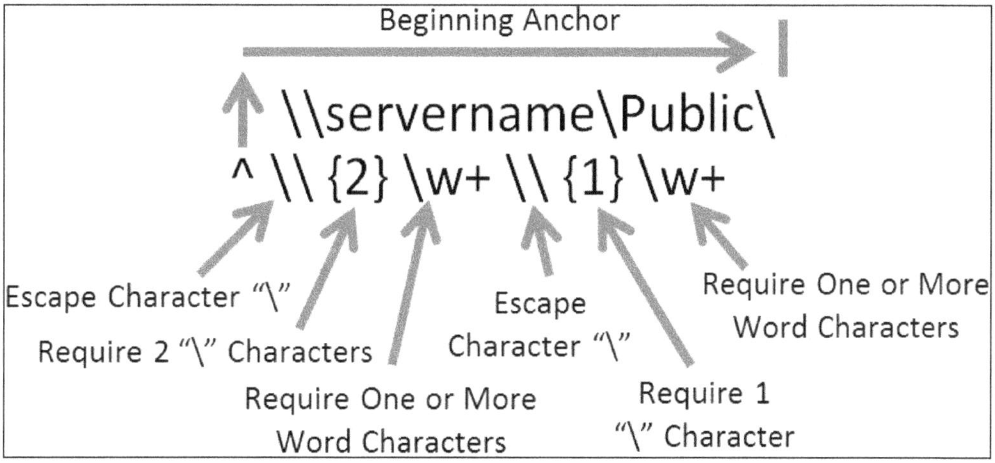

The following syntax is used to validate a UNC path:

```
"\\servername\Public\" -match "^\\{2}\w+\\{1}\w+"
```

The output of this is shown in the following screenshot:

The preceding example displays how to validate a UNC path by leveraging regular expressions. This expression leverages the `-match` comparison operator to evaluate whether `\\servername\Public\` matches the expression of `^\\{2}\w+\\{1}\w+`. You will use the `-match` operator over the `-cmatch` operator as UNC paths are not case-sensitive. When you break down the expression it starts by using the anchor of `^` to start evaluating from the beginning. It then uses the escape character of `\` to escape the backslash character. You then use a quantifier of `{2}` to require two backslashes. The expression will continue reading forward to the `\w+` expression, which will require one or more word characters. You escape the `\` character again followed by the quantifier of `{1}` to only require one backslash this time. Finally, you end the sequence with `\w+\` which requires one or more word characters to follow. When the expression evaluates the string as `\\servername\Public\`, it will return `True`. This is a result of the expression seeing two backslashes and then a set of word characters, followed by another backslash, and more word characters. While this doesn't validate the complete UNC path, it is a quick method to verify that the beginning of the UNC path is correct.

The following diagram shows how to create a number in the **ICANN** format:

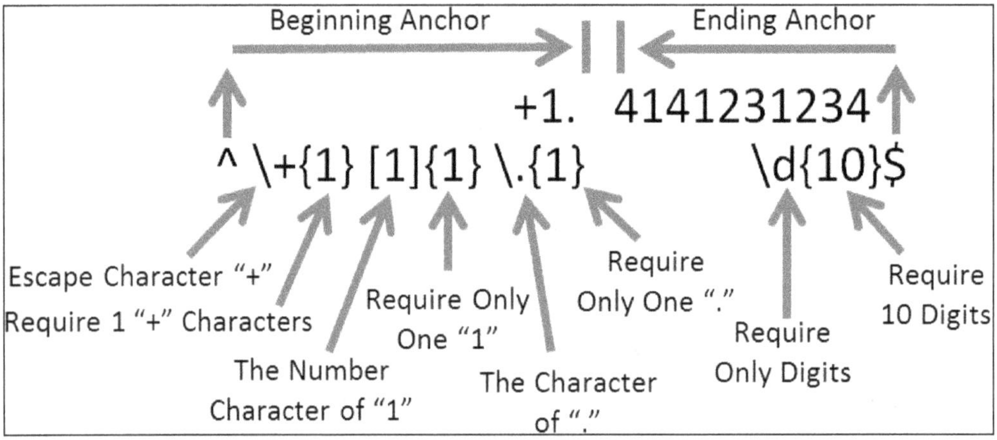

To test a number, the following syntax is used:

```
"+1.4141231234" -cmatch "^\+{1}[1]{1}\.{1}\d{10}$"
```

The output of this is shown in the following screenshot:

```
PS C:\> "+1.4141231234" -cmatch "^\+{1}[1]{1}\.{1}\d{10}$"
True
```

When the **Internet Corporation for Assigned Names and Numbers** (**ICANN**) changed their policy on WHOIS validation and made it mandatory from January 1, 2014, the most notable change was with the formatting of phone numbers. This example displays how to validate numbers for the ICANN standard for a United States number. This expression leverages the `-cmatch` comparison operator to evaluate whether `+1.4141231234` matches the expression of `^\+{1}[1]{1}\.{1}\d{10}$`. When you break down the expression, it starts by using the anchor of `^` to start evaluating from the beginning. It then uses the escape character of `\` to escape the `+` character. You then use a quantifier of `{1}` to require one `+` characters. The expression will continue reading forward to the `[1]{1}` expression which uses a quantifier to require one `1` character. You escape the `.` character followed by the quantifier of `{1}` to only require one `.` character. You then use an ending character of `$` to evaluate the expression of `\d`, which requires all digits, and the quantifier of `{10}`, which makes 10 digits mandatory. When the expression evaluates the string as `+1.4141231234`, it will return `True`. This is a result of the expression seeing the character `+`, followed by number character `1`, a `.` character, and ending with 10 digits.

Summary

This chapter explained the basics of regular expressions and showed how to integrate them with PowerShell. It explained that if you are using regular expressions, you should fully comment on the code to allow other developers to read your expressions easily. This chapter further explained that PowerShell uses the `-match`, `-cmatch`, and `-replace` operators with regular expressions to evaluate criteria for strings. You also saw the most common metacharacters and how to use them in expressions. You also learned how to use grouping constructs, ranges, and qualifiers. This chapter discussed the most common anchors and concluded by providing examples of regular expressions that you may use in your scripts. These examples included a regular expression to validate a MAC address, UNC Path, and an ICANN formatted United States telephone number. In the next chapter, you will explore error and exception handling and find out about techniques for handling errors in your scripts. The next chapter will also leverage the concepts learned in the previous chapters in order to provide robust and reliable scripts.

6

Error and Exception Handling and Testing Code

One of the most important components for creating PowerShell scripts is error and exception handling. Error and exception handling is often a forgotten component of scripting because it's common to feel that the code should always execute linearly and in an implicit fashion. While small scripts may provide low risk opportunities to not use error and exception handling, it is still recommended to use some level of error and exception handling. This is due to the common practice of taking the small scripts and using them as starting points for more complex scripts. The more complex you build your scripts, the higher the probability of failure and unexpected results.

In this chapter, you will learn the following concepts:

- Error and exception handling with parameters
- Error and exception handling with `Try/Catch`
- Error and exception handling with legacy exception handling
- Methodologies for testing code
- Where to test code

Utilization of strategies for testing code is an equally important component while you are developing scripts. While most developers test their code when they develop, testing the entire solution and validating the scripts are often forgotten. The more time you put into testing scenarios, the more reliable your scripts will be while they're being used in the environment. While there are many different testing strategies, any strategy is better than no strategy at all.

PowerShell has two different types of errors which are terminating and non-terminating. Terminating errors will stop the script from executing further commands. The non-terminating errors will call the `write-error` cmdlet, print an error to the screen, and continue. You will learn how to handle these different types of errors in this chapter.

Error and exception handling – parameters

PowerShell offers several different options to achieve error and exception handling. The most popular method used to catch non-terminating errors is bypassing error and exception handling parameters while executing PowerShell cmdlets. If a cmdlet detects a non-terminating error during runtime, the PowerShell **Common Language Runtime** (**CLR**) has the ability to store the error information in variables. You can then call the error variable and execute other actions based on the contents of the `$error` variable.

The PowerShell parameters that handle error and exceptions are `-WarningAction` and `-ErrorAction`. When an issue occurs with your script, the PowerShell CLR will reference the `-ErrorAction` and `-WarningAction` arguments to determine what the next step for the script is.

There are five actions that are supported within PowerShell. The `SilentlyContinue` action will suppress the error and warning information, populate the error variables, and continue. The `Ignore` action will suppress the warning and error message and not populate any specified variables. The `Continue` action will write to the screen the warning and error information and attempt to continue with the script. The `Stop` action will write the warning and error information stop execution of the script. The `Inquire` action will prompt the end user if they want to `Halt`, `Suspend`, `Accept the Error`, or `Accept All Errors`.

The two global variables that you can set so that they provide a default error and warning action for your script are `$errorActionPreference` and `$warningActionPreference`. When you set these variables to one of the above actions, it will always default to this action for errors and warnings. By default, PowerShell is set to `Continue`, however, you can set the `$errorActionPreference` and `$warningActionPreference` to different values for different default actions.

For the warning and error actions that can place error details in a variable, the -`ErrorVariable` and `-WarningVariable` parameters can be used in conjunction with a variable name to store the error information. Proper use of these parameters would look like `-ErrorVariable err` and `-WarningVariable war`. Subsequently, the error information would be available in the `$err` variable, and the warning information would be placed in the `$war` variable.

To use cmdlet error handling, do the following action:

```
Function serviceExample($svcName) {
Get-service $svcName -ErrorAction SilentlyContinue -ErrorVariable err

    If ($err) {
      Write-host "Error! Error Details: $err"
        return
    }

    Write-host "Successfully Retrieved Service Information for $svcName.
"
}
ServiceExample "Windows Update"
Write-host ""
ServiceExample "Does Not Exist"
```

The output of this is shown in the following screenshot:

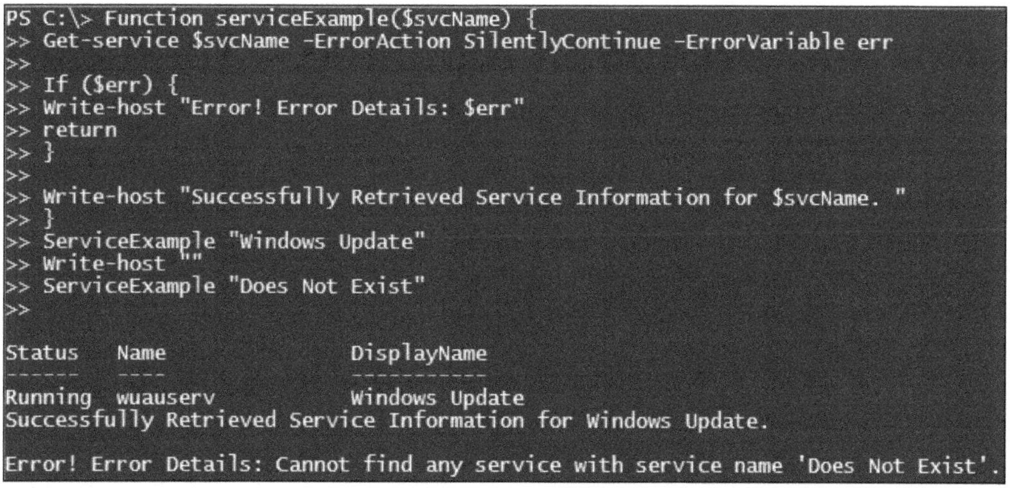
PS C:\> Function serviceExample($svcName) {
>> Get-service $svcName -ErrorAction SilentlyContinue -ErrorVariable err
>>
>> If ($err) {
>> Write-host "Error! Error Details: $err"
>> return
>> }
>>
>> Write-host "Successfully Retrieved Service Information for $svcName. "
>> }
>> ServiceExample "Windows Update"
>> Write-host ""
>> ServiceExample "Does Not Exist"
>>
Status Name DisplayName
------ ---- -----------
Running wuauserv Windows Update
Successfully Retrieved Service Information for Windows Update.
Error! Error Details: Cannot find any service with service name 'Does Not Exist'.

The preceding script displays the best method to leverage the built-in cmdlet support for error and exception handling. In this example, you create a new function named `serviceExample`. You also allow for the argument of `$svcName`. When you enter the script, you leverage the `get-service` cmdlet to query the server to see whether the data within the `$svcName` variable is a service on the system. You also pass the `-ErrorAction SilentlyContinue` to suppress messages on the screen and continue. You then specify `-ErrorVariable err` to pass any error details into the `$err` variable. If the `$err` variable has data in it or is implied true, the script will write to the console `Error! Error Details: $err` followed by `return`, which will exit out of the function. If the `$err` variable doesn't have any error details, it will proceed to write to the console `Successfully Retrieved Service Information for $svcName`. In this example, you use the `serviceExample` function to query if the `Windows Update` service exists. You will determine that the service does exist and the console will print the information about the service in addition to printing `Successfully Retrieved Service Information for Windows Update`.

You will then use the `serviceExample` function again to query if the `Does Not Exist` service exists. You will determine that the service does not exist and the script will write to the console the message `Error! Error Details: Cannot find any service with service name 'Does Not Exist'`.

> When you are using `-ErrorVariable` and `-WarningVariable`, it is common to want to declare a variable name including the dollar sign ($). It is important to remember that you need to declare what the variable name will be but omit the dollar sign ($). PowerShell will create the variable anew or reuse an existing variable and then populate the error data within it.

Error and exception handling – Try/Catch

One of the more popular error and exception handling techniques is leveraging `Try/Catch` methodology. The `Try/Catch` block is used for handling terminating errors and has a very simple structure. You first use the `Try { }` section of code and then use `Catch { }` to catch any errors and perform actions based on the errors. In the instance that you catch an error, you can access the exception object by declaring `$_`. The `$_` refers to what is in the current pipeline. Since an error occurred during the `Try` sequence, the data in the pipeline is the actual error information.

To use the `Try/Catch` block, do the following action:

```
Try {
    1+ "abcd"
}
Catch {
  Write-host "Error Processing the Command: $_"
}
Write-host ""
Write-host "Attempting to Add a String without Exception Handling:"
1+ "abcd"
```

The output of this is shown in the following screenshot:

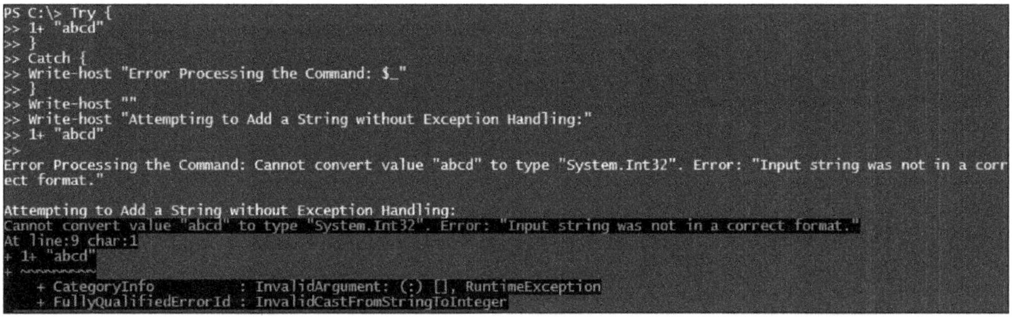
PS C:\> Try {
>> 1+ "abcd"
>> }
>> Catch {
>> Write-host "Error Processing the Command: $_"
>> }
>> Write-host ""
>> Write-host "Attempting to Add a String without Exception Handling:"
>> 1+ "abcd"
>>
Error Processing the Command: Cannot convert value "abcd" to type "System.Int32". Error: "Input string was not in a corr
ect format."
Attempting to Add a String without Exception Handling:
Cannot convert value "abcd" to type "System.Int32". Error: "Input string was not in a correct format."
At line:9 char:1
+ 1+ "abcd"
+ ~~~~~~~~~
+ CategoryInfo : InvalidArgument: (:) [], RuntimeException
+ FullyQualifiedErrorId : InvalidCastFromStringToInteger

The preceding example shows how you have the ability to leverage the `Try/Catch` block during runtime. In this example, you enter the `Try` block by declaring `Try {`. You then attempt to add a number value to a string. Since these are two different data types, the action will throw an exception. The `Catch` block is then declared with `Catch {`. It will handle the error and write the `Error Processing the Command: $_` error to the console. `$_` is replaced with the current pipeline, which in this case is the error message. The console will read `Error Processing the Command: Cannot convert value "abcd" to type "System.Int32". Error: "Input string was not in a correct format."`.

In the second part of this script, you write a line separator with `write-host ""` and write to the console `Attempting to Add a String without Exception Handling:`. You then attempt to add a number value to a string outside of the `Try/Catch` block. When you perform this outside of the `Try/Catch` block, you still receive the same error details. In addition to this, you see all of the other properties associated with the exception that was thrown. From what you see on the screen, when you leverage the `Try/Catch` block, it will much more gracefully handle the exception.

Error and exception handling –Try/Catch with parameters

One of the best practice techniques for error and exception handling is to combine the use of the `Try/Catch` block and cmdlet parameters. This is due to PowerShell being able to gracefully handle terminating and non-terminating error scenarios. For instance, if you execute a line of code that throws a warning message but doesn't generate a terminating error, you can catch the warning and perform actions based on that warning. In that same instance, if the syntax of the cmdlet is incorrect, the `Try/Catch` block will be able to handle the terminating error due to the cmdlet throwing the exception and the catch method handling the terminating error. When you leverage both the handling techniques, you have a more robust solution to exception handling.

To use cmdlet error handling with the `Try/Catch` block, do the following action:

```
Try {
    Get-process "Doesn't Exist" -ErrorAction SilentlyContinue     -
ErrorVariable err
}
Catch {
  Write-host "Try/Catch Exception Details: $_"
}
if ($err) {
  Write-host "Cmdlet Error Handling Error Details: $err"
}
```

The output of this is shown in the following screenshot:

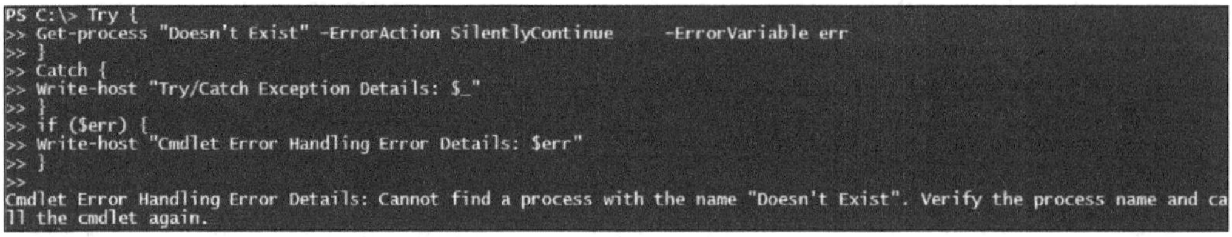
PS C:\> Try {
>> Get-process "Doesn't Exist" -ErrorAction SilentlyContinue   -ErrorVariable err
>> }
>> Catch {
>> Write-host "Try/Catch Exception Details: $_"
>> }
>> if ($err) {
>> Write-host "Cmdlet Error Handling Error Details: $err"
>> }
>>
Cmdlet Error Handling Error Details: Cannot find a process with the name "Doesn't Exist". Verify the process name and ca
ll the cmdlet again.

The preceding example displays the proper method used to incorporate both the exception handling techniques with the `get-service` cmdlet. You first start by calling the `Try` block in use with the `get-service` cmdlet to retrieve information about a service named `Doesn't Exist`. You then tell the cmdlet to `SilentlyContinue` as `ErrorAction` and store the error details in a variable named `Err`. You then declare the `Catch` block, which will catch the output of any errors that occur during the execution of `get-service`. If an exception occurs, write to the console `Try/Catch Exception Details: $_`. You also create an `If` statement "if the `$err` variable contains data, write to the console `Cmdlet Error Handling Error Details: $err`, where `$err` contains the error information.

When you execute the script, you see that the `Catch` method doesn't catch the error message from the `get-service` cmdlet. This is due to the error being a non-terminating error, and so it doesn't invoke the `Try/Catch` block. When you run the script however, the cmdlet properly handles the error and places the error details in the `$err` variable. The script prints the message `Cmdlet Error Handling Error Details: Cannot find a process with the name "Doesn't Exist". Verify the process name and call the cmdlet again.` to the console.

Error and exception handling – legacy exception handling

When you are developing your scripts, you may run into command-line tools that don't have a built-in exception handling function. This is common for third-party tools that only output the debugging information to the screen, and do not properly handle the exception. One of the most common methods to handle legacy command-based applications is by the use of variables. When you execute a command, you have the ability to check the output from that command. If the output is something other than what you expect, you have the ability to throw an exception.

For example, the `netsh` command has the ability to add firewall rules to your system. When you successfully add a firewall rule to a system, the response to the console is `Ok.`. By leveraging a variable, you have the ability to catch the response from this command. If the response is anything other than `Ok.`, you have the ability to write to the console the data contained in the variable.

> To add a firewall rule on a system using the `netsh` command, you need to open PowerShell with the **Run as Administrator** option.

To catch a legacy command, you can perform the following action:

```
$err = netsh advfirewall firewall add rule name="Test Allow 12345"
protocol=TCP dir=out localport=12345 action=Allow
If ($err -notlike "Ok.") {
  Write-host "Error Processing netsh command: $err"
}
Write-host "Data Contained in the Variable Err is $err"
```

The output of this is shown in the following screenshot:

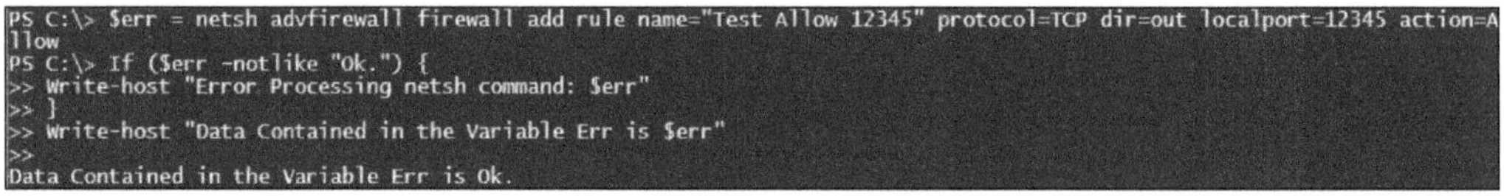
PS C:\> $err = netsh advfirewall firewall add rule name="Test Allow 12345" protocol=TCP dir=out localport=12345 action=A
llow
PS C:\> If ($err -notlike "Ok.") {
>> Write-host "Error Processing netsh command: $err"
>> }
>> Write-host "Data Contained in the Variable Err is $err"
>>
Data Contained in the Variable Err is Ok.

The preceding script shows how to properly catch the output of a firewall rule addition from a legacy command-line tool of `netsh`. You first start the script by declaring a variable which is used to capture the output from the `netsh` command. PowerShell will then process the command of `netsh advfirewall firewall add rule name="Test Allow 12345" protocol=TCP dir=out localport=12345 action=Allow`. The output of that command is set in the `$err` variable. You then create the `IF` statement to throw an exception if the `$err` variable is not like the output of `Ok.`. In this instance, the command is successful and the `$err` variable is set to `Ok.`. At the end of the script, you then write to the console `Data Contained in the Variable Err is $err`, where `$err` is the output from the `netsh` command. The result that is printed to the console is `Data Contained in the Variable Err is Ok.`.

To catch a legacy command, perform the following action:

```
$err = netsh advfirewall firewall add rule name="Test Allow 12345"
protocol=TCP dir=out localport=1234567 action=Allow
If ($err -notlike "Ok.") {
  Write-host "Error Processing netsh command: $err"
}
```

The output of this is shown in the following screenshot:

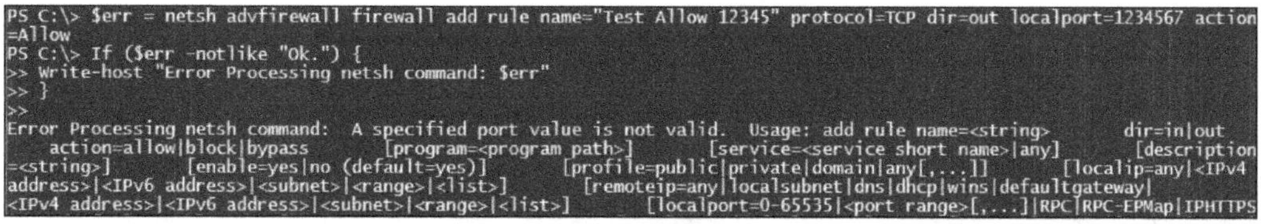
PS C:\> $err = netsh advfirewall firewall add rule name="Test Allow 12345" protocol=TCP dir=out localport=1234567 action
=Allow
PS C:\> If ($err -notlike "Ok.") {
>> Write-host "Error Processing netsh command: $err"
>> }
>>
Error Processing netsh command: A specified port value is not valid. Usage: add rule name=<string> dir=in|out
action=allow|block|bypass [program=<program path>] [service=<service short name>|any] [description
=<string>] [enable=yes|no (default=yes)] [profile=public|private|domain|any[,...]] [localip=any|<IPv4
address>|<IPv6 address>|<subnet>|<range>|<list>] [remoteip=any|localsubnet|dns|dhcp|wins|defaultgateway|
<IPv4 address>|<IPv6 address>|<subnet>|<range>|<list>] [localport=0-65535|<port range>[,...]|RPC|RPC-EPMap|IPHTTPS

In this script, you attempt to perform a `netsh` command to add an additional firewall rule. This time, however, you try to add a rule with an invalid port number of `1234567`. When the `netsh` command processes the command of `netsh advfirewall firewall add rule name="Test Allow 12345" protocol=TCP dir=out localport=1234567 action=Allow`, it throws an exception to the console. This exception is caught in the `$err` variable. When the command evaluates the `IF` statement, it determines that `$err` is not like `Ok.`. The script will then print to the screen `Error Processing netsh command: $err`, where `$err` is an array of strings comprising the error message.

When the error message outputs to the screen, you will see that the full exception is an array of strings that is very lengthy. This is a result of the `netsh` command providing detailed help information inclusive of the error message. Fortunately, when any command-line tool outputs multiple lines of text, the `$err` variable is automatically converted to an array. This means that each line in the error message becomes a different item in an array object, and you can reference these individual lines for error information.

To print the legacy error array to the screen, perform the following action:

```
$err = netsh advfirewall firewall add rule name="Test Allow 12345"
protocol=TCP dir=out localport=1234567 action=Allow
If ($err -notlike "Ok.") {
  Write-host "Array Line 0: " $err[0]
  Write-host "Array Line 1: " $err[1]
  Write-host "Array Line 2: " $err[2]
  Write-host "Array Line 3: " $err[3]
  Write-host ""
  Write-host "Error Processing netsh command:" $err[1]
}
```

The output of this is shown in the following screenshot:

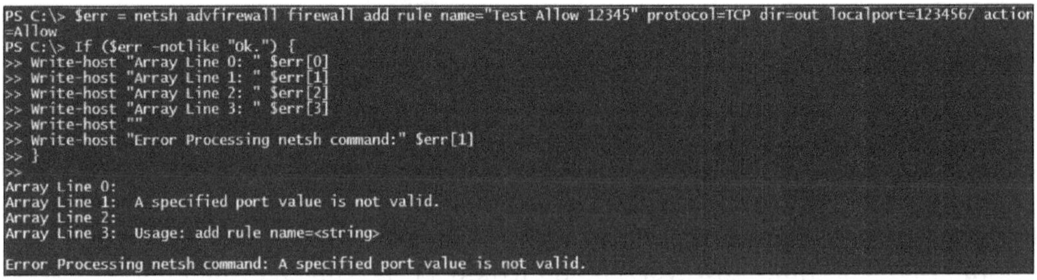

```
PS C:\> $err = netsh advfirewall firewall add rule name="Test Allow 12345" protocol=TCP dir=out localport=1234567 action
=Allow
PS C:\> If ($err -notlike "Ok.") {
>> Write-host "Array Line 0: " $err[0]
>> Write-host "Array Line 1: " $err[1]
>> Write-host "Array Line 2: " $err[2]
>> Write-host "Array Line 3: " $err[3]
>> Write-host ""
>> Write-host "Error Processing netsh command:" $err[1]
>> }
>>
Array Line 0:
Array Line 1:  A specified port value is not valid.
Array Line 2:
Array Line 3:  Usage: add rule name=<string>

Error Processing netsh command: A specified port value is not valid.
```

The preceding example provides a deeper look into how PowerShell automatically converts the `$err` variable into an array. The conversion occurs after the `netsh` command writes more than one line of exception information into the `$err` array.

You will see that the first value `$err[0]` contains blank information. The second line `$err[1]` contains useable error details with the message `A specified port value is not valid.`. The third line `$err[2]` contains blank information. The fourth line that you output provides the start of the detailed help information. As the second line `$err[1]` contains the useful error information, you can print to the screen the message `Error Processing netsh command:" $err[1]`. This will write `Error Processing netsh command: A specified port value is not valid.` to the console.

Methodologies for testing code

When you are creating PowerShell Scripts, it is imperative that you test your code along the way. While there are many different development standards which you can follow such as Scrum and Agile, they all have the same premise of "test often". This section will explore recommendations for testing your code as you are developing it so that you can provide more reliable scripts.

Testing the –WhatIf argument

PowerShell offers the ability to test the cmdlet's code without actually running them. This is done by the use of the `-WhatIf` argument. The `-WhatIf` argument will simulate the action that the cmdlet will take on a system without actually executing the command itself. This can assist you in determining if you have the right syntax for a command. This can also benefit you if you're getting large content from a file and need to verify that the individual items in the file won't crash your script.

To use the `-WhatIf` argument, perform the following action:

```
Get-service "Windows Update"
Stop-service "Windows Update" -WhatIf
Get-service "Windows Update"
```

The output of this is shown in the following screenshot:

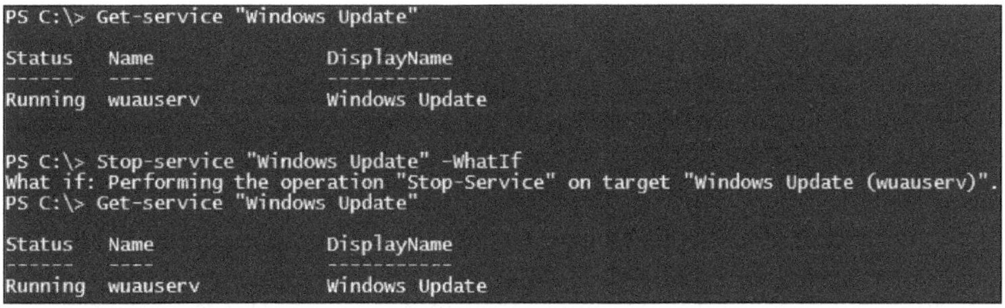
PS C:\> Get-service "Windows Update"
Status Name DisplayName
Running wuauserv Windows Update
PS C:\> Stop-service "Windows Update" -WhatIf
What if: Performing the operation "Stop-Service" on target "Windows Update (wuauserv)".
PS C:\> Get-service "Windows Update"
Status Name DisplayName
Running wuauserv Windows Update

The preceding script displays the proper use of the `-Whatif` argument. You first start by calling the `get-service` cmdlet to retrieve information about the Windows Update Service. From running this command you determine that the Windows Update Service is currently in a running state. You then test execute the cmdlet of `stop-service` with `Windows Update` and the `-WhatIf` argument. Normally, the `Stop-service` command would attempt to stop the service. Instead, it outputs to the console `What if: Performing the operation "Stop-Service" on Target "Windows Update (wuaserv)"`. When you call `get-service` again, you determine that the command didn't actually run; rather it successfully tested the command.

Testing the frequency

It is important to test your code as you are developing it. When you complete a small section of code, it is recommended to test that section of code independent of the entire script. The following is a list of items that should trigger the testing of your code:

- **Creation of a function or method**: When you complete a function or a method, you should always test it separately from the entire script. During scripting runtime, when you call a function, PowerShell will jump to that function or method in your script. After execution, the script will jump back to the current position in the script. The movement between the declared function and method, and the current position in the script, may cause issues with processing the subsequent code in your script. This is because the output from the functions and the methods may not be expected for subsequent steps in your script. Testing your newly created functions and methods independently and inline are essential to coding success.

- **Changes to container names in your script**: There are times where you may change the name of a variable or an array to better describe what the container is storing. When you change container names, there are instances where you might misspell or forget to update one of the containers in the full script. This is why upon changing the naming of a variable or array, you should test the script to ensure proper execution.
- **New or updated datasets**: One of the most forgotten testing requirements is when you are leveraging a new or updated dataset such as a CSV or XML file. While your PowerShell code may not have changed, the application that generated the dataset may have values that you didn't anticipate. This could be due to the the dataset being corrupt or incomplete, or due to new values that you are not expecting in that dataset. This is why it is recommended that you test after you update a dataset.
- **Completion of a script**: When you complete a script, you should test the script in totality. While each of the individual parts of the script may execute successfully, the script may not execute in its entirety. This is why it is recommended to test the full script prior to running it on production systems.

Hit testing containers

As you are developing your scripts, it is common to create a large number of variables and arrays. As you are creating your scripts, it is also common to reuse these variables and arrays in the same script. When you are working with your scripts, it is recommended to test each of these containers to ensure that they have the data you are expecting.

To create an array and test proper formatting of the container, do the following action:

```
$array = "user.name", "joe.user", "jane.doe"
$array
```

The output of this is shown in the following screenshot:

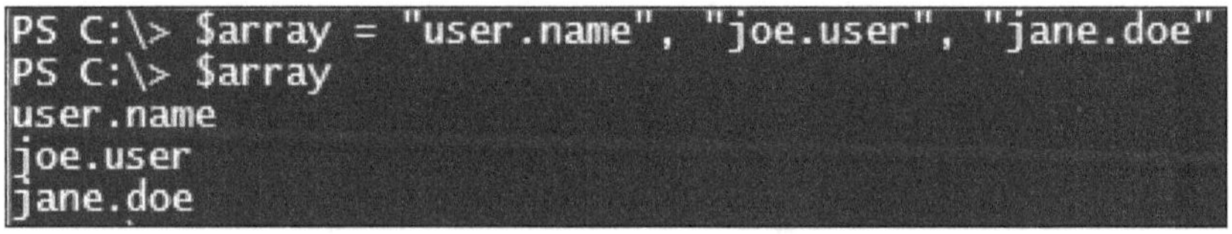

In the preceding example, you create an array `$array` full of usernames and test that the output of `$array` displays the usernames properly. You should open a PowerShell window and call the `$array` array to ensure the array is populated properly with usernames. This will help minimize the risk of your array being populated with erroneous information.

To view the number of services on your system, do the following action:

```
$services = get-service
$service.count
$services.count
```

The output of this is shown in the following screenshot:

PS C:\> $services = get-service
PS C:\> $service.count
0
PS C:\> $services.count
188

Another technique to test containers is through the use of the `count` method. When you are grabbing a large dataset from a system, you should test and count the number of items in the dataset as you are working with them. The preceding script displays why it's important to use the `count` method to test your script. You first start by declaring a variable of `$services` and by using the `get-service` cmdlet to gather all of the services on the system. You then erroneously try to count a variable named `$service` with the use of `$service.count`. The result returns `0`. Since this is obviously not the variable you used to catch the `get-service` object, you can now dig deeper into the script to determine your error. You will see that you executed the `count` method on the variable named `$services`, and it returns `204` services.

Hit testing becomes more important when you are leveraging external data sources such as CSV or XML files as the margin for error becomes greater. This is why it is recommended that you hit test and validate your variables and arrays as you go along to ensure the quality of your scripts.

Don't test in production

Testing your code on production systems is something that should never be done. The truth is, however, that many people still do test their code on production systems. Whether it is the lack of a testing platform or tight timelines, most people ignore the level of risk to complete the task at hand.

If it is absolutely necessary that you need to test your code on production systems, there are a few things that you can do to lower the overall risk:

- **Create an isolated environment to test**: On the production systems, if possible, create a segregated zone against which you can execute the PowerShell script. While you may still be leveraging production systems, you minimize the impact to the global system by segregating the script execution. For example, if you are creating a script to migrate a large quantity of users into Active Directory, create a test organizational unit into which you can populate the new users. This will minimize the risks without impacting production organizational units.
- **Clone your production system**: Virtualization provides the ability to quickly clone and create new virtual systems. If your production system is virtual, it might be possible to clone the production system and use the cloned system for testing. You also may have the ability to isolate this cloned system to a test environment to ensure that if something doesn't function properly, you don't impact the rest of your environment.
- **Leverage the -WhatIf argument**: Before you execute the commands on the production systems, try to leverage the `-WhatIf` argument. This will potentially vet out issues that will occur during the execution of your scripts.
- **Utilize write-debug**: In situations where you are running command-line tools that are not PowerShell cmdlets, you can leverage `write-debug`. If you put `write-debug` with the command-line tool parameters in quotations, you have the ability to print to the console the full syntax for the execution of that command-line tool. This will ensure that all variables are being populated properly for execution of that command. This will help you vet out any misspelled variables and ensure the command syntax is correct.
- **Use a small dataset for testing**: If you are executing a script that uses a dataset for execution (such as a list of users), it is recommended to break off a part of that dataset and use that small section for testing. This will ensure that if something doesn't function properly during execution, you will minimize its impact on the production systems.

Summary

This chapter displays how to properly incorporate error and exception handling in your scripts. You explored how to leverage built-in cmdlet parameters for error and exception handling, and how to work with warnings and errors in your scripts. You also learned the `Try/Catch` block and how to use that to catch errors outside of what cmdlets can handle. You also learned how to use the cmdlet parameter for error and exception handling in conjunction with the `Try/Catch` block to provide robust solutions for catching issues in your scripts.

This chapter also explored methods with which you can work with legacy command-line tools and catch error messages from these tools. You learned that while the legacy tools may not have robust exception handling, PowerShell is dynamic enough to catch the errors and parse it for use in your scripts. You learned that PowerShell will automatically take multiple lines from an error message from a legacy command-line tool and place them as new items in an array.

Finally, this chapter ended with offering recommendations and methodologies for testing your PowerShell code. You learned that PowerShell has a `-WhatIf` argument which allows you to test the output from PowerShell cmdlets without actually executing them. You discovered that there are four main triggers available to test your scripts. These can be used after the creation of a function or a method, after changing container names in your script, updates in existing datasets or new datasets, and after the completion of a script. You also explored that you should always test your containers as you are building them as it will reduce typographic errors in the container names themselves. You completed this chapter by learning that you shouldn't test your code on production systems. If you need to, however, you have the ability to lower the risk by creating an isolated environment, cloning production systems, leveraging the `-WhatIf` argument, utilizing `write-host` and `write-debug`, and using small datasets for testing. In the next chapter, you will dive into the process of remotely executing PowerShell commands on systems. It will show you how to perform session-based remote management.

7
Session-based Remote Management

When you are developing your scripts, you may run into situations where you need to configure remote systems. While a lot of command-line programs provide the ability to execute remote commands, PowerShell provides **Common Information Model (CIM)** cmdlets allowing the scripts to be executed on remote systems over a session. The CIM cmdlet brokers the communications which provides improved performance and reliability while executing a group of commands on multiple remote systems.

Microsoft's implementation of the CIM cmdlets was derived from the need to communicate with both Windows and non Windows systems from a singular command base. Microsoft initially created **Web Services for Management (WS-Man)**, which allows communications to non Windows systems. This was problematic due to the protocol being SOAP-based and made it difficult to quickly create PowerShell scripts to communicate with these systems.

With the release of PowerShell 2.0, Microsoft developed **Windows Remote Management (WinRM)**, which created a wrapper around the WS-Man protocol known as CIM cmdlets. This greatly simplifies the communication structure and reduces the size of your scripts. CIM cmdlets communicate over port number `5985` for HTTP and `5986` for HTTPS. This is one of the biggest benefits over **Remote Procedure Call (RPC)**-based programs, due to the large quantity of upper port ranges that are required to be opened for RPC communications.

In this chapter you will learn the following concepts:

- Utilizing CIM sessions
- Creating a session
- Creating a session with session options
- Using sessions for remote management
- Removing sessions

> To follow the examples in this book, it is recommended that you start by executing the code on two to three systems that are on the same domain and same subnet and have the firewalls disabled. You will also need to start the **Windows Remote Management Service** (**WS-Management**) service. The commands should be executed with the administrator accounts, and all systems should have Windows Management Framework 4.0 for PowerShell 4.0. This will reduce the complexities around permissions and port configurations.

Utilizing CIM sessions

The `new-cimsession` cmdlet leverages two different protocols for communication with local and remote systems. Communications to the local system leverages the **Distributed Component Object Model** (**DCOM**) protocol, and remote sessions leverage the WS-Man protocol. Remote systems will need to have port `5985` for HTTP and `5986` for HTTPS opened on their firewalls to enable proper communications over WinRM. While DCOM is the default communication protocol for a local system, you can use the `- CIMSessionOptions` parameter to force WS-Man communications.

In addition to opening firewall ports, you also need to enable the WS-Management Service on the system that you are executing the commands on and the system you are remoting to as well. On most systems, this service will be set to "manual" and will not be in a running state.

The last requirement for proper communications is configuring the WinRM service. Before configuring these options, you should be aware of the security implications. When you allow all systems or a range of IPs to leverage the WinRM service, you may be putting your system at risk. Always choose options that will enable the least amount of privilege necessary to complete the task.

One method to manually configure the WinRM service includes performing the following steps:

1. Configure the Local Account Token Filter Policy in the registry. This is done by setting the `HKEY_LOCAL_MACHINE\SOFTWARE\Microsoft\Windows\CurrentVersion\Policies\system\LocalAccountTokenFilterPolicy` key equal to `1`.
2. Enable Kerberos for use with the WinRM service. This is done with the command of:

   ```
   winrm set winrm/config/service/auth @{Kerberos="true"}
   ```

3. Create a listener to accept requests on an IP address on the system via HTTP or HTTPS, as shown here:
   - For HTTP this is performed through this:

     ```
     winrm create winrm/config/Listener?Address=*+Transport=HTTP
     ```

   - For HTTPS this is performed through this:

     ```
     winrm create winrm/config/Listener?Address=*+Transport=HTTPS
     @{Hostname="Host Computer";CertificateThumbprint=" 40-digit
     hex string thumbprint"}
     ```

The syntax for both of these commands will allow WinRM communications on all IP addresses on the local system. If you want to restrict to only specific interfaces / IP addresses, replace the `*` with an IP address.

You may also choose to configure an Active Directory group policy that will enable the use of WinRM in your environment. The primary Windows Remote Management and Windows Remote Shell policies can be found under Windows Components and Administrative Templates in group policy.

An alternative method to configure a system for WinRM is by leveraging the `set-WSManQuickConfig` cmdlet. This configures all of the required settings from a single command. While this may be convenient, its down side is that it automatically configures less restrictive policies than what can be set manually. It is common for people to use a blend of the automated configuration, manual configuration, and group policy configuration.

To leverage the quick configuration, do the following action:

```
Set-WsManQuickConfig
```

The output of this is shown in the following screenshot:

```
PS C:\> Set-WSManQuickConfig

WinRM Quick Configuration
Running the Set-WSManQuickConfig command has significant security implications, as it enables remote management through
 the WinRM service on this computer.
This command:
 1. Checks whether the WinRM service is running. If the WinRM service is not running, the service is started.
 2. Sets the WinRM service startup type to automatic.
 3. Creates a listener to accept requests on any IP address. By default, the transport is HTTP.
 4. Enables a firewall exception for WS-Management traffic.
 5. Enables Kerberos and Negotiate service authentication.
Do you want to enable remote management through the WinRM service on this computer?
[Y] Yes  [N] No  [S] Suspend  [?] Help (default is "Y"): Y
WinRM is already set up to receive requests on this computer.
WinRM has been updated for remote management.
Created a WinRM listener on HTTP://* to accept WS-Man requests to any IP on this machine.
WinRM firewall exception enabled.
Configured LocalAccountTokenFilterPolicy to grant administrative rights remotely to local users.
```

The preceding command displays the quick configuration of WinRM using a PowerShell window running as Administrator. When you enter the `set-WSManQuickConfig` command and select `Y` as the option, the cmdlet will automatically configure the system for using WinRM. The cmdlet will check the WinRm Service and ensure that it's running, set the startup of the service to automatic, create a listener for all IP addresses assigned to the system over HTTP, enable the firewall exceptions, set up the computer for Kerberos, and negotiate service authentication.

> It is important to note that while using `Set-WsManQuickConfig`, the cmdlet requires that all network interfaces should not be in *Public Mode*. The interface will need to be set to either *Work Mode* or *Home Mode*. The cmdlet will throw an error message that the WinRM Firewall exception will not work on public networks. To get around this issue, disable the network interface that is set to "public" and try to run the command again. This is by design a security precaution to ensure that people on the public interfaces don't attempt to remotely manage your system in an unauthorized manner.

An alternative to enable WinRM on a system is to leverage the `Enable-PSRemoting` cmdlet. This cmdlet will configure the necessary components on a client machine to receive commands. There are several common parameters that can be used in conjunction with the `Enable-PSRemoting` cmdlet, which include the `-SkipNetworkProfileCheck` parameter which skips the *Public Mode* check. You may also leverage the `-force` parameter which suppresses all prompts while enabling WinRM on a system.

If you want to disable WS-Management on a system, you can leverage the `disable-PSremoting` cmdlet. This also accepts the `-force` parameter to suppress all prompts while disabling WinRM on a system.

To leverage the `Enable-PSRemoting` CMDlet, do the following action:

```
Enable-PSRemoting -SkipNetworkProfileCheck -Force
Disable-PSRemoting -force
```

The output of this is shown in the following screenshot:

```
PS C:\> Enable-PSRemoting -SkipNetworkProfileCheck -Force
WinRM is already set up to receive requests on this computer.
WinRM is already set up for remote management on this computer.
PS C:\> Disable-PSRemoting -force
WARNING: Disabling the session configurations does not undo all the changes made by the Enable-PSRemoting or
Enable-PSSessionConfiguration cmdlet. You might have to manually undo the changes by following these steps:
    1. Stop and disable the WinRM service.
    2. Delete the listener that accepts requests on any IP address.
    3. Disable the firewall exceptions for WS-Management communications.
    4. Restore the value of the LocalAccountTokenFilterPolicy to 0, which restricts remote access to members of the
Administrators group on the computer.
```

The preceding example displays how to enable and disable `PSRemoting` on a system. You first start by calling `Enable-PSRemoting` with the `-SkipNetworkProfileCheck` and `-Force` parameters. As shown in this example, the `Enable-PSRemoting` cmdlet can detect that WinRM is partially configured. In this case, it will only enable the components that are required for the service to start working properly. After executing this command, WinRM is ready to start accepting commands over WinRM.

In the second part of this example, you leverage the `Disable-PSRemoting` cmdlet with the `-Force` trigger to disable WinRM. After executing the command, WinRM will no longer accept commands on a system.

> After leveraging the `Disable-PSRemoting` cmdlet , you may still need to manually disable other components of WinRM to fully disable it on a system. To do this, you can reverse the manual configuration settings described earlier, which will disable the remaining components that the `Disable-PSRemoting` cmdlet doesn't disable.

Creating a session

When you first want to establish a connection with a local or remote system, you have to create a new session. The `new-cimsession` cmdlet provides the ability to create a new session with these resources. After you create the session, all communications leveraging the CIM session to the remote systems are tunnelled through this RPC session.

To create a new CIM session, do the following action:

```
new-cimsession
```

The output of this is shown in the following screenshot:

PS C:\> new-cimsession
Id : 1
Name : CimSession1
InstanceId : eb369bdd-9c9d-4c2f-852c-801165e86542
ComputerName : localhost
Protocol : DCOM

The preceding example displays how to create a new CIM session. You first create a session by calling just the `new-cimsession` cmdlet. You will see that the session is assigned `ID`, `Name`, and `InstanceID`. The `ID` is an incremental quantifier attribute that can be referenced to execute commands with that specific session. This typically represents the number of CIM sessions that you've created in that instance of the PowerShell command window. Subsequently, you can also reference the session by its `Name` attribute which provides a clear text way to reference a session. The `InstanceID` attribute is generated upon creation of the cmdlet. The `InstanceID` attribute is unique to only this session. The `ComputerName` attribute will reference what systems are connected to that session. The `Protocol` attribute displays that it is leveraging the `DCOM` protocol for local communications.

If you want to create a session with a specific computer to have a connection with that, you can leverage the `-computername` parameter. This allows you to create sessions to one or multiple systems separated by commas. You also have the ability to create a clear text name for the cmdlet. By leveraging the `-name` parameter, you have the ability to name the group of session in a friendly manner.

To create a new CIM session with multiple systems, do the following action:

```
new-cimsession -computername Localhost,localhost,localhost -name
LocalSessions
```

The output of this is shown in the following screenshot:

```
PS C:\> new-cimsession -computername Localhost,localhost,localhost -name LocalSessions

Id           : 1
Name         : LocalSessions
InstanceId   : 1a242023-7f4d-4d65-b2c6-60731c1a5178
ComputerName : localhost
Protocol     : WSMAN

Id           : 2
Name         : LocalSessions
InstanceId   : bf308272-58f3-4f4b-abde-7a73ddfeeb52
ComputerName : Localhost
Protocol     : WSMAN

Id           : 3
Name         : LocalSessions
InstanceId   : 86b9c4d4-046d-4ff7-ba0a-ac70a5718c85
ComputerName : localhost
Protocol     : WSMAN
```

In this example, you leverage the `new-cimsession` cmdlet to create three sessions. By leveraging the `-computername` parameter, you create three remote sessions with three computers named `localhost`. As you are calling remote computer names by utilizing the `-computername` parameter, the default protocol is `WSMAN` instead of `DCOM`. By calling the `-name` parameter, you are able to assign the group of sessions a single session name to work with the full group of sessions. You will also see that each session is assigned a unique `ID` and `Instance ID`.

Creating a session with session options

When you are creating a session, there are times where you need to configure advanced options for communication. To do this, the `new-cimsessionoption` cmdlet can be leveraged to set advanced connection options for a CIM session.

Some of these additional parameters include:

- `Protocol`: The `Protocol` parameter allows you to override the default setting for the protocol being used. This value can be either `DCOM` or `WSMAN`.
- `ProxyAuthentication`: The `ProxyAuthentication` parameter allows you to specify the authentication mechanism to the remote system. The valid values for this parameter are `Default` (none), `Digest`, `Negotiate`, `Basic`, `Kerberos`, `NTLMDomain`, and `CredSSP`.

- `ProxyCredential`: The `ProxyCredential` parameter allows you to specify credentials to authenticate to a remote system. To use the `ProxyCredential` parameter, you must access the `PSCredential` object and set this to a variable. The best way to create the `PSCredential` object is through the use of the `get-credential` PowerShell cmdlet. You can then use this `PSCredential` object with the `ProxyCredential` parameter to authenticate with different credentials.
- `UseSSL`: The `UseSSL` parameter forces the use of SSL for remote communications.
- `NoEncryption`: The `NoEncryption` parameter will override the default encryption values to force no encryption in communication with a remote system.

To use the `new-cimsessionoption` cmdlet, you first need to declare a variable to place the options into, followed by the options you want to create for a session. You then use the `new-cimsessionoption` variable with the `new-cimsession` command and the `-sessionoption` parameter to create the session.

To create a new CIM session with session options, do the following action:

```
$sessionoptions = new-cimsessionoption -protocol DCOM
New-cimsession -sessionoption $sessionoptions -computername
Localhost,localhost,localhost -name LocalSessions
```

The output of this is shown in the following screenshot:

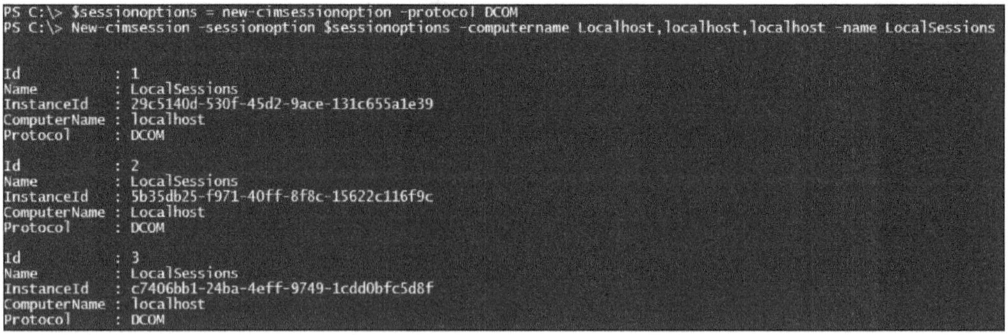
PS C:\> $sessionoptions = new-cimsessionoption -protocol DCOM
PS C:\> New-cimsession -sessionoption $sessionoptions -computername Localhost,localhost,localhost -name LocalSessions
Id : 1
Name : LocalSessions
InstanceId : 29c5140d-530f-45d2-9ace-131c655a1e39
ComputerName : localhost
Protocol : DCOM
Id : 2
Name : LocalSessions
InstanceId : 5b35db25-f971-40ff-8f8c-15622c116f9c
ComputerName : Localhost
Protocol : DCOM
Id : 3
Name : LocalSessions
InstanceId : c7406bb1-24ba-4eff-9749-1cdd0bfc5d8f
ComputerName : localhost
Protocol : DCOM

The preceding example displays how to properly create a CIM session with the use of the `new-cimsessionoption` cmdlet. You first start by creating a new CIM session option for forcing the communication protocol to `DCOM` and placing the session object to the `$sessionoptions` variable. You then use the `new-cimsession` cmdlet and the `-sessionoption` parameter to force new session options for the remote communication. You then call the `-computername` parameter to specify three remote computers and the `-name` parameter to group the three sessions into one session `Name` of `LocalSessions`. You will see that the output from the `new-cimsession` cmdlet will be very similar to the previous example; however, the `Protocol` is now forced to `DCOM`.

Using sessions for remote management

Now that you know how to create sessions, you will want to be able to leverage these newly created sessions to execute remote tasks. To be able to use a CIM session, you have to call the session by the `get-cimsession` cmdlet and then putting that session object into a variable. This is done by declaring a variable and setting it equal to the results of the `get-cimsession` command. The session object will then be contained in that variable.

To create and get a new CIM session, do the following action:

```
New-cimsession
$newsession = get-cimsession
$newsession
```

The output of this is shown in the following screenshot:

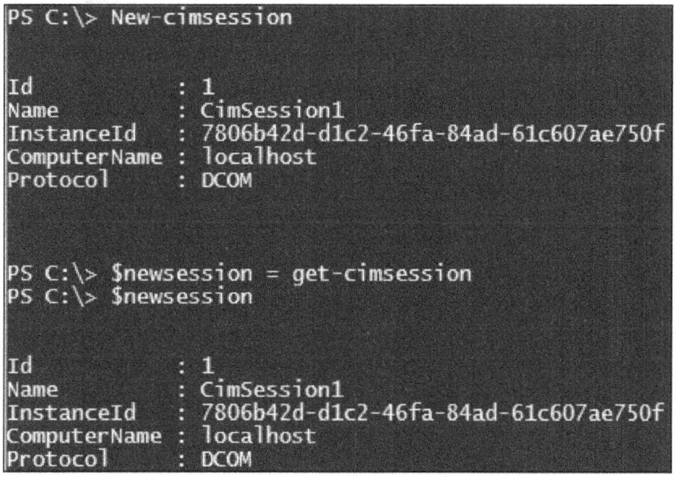

PS C:\> New-cimsession
Id   : 1
Name   : CimSession1
InstanceId   : 7806b42d-d1c2-46fa-84ad-61c607ae750f
ComputerName : localhost
Protocol   : DCOM
PS C:\> $newsession = get-cimsession
PS C:\> $newsession
Id   : 1
Name   : CimSession1
InstanceId   : 7806b42d-d1c2-46fa-84ad-61c607ae750f
ComputerName : localhost
Protocol   : DCOM

This example displays how to create a new session and place that new session object into a variable. You first start by creating the new session with the `new-cimsession` cmdlet. You then call the new session through the `get-cimsession` command and by setting that session object to the variable named `$newsession`. When you call just the `$newsession` variable, you will see the session object contained in that variable.

Once you capture the session object in a variable, you have the ability to interact with that session with the use of other PowerShell cmdlets. While CIM sessions aren't supported by all of the PowerShell cmdlets, there are a variety of CIM cmdlets that do support CIM sessions. To execute a command over a CIM session, you declare the `-CIMSession` parameter with a PowerShell cmdlet and it will remotely execute this command over that session.

One of the CIM commands that you can leverage `CimSessions` with is the `Invoke-Cimmethod` cmdlet. This cmdlet has the ability to invoke methods on a system like launching an application. The syntax of this command is calling `invoke-cimmethod` followed by the `-cimsession` parameter. You then call the Windows process class by using `-class win32_process`. You then create a new process by typing `-MethodName Create`. You finally issue the `-argument` parameter and issue the command-line arguments in the format of `@{CommandLine='programname.exe';CurrentDirectory="c:\DirectoryOfProg"}`.

To create a new CIM session and use the `invoke-cimmethod` cmdlet, do the following action:

```
New-cimsession -name MyComputer

$newsession = get-cimsession -Name MyComputer

Invoke-cimmethod -cimsession $newsession -class win32_process -MethodName
Create -Argument @{CommandLine='calc.exe';CurrentDirectory="c:\windows\
system32"}
```

The output of this is shown in the following screenshot:

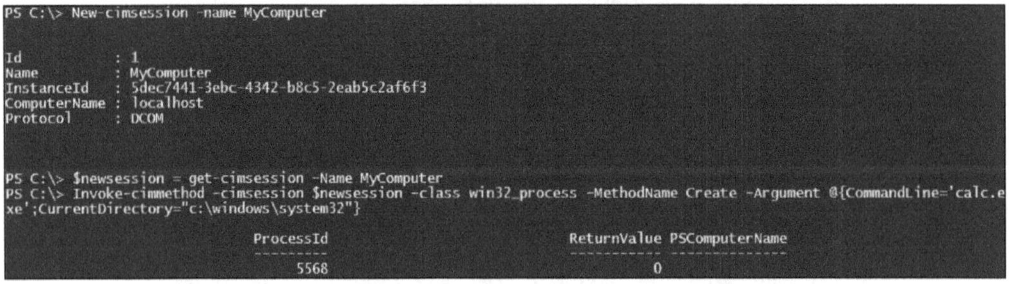
PS C:\> New-cimsession -name MyComputer
Id : 1
Name : MyComputer
InstanceId : 5dec7441-3ebc-4342-b8c5-2eab5c2af6f3
ComputerName : localhost
Protocol : DCOM
PS C:\> $newsession = get-cimsession -Name MyComputer
PS C:\> Invoke-cimmethod -cimsession $newsession -class win32_process -MethodName Create -Argument @{CommandLine='calc.e
xe';CurrentDirectory="c:\windows\system32"}
ProcessId
5568
ReturnValue PSComputerName
0

The preceding example displays how to create a new session, place that session in an object, and invoke a new calculator instance on a remote system. You first start by declaring `new-cimsession` with the name of `MyComputer`. You then use the `get-cimsession` cmdlet to place the CIM session object into the `$newsession` variable. You use the `invoke-cimmethod` cmdlet with the `-cimsession` parameter referencing the `$newsession` variable. You follow this by calling the `-class` parameter of `win32_process` and the `-MethodName` parameter referencing the `Create` method. Finally, you pass in the arguments for the calculator instance of `@{CommandLine='calc.exe';CurrentDirectory="c:\windows\system32"}`. This will successfully launch the calculator program on a remote system.

Removing sessions

When you are working with sessions from a singular system, it is important to remember that the sessions stay alive until you close the PowerShell window or until you remove the CIM session from memory. While it may be easier to close the PowerShell window, in instances of systems that are running batch configuration jobs, you may at any point in time open thousands of CIM sessions from a singular system. This not only causes derogated performance on the originating system but also opens up opportunities for security vulnerabilities. Since it is strongly recommended to close all open sessions on a system, you can leverage the `remove-cimsession` cmdlet to close sessions after you are done with using them.

The `remove-cimsession` cmdlet can leverage any of the session identifiers to close sessions. You can use the `-Name` parameter to close sessions by `Name`, the `-ID` parameter to close by `ID`, the `-InstanceID` parameter to close by `InstanceID`, and the `-ComputerName` parameter to close by `ComputerName`.

To create and remove a CIM session, do the following action:

```
new-cimsession -Name MySession
remove-cimsession -Name MySession
get-cimsession
```

The output of this is shown in the following screenshot:

PS C:\> new-cimsession -Name MySession
Id : 1
Name : MySession
InstanceId : c0a271c9-6f9a-44bf-85ca-31ead11e118d
ComputerName : localhost
Protocol : DCOM
PS C:\> remove-cimsession -Name MySession
PS C:\> get-cimsession

In the preceding example, you use the `new-cimsession` cmdlet to create a new session with the name of `MySession`. You then run the `remove-cimession` cmdlet with the `-name` parameter to remove the session with a name of `MySession`. Finally, you run the `get-cimsession` cmdlet to verify that there are no active sessions on the system. You will then see that after you run the `remove-cimsession` cmdlet, there are no active sessions remaining.

Summary

This chapter explained how to properly manage systems by utilizing sessions. The chapter started by explaining the prerequisites to enable the use of Windows Remote Management in your environment. This includes port numbers, security permissions, and services. The chapter also explained that you can use the quick configuration on systems, though it can be less secure than the manual configuration of WinRm.

The chapter then proceeded to explain how to create sessions through the use of the `new-cimsession` cmdlet. It also explained that you can create session options to change the connection parameters to remote systems with the `new-cimsessionoption` cmdlet. It explained that the most popular session options are `Protocol`, `ProxyAuthentication`, `ProxyCredential`, `UseSSL`, and `NoEncryption`. The chapter then highlighted that you have to set the session options object a variable prior to using them with a new CIM session.

This chapter also showed how to set a session to an object using the `get-cimsession` cmdlet. It explained how to use this session object in conjunction with the `invoke-cimmethod` to launch `calc.exe` on a remote system. The chapter ends by explaining how to close sessions with the use of `remove-cimsession` cmdlet and how to verify that all of the sessions are closed. In the next chapter, you will be exploring file, folder, and registry items with PowerShell. You will learn how to create, view, modify, and delete these items using a small set of cmdlets.

8
Managing Files, Folders, and Registry Items

When you are automating tasks on servers and workstations, you will frequently run into situations where you need to manage files, folders, and registry items. PowerShell provides a wide variety of cmdlets that enable you to create, view, modify, and delete items on a system.

In this chapter, you will learn many techniques to interact with files, folders, and registry items. These techniques and items include:

- Registry provider
- Creating files, folders, registry keys, and registry named values
- Adding named values to registry keys
- Verifying the existence of item files, folders, and registry keys
- Renaming files, folders, registry keys, and named values
- Copying and moving files and folders
- Deleting files, folders, registry keys, and named values

> To properly follow the examples in this chapter, you will need to sequentially execute the examples. Each example builds on the previous examples, and some of these examples may not function properly if you do not execute the previous steps.

Registry provider

When you're working with the registry, PowerShell interprets the registry in the same way it does files and folders. In fact, the cmdlets that you use for files and folders are the same that you would use for registry items. The only difference with the registry is the way in which you call the registry path locations. When you want to reference the registry in PowerShell, you use the `[RegistryLocation]:\Path\` syntax. This is made available through the PowerShell Windows Registry Provider.

While referencing `[RegistryLocation]:\Path\`, PowerShell provides you with the ability to use registry abbreviations pertaining to registry path locations. Instead of referencing the full path of `HKEY_LOCAL_MACHINE`, you can use the abbreviation of `HKLM`. Some other abbreviations include:

- HKLM: Abbreviation for `HKEY_LOCAL_MACHINE` hive
- HKCU: Abbreviation for `HKEY_CURRENT_USER` hive
- HKU: Abbreviation for `HKEY_USERS` hive
- HKCR: Abbreviation for `HKEY_CLASSES_ROOT` hive
- HKCC: Abbreviation for `HKEY_CURRENT_CONFIG` hive

For example, if you wanted to reference the named values in the `Run` registry key for programs that start up on boot, the command line syntax would look like this:

```
HKLM:\Software\Microsoft\Windows\CurrentVersion\Run
```

While it is recommended that you don't use cmdlet aliases in your scripts, it is recommended, and a common practice, to use registry abbreviations in your code. This not only reduces the amount of effort to create the scripts but also makes it easier for others to read the registry locations.

Creating files, folders, and registry items with PowerShell

When you want to create a new file, folder, or registry key, you will need to leverage the `new-item` cmdlet. The syntax of this command is `new-item`, calling the `-path` argument to specify the location, calling the `-name` argument to provide a name for the item, and the `-ItemType` argument to designate whether you want a file or a directory (folder). When you are creating a file, it has an additional argument of `-value`, which allows you to prepopulate data into the file after creation. When you are creating a new registry key in PowerShell, you can omit the `-ItemType` argument as it is not needed for registry key creation. PowerShell assumes that when you are interacting with the registry using `new-item`, you are creating registry keys. The `new-item` command accepts the `-force` argument in the instance that the file, folder, or key is being created in a space that is restricted by **User Account Control** (**UAC**).

To create a new folder and registry item, do the following action:

```
New-item -path "c:\Program Files\" -name MyCustomSoftware -ItemType
Directory
New-item -path HKCU:\Software\MyCustomSoftware\ -force
```

The output of this is shown in the following screenshot:

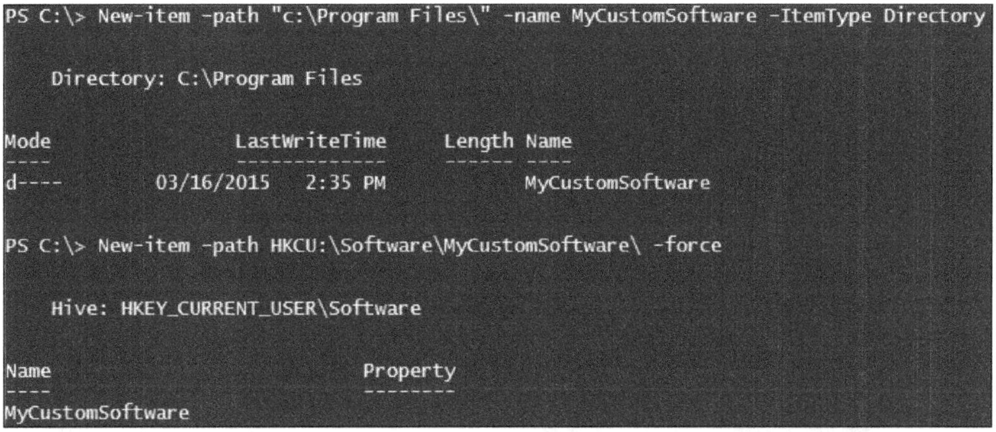

PS C:\> New-item -path "c:\Program Files\" -name MyCustomSoftware -ItemType Directory
Directory: C:\Program Files
Mode
LastWriteTime
Length Name
d----
03/16/2015 2:35 PM
MyCustomSoftware
PS C:\> New-item -path HKCU:\Software\MyCustomSoftware\ -force
Hive: HKEY_CURRENT_USER\Software
Name
Property
MyCustomSoftware

The preceding example shows how you can create folders and registry keys for a custom application. You first create a new folder in `c:\Program Files\` named `MyCustomSoftware`. You then create a new registry key in `HKEY_CURRENT_USER:\Software\` named `MyCustomSoftware`.

You start by issuing the `new-item` cmdlet followed by the `-path` argument to designate that the new folder should be placed in `c:\Program Files\`. You then call the `-name` argument to specify the name of `MyCustomSoftware`. Finally, you tell the cmdlet that the `-ItemType` argument is `Directory`. After executing this command you will see a new folder in `c:\Progam Files\` named `MyCustomSoftware`.

You then create the new registry key by calling the `new-item` cmdlet and issuing the `-path` argument and then specifying the `HKCU:\Software\MyCustomSoftware\` key location, and you complete it with the `-force` argument to force the creation of the key. After executing this command, you will see a new registry key in `HKEY_CURRENT_USER:\Software\` named `MyCustomSoftware`.

One of the main benefits of PowerShell breaking apart the `-path`, `-name`, and `-values` arguments is that you have the ability to customize each of the values before you use them with the `new-item` cmdlet. For example, if you want to name a log file with the date stamp, add that parameter into a string and set the `-name` value to a string.

To create a log file with a date included in the filename, do the following action:

```
$logpath = "c:\Program Files\MyCustomSoftware\Logs\"
New-item -path $logpath -ItemType Directory | out-null
$itemname = (get-date -format "yyyyMMddmmss") + "MyLogFile.txt"
$itemvalue = "Starting Logging at: " + " " + (get-date)
New-item -path $logpath -name $itemname -ItemType File -value $itemvalue
$logfile = $logpath + $itemname
$logfile
```

The output of this is shown in the following screenshot:

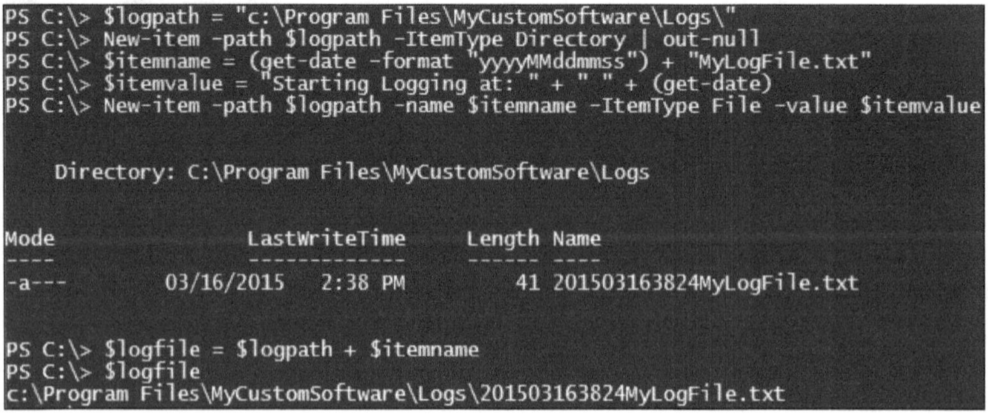
PS C:\> $logpath = "c:\Program Files\MyCustomSoftware\Logs\"
PS C:\> New-item -path $logpath -ItemType Directory | out-null
PS C:\> $itemname = (get-date -format "yyyyMMddmmss") + "MyLogFile.txt"
PS C:\> $itemvalue = "Starting Logging at: " + " " + (get-date)
PS C:\> New-item -path $logpath -name $itemname -ItemType File -value $itemvalue
Directory: C:\Program Files\MyCustomSoftware\Logs
Mode LastWriteTime Length Name
---- ------------- ------ ----
-a--- 03/16/2015 2:38 PM 41 201503163824MyLogFile.txt
PS C:\> $logfile = $logpath + $itemname
PS C:\> $logfile
c:\Program Files\MyCustomSoftware\Logs\201503163824MyLogFile.txt

The content of the log file is shown in the following screenshot:

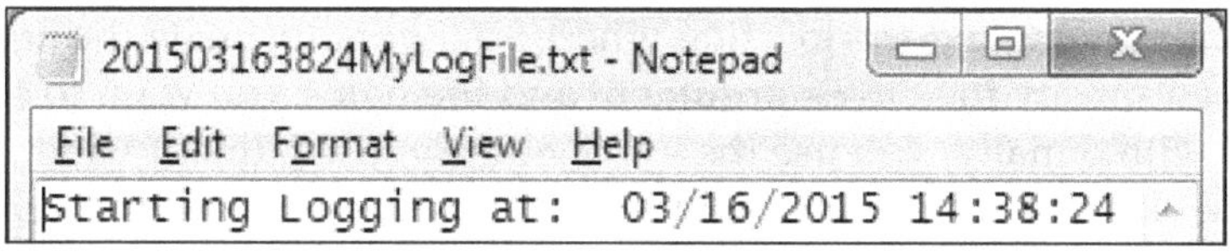

The preceding example displays how you can properly create a new log file with a date time path included in the log file name. It also shows how to create a new directory for the logs. It then displays how to include text inside the log file, designating the start of a new log file. Finally, this example displays how you can save the log file name and path in a variable to use later in your scripts.

You first start by declaring the path of `c:\Program Files\MyCustomSoftware\Logs\` in the `$logpath` variable. You then use the `new-item` cmdlet to create a new folder in `c:\Program Files\MyCustomSoftware\` named `Logs`. By piping the command to `out-null`, the default output of the directory creation is silenced. You then declare the name that you want the file to be by using the `get-date` cmdlet, with the `-format` argument set to `yyyyMMddmmss`, and by adding `mylogfile.txt`. This will generate a date time stamp in the format of `4` digits including year, month, day, minutes, seconds, and `mylogfile.txt`. You then set the name of the file to the `$itemname` variable. Finally, you declare the `$itemvalue` variable which contains `Starting Log at:` and the standard PowerShell date time information. After the variables are populated, you issue the `new-item` command, the `-path` argument referencing the `$logpath` variable, the `-name` argument referencing the `$itemname` variable, the `-ItemType` referencing `File`, and the `-value` argument referencing the `$itemvalue` variable. At the end of the script, you will take the `$logpath` and `$itemname` variables to create a new variable of `$logfile`, which contains the location of the log file. As you will see from this example, after you execute the script the log file is populated with the value of `Starting Logging at:  03/16/2015 14:38:24`.

Adding named values to registry keys

When you are interacting with the registry, you typically view and edit named values or properties that are contained with in the keys and sub-keys. PowerShell uses several cmdlets to interact with named values. The first is the `get-itemproperty` cmdlet which allows you to retrieve the properties of a named value. The proper syntax for this cmdlet is to specify `get-itemproperty` to use the `-path` argument to specify the location in the registry, and to use the `-name` argument to specify the named value.

The second cmdlet is `new-itemproperty`, which allows you to create new named values. The proper syntax for this cmdlet is specifying `new-itemproperty`, followed by the `-path` argument and the location where you want to create the new named value. You then specify the `-name` argument and the name you want to call the named value with. Finally, you use the `-PropertyType` argument which allows you to specify what kind of registry named value you want to create. The `PropertyType` argument can be set to `Binary`, `DWord`, `ExpandString`, `MultiString`, `String`, and `Qword`, depending on what your need for the registry value is. Finally, you specify the `-value` argument which enables you to place a value into that named value. You may also use the `-force` overload to force the creation of the key in the instance that the key may be restricted by UAC.

To create a named value in the registry, do the following action:

```
$regpath = "HKCU:\Software\MyCustomSoftware\"
$regname = "BuildTime"
$regvalue = "Build Started At: " + " " + (get-date)
New-itemproperty -path $regpath -name $regname -PropertyType String -
value $regvalue
$verifyValue = Get-itemproperty -path $regpath -name $regname
Write-Host "The $regName named value is set to: " $verifyValue.$regname
```

The output of this is shown in the following screenshot:

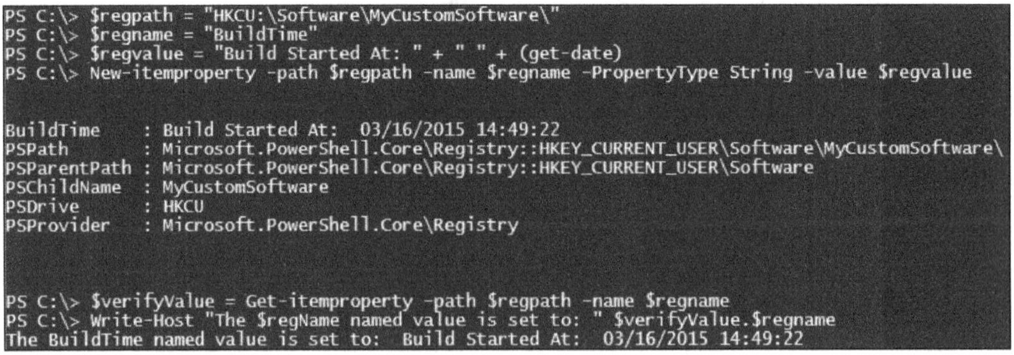
PS C:\> $regpath = "HKCU:\Software\MyCustomSoftware\"
PS C:\> $regname = "BuildTime"
PS C:\> $regvalue = "Build Started At: " + " " + (get-date)
PS C:\> New-itemproperty -path $regpath -name $regname -PropertyType String -value $regvalue
BuildTime : Build Started At: 03/16/2015 14:49:22
PSPath : Microsoft.PowerShell.Core\Registry::HKEY_CURRENT_USER\Software\MyCustomSoftware\
PSParentPath : Microsoft.PowerShell.Core\Registry::HKEY_CURRENT_USER\Software
PSChildName : MyCustomSoftware
PSDrive : HKCU
PSProvider : Microsoft.PowerShell.Core\Registry
PS C:\> $verifyValue = Get-itemproperty -path $regpath -name $regname
PS C:\> Write-Host "The $regName named value is set to: " $verifyValue.$regname
The BuildTime named value is set to: Build Started At: 03/16/2015 14:49:22

After executing the script, the registry will look like the following screenshot:

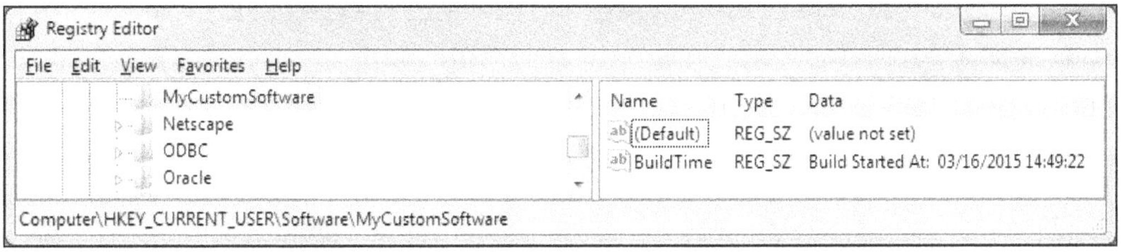

This script displays how you can create a registry named value in a specific location. It also displays how you can retrieve a value and display it in the console. You first start by defining several variables. The first variable `$regpath` defines where you want to create the new named value which is in the `HKCU:\Software\MyCustomSoftware\` registry key. The second variable `$regname` defines what you want the new named value to be named, which is `BuildTime`. The third variable defines what you want the value of the named value to be, which is `Build Started At:` with the current date and time. The next step in the script is to create the new value. You first call the `new-itemproperty` cmdlet with the `-path` argument and specify the `$regpath` variable. You then use the `-name` argument and specify `$regname`. This is followed by specifying the `-PropertyType` argument and by specifying the string `PropertyType`. Finally, you specify the `-value` argument and use the `$regvalue` variable to fill the named value with data.

Proceeding forward in the script, you verify that the named value has proper data by leveraging the `get-itemproperty` cmdlet. You first define the `$verifyvalue` variable that captures the data from the cmdlet. You then issue `get-itemproperty` with the `-path` argument of `$regpath` and the `-name` argument of `$regname`. You then write to the console that the `$regname` named value is set to `$verifyvalue.$regname`. When you are done with script execution, you should have a new registry named value of `BuildTime` in the `HKEY_CURRENT_USER:\Software\MyCustomSoftware\` key with a value similar to `Build Started At: 03/16/2015 14:49:22`.

Verifying files, folders, and registry items

When you are creating and modifying objects, it's important to make sure that the file, folder, and registry items don't exist prior to creating and modifying them. The `test-path` cmdlet allows you to test to see if a file, folder, or registry item exists prior to working with it. The proper syntax for this is first calling `test-path` and then specifying a file, folder, or registry location. The result of the `test-path` command is `True` if the object exists or `False` if the object doesn't exist.

To verify if files, folders, and registry entries exist, do the following action:

```
$testfolder = test-path "c:\Program Files\MyCustomSoftware\Logs"
#Update The Following Line with the Date/Timestamp of your file
$testfile = test-path "c:\Program Files\MyCustomSoftware\
Logs\201503163824MyLogFile.txt"
$testreg = test-path "HKCU:\Software\MyCustomSoftware\"
If ($testfolder) { write-host "Folder Found!" }
If ($testfile) { write-host "File Found!" }
If ($testreg) { write-host "Registry Key Found!" }
```

The output is shown in the following screenshot:

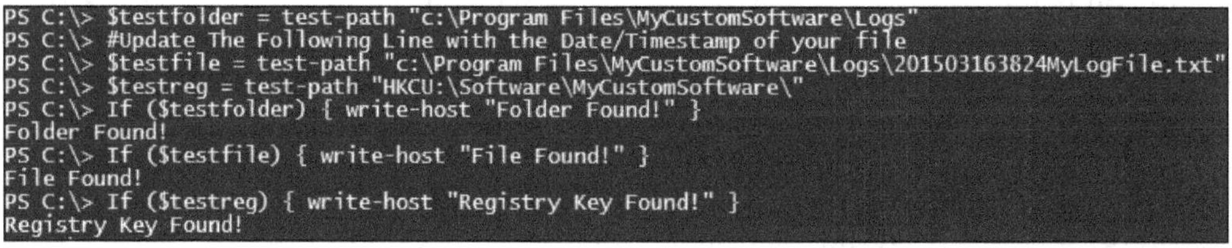

```
PS C:\> $testfolder = test-path "c:\Program Files\MyCustomSoftware\Logs"
PS C:\> #Update The Following Line with the Date/Timestamp of your file
PS C:\> $testfile = test-path "c:\Program Files\MyCustomSoftware\Logs\201503163824MyLogFile.txt"
PS C:\> $testreg = test-path "HKCU:\Software\MyCustomSoftware\"
PS C:\> If ($testfolder) { write-host "Folder Found!" }
Folder Found!
PS C:\> If ($testfile) { write-host "File Found!" }
File Found!
PS C:\> If ($testreg) { write-host "Registry Key Found!" }
Registry Key Found!
```

This example displays how to verify if a file, folder, and registry item exists. You first start by declaring a variable to catch the output from the `test-path` cmdlet. You then specify `test-path`, followed by a file, folder, or registry item whose existence you want to verify.

In this example, you start by using the `test-path` cmdlet to verify if the `Logs` folder is located in the `c:\Program Files\MyCustomSoftware\` directory. You then store the result in the `$testfolder` variable. You then use the `test-path` cmdlet to check if the file located at `c:\Program Files\MyCustomSoftware\Logs\201503163824MyLogFile.txt` exists. You then store the result in the `$testfile` variable. Finally, you use the `test-path` cmdlet to see if the registry key of `HKCU:\Software\MyCustomSoftware\` exists. You then store the result in the `$testreg` variable. To evaluate the variables, you create `IF` statements to check whether the variables are `True` and write to the console if the items are found. After executing the script, the console will output the messages `Folder Found!`, `File Found!`, and `Registry Key Found!`.

Copying and moving files and folders

When you are working in the operating system, there may be instances where you need to copy or move files and folders around on the operating system. PowerShell provides two cmdlets to copy and move files. The `copy-item` cmdlet allows you to copy a file or a folder from one location to another. The proper syntax of this cmdlet is calling `copy-item`, followed by `-path` argument for the source you want to copy and the `-destination` argument for the destination of the file or folder. The `copy-item` cmdlet also has the `-force` argument to write over a read-only or hidden file. There are instances when read-only files cannot be overwritten, such as a lack of user permissions, which will require additional code to change the file attributes before copying over files or folders. The `copy-item` cmdlet also has a `-recurse` argument, which allows you to recursively copy the files in a folder and its subdirectories.

> A common trick to use with the `copy-item` cmdlet is to rename during the copy operation. To do this, you change the destination to the desired name you want the file or folder to be. After executing the command, the file or folder will have a new name in its destination. This reduces the number of steps required to copy and rename a file or folder.

The `move-item` cmdlet allows you to move files from one location to another. The `move-item` cmdlet has the same syntax as the `copy-item` cmdlet. The proper syntax of this cmdlet is calling `move-item`, followed by the `-path` argument for the source you want to move and the `-destination` argument for the destination of the file or folder. The `move-item` cmdlet also has the `-force` overload to write over a read-only or hidden file. There are also instances when read-only files cannot be overwritten, such as a lack of user permissions, which will require additional code to change the file attributes before moving files or folders. The `move-item` cmdlet does not, however, have a `-recurse` argument. Also, it's important to remember that the `move-item` cmdlet requires the destination to be created prior to the move. If the destination folder is not available, it will throw an exception. It's recommended to use the `test-path` cmdlet in conjunction with the `move-item` cmdlet to verify that the destination exists prior to the move operation.

> PowerShell has the same file and folder limitations as the core operating system it is being run on. This means that file paths that are longer than 256 characters in length will receive an error message during the copy process. For paths that are over 256 characters in length, you need to leverage `robocopy.exe` or a similar file copy program to copy or move files.
>
> All `move-item` operations are recursive by default. You do not have to specify the `-recurse` argument to recursively move files. To copy files recursively, you need to specify the `-recurse` argument.

To copy and move files and folders, do the following action:

```
New-item -path "c:\Program Files\MyCustomSoftware\AppTesting" -ItemType
Directory | Out-null

New-item -path "c:\Program Files\MyCustomSoftware\AppTesting\Help"
-ItemType Directory | Out-null

New-item -path "c:\Program Files\MyCustomSoftware\AppTesting\" -name
AppTest.txt -ItemType File | out-null

New-item -path "c:\Program Files\MyCustomSoftware\AppTesting\Help\" -name
HelpInformation.txt -ItemType File | out-null

New-item -path "c:\Program Files\MyCustomSoftware\" -name ConfigFile.txt
-ItemType File | out-null

move-item -path "c:\Program Files\MyCustomSoftware\AppTesting" -
destination "c:\Program Files\MyCustomSoftware\Archive" -force

copy-item -path "c:\Program Files\MyCustomSoftware\ConfigFile.txt" "c:\
Program Files\MyCustomSoftware\Archive\Archived_ConfigFile.txt" -force
```

The output of this is shown in the following screenshot:

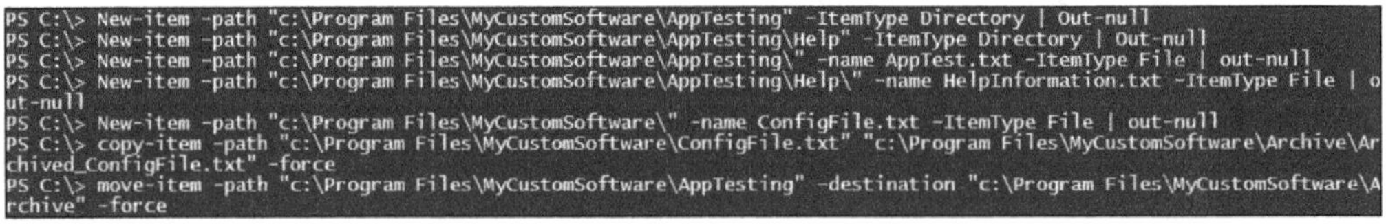
PS C:\> New-item -path "c:\Program Files\MyCustomSoftware\AppTesting" -ItemType Directory | Out-null
PS C:\> New-item -path "c:\Program Files\MyCustomSoftware\AppTesting\Help" -ItemType Directory | Out-null
PS C:\> New-item -path "c:\Program Files\MyCustomSoftware\AppTesting\" -name AppTest.txt -ItemType File | out-null
PS C:\> New-item -path "c:\Program Files\MyCustomSoftware\AppTesting\Help\" -name HelpInformation.txt -ItemType File | o
ut-null
PS C:\> New-item -path "c:\Program Files\MyCustomSoftware\" -name ConfigFile.txt -ItemType File | out-null
PS C:\> copy-item -path "c:\Program Files\MyCustomSoftware\ConfigFile.txt" "c:\Program Files\MyCustomSoftware\Archive\Ar
chived_ConfigFile.txt" -force
PS C:\> move-item -path "c:\Program Files\MyCustomSoftware\AppTesting" -destination "c:\Program Files\MyCustomSoftware\A
rchive" -force

This example displays how to properly use the `copy-item` and `move-item` cmdlets. You first start by using the `new-item` cmdlet with the `-path` argument set to `c:\Program Files\MyCustomSoftware\AppTesting` and the `-ItemType` argument set to `Directory`. You then pipe the command to `out-null` to suppress the default output. This creates the `AppTesting` sub directory in the `c:\Program Files\MyCustomSoftware\` directory. You then create a second folder using the `new-item` cmdlet with the `-path` argument set to `c:\Program Files\MyCustomSoftware\AppTesting\Help` and the `-ItemType` argument set to `Directory`. You then pipe the command to `out-null`. This creates the `Help` sub directory in the `c:\Program Files\MyCustomSoftware\AppTesting` directory.

After creating the directories, you create a new file using the `new-item` cmdlet with the path of `c:\Program Files\MyCustomSoftware\AppTesting\`, the `-name` argument set to `AppTest.txt`, the `-ItemType` argument set to `File`; you then pipe it to `out-null`. You create a second file by using the `new-item` cmdlet with the path of `c:\Program Files\MyCustomSoftware\AppTesting\Help`, the `-name` argument set to `HelpInformation.txt` and the `-ItemType` argument set to `File`, and then piping it to `out-null`. Finally, you create a third file using the `new-item` cmdlet with the path of `c:\Program Files\MyCustomSoftware`, the `-name` argument set to `ConfigFile.txt` and the `-ItemType` argument set to `File`, and then pipe it to `out-null`.

After creating the files, you are ready to start copying and moving files.

You first move the `AppTesting` directory to the `Archive` directory by using the `move-item` cmdlet and then specifying the `-path` argument with the value of `c:\Program Files\MyCustomSoftware\AppTesting` as the source, the `-destination` argument with the value of `c:\Program Files\MyCustomSoftware\Archive` as the destination, and the `-force` argument to force the move if the directory is hidden. You then copy a configuration file by using the `copy-item` cmdlet, using the `-path` argument with `c:\Program Files\MyCustomSoftware\ConfigFile.txt` as the source, and then specifying the `-destination` argument with `c:\Program Files\MyCustomSoftware\Archive\Archived_ConfigFile.txt` as the new destination with a new filename;, you then leverage the `-force` argument to force the copy if the file is hidden.

This follow screenshot displays the file folder hierarchy after executing this script:

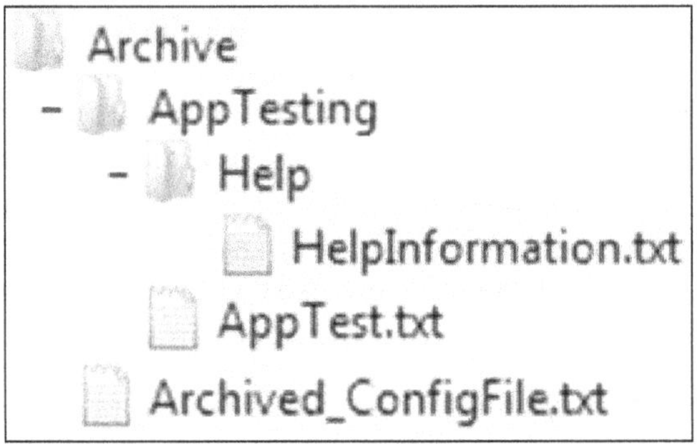

After executing this script, the file folder hierarchy should be as displayed in the preceding screenshot. This also displays that when you move the `AppTesting` directory to the `Archive` folder, it automatically performs the move recursively, keeping the file and folder structure intact.

Renaming files, folders, registry keys, and named values

When you are working with PowerShell scripts, you may have instances where you need to rename files, folders, and registry keys. The `rename-item` cmdlet can be used to perform renaming operations on a system. The syntax for this cmdlet is `rename-item` and specifying the `-path` argument with path to the original object, and then you call the `-newname` argument with a full path to what you want the item to be renamed to. The `rename-item` has a `-force` argument to force the rename in instances where the file or folder is hidden or restricted by UAC or to avoid prompting for the rename action.

To copy and rename files and folders, do the following action:

```
New-item -path "c:\Program Files\MyCustomSoftware\OldConfigFiles\" -
ItemType Directory | out-null

Rename-item -path "c:\Program Files\MyCustomSoftware\OldConfigFiles" -
newname "c:\Program Files\MyCustomSoftware\ConfigArchive" -force

copy-item -path "c:\Program Files\MyCustomSoftware\ConfigFile.txt" "c:\
Program Files\MyCustomSoftware\ConfigArchive\ConfigFile.txt" -force

Rename-item -path "c:\Program Files\MyCustomSoftware\ConfigArchive\
ConfigFile.txt" -newname "c:\Program Files\MyCustomSoftware\
ConfigArchive\Old_ConfigFile.txt" -force
```

The output of this is shown in the following screenshot:

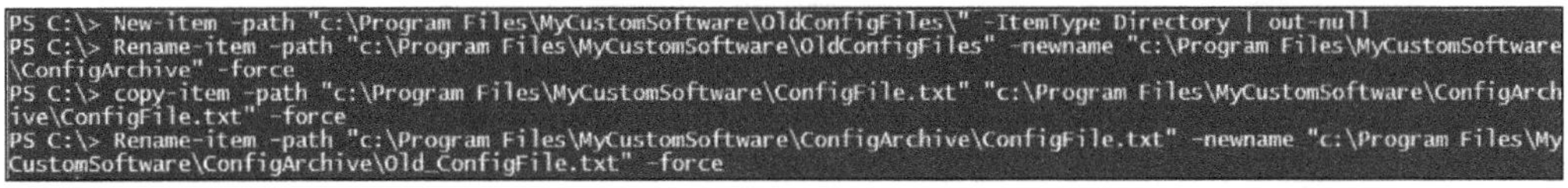
PS C:\> New-item -path "c:\Program Files\MyCustomSoftware\OldConfigFiles\" -ItemType Directory | out-null
PS C:\> Rename-item -path "c:\Program Files\MyCustomSoftware\OldConfigFiles" -newname "c:\Program Files\MyCustomSoftware\ConfigArchive" -force
PS C:\> copy-item -path "c:\Program Files\MyCustomSoftware\ConfigFile.txt" "c:\Program Files\MyCustomSoftware\ConfigArchive\ConfigFile.txt" -force
PS C:\> Rename-item -path "c:\Program Files\MyCustomSoftware\ConfigArchive\ConfigFile.txt" -newname "c:\Program Files\MyCustomSoftware\ConfigArchive\Old_ConfigFile.txt" -force

In this example, you create a script that creates a new folder and a new file, and then renames the file and the folder. To start, you leverage the `new-item` cmdlet which creates a new folder in `c:\Program Files\MyCustomSoftware\` named `OldConfigFiles`. You then pipe that command to `Out-Null`, which silences the standard console output of the folder creation. You proceed to rename the folder `c:\Program Files\MyCustomSoftware\OldConfigFiles` with the `rename-item` cmdlet using the `-newname` argument to `c:\Program Files\MyCustomSoftware\ConfigArchive`. You follow the command with the `-force` argument to force the renaming of the folder.

You leverage the `copy-item` cmdlet to copy the `ConfigFile.txt` into the `ConfigArchive\` directory. You first start by specifying the `copy-item` cmdlet with the `-path` argument set to `c:\Program Files\MyCustomSoftware\ConfigFile.txt` and the destination set to `c:\Program Files\MyCustomSoftware\ConfigArchive\ConfigFile.txt`. You include the `-Force` argument to force the copy.

After moving the file, leverage the `rename-item` cmdlet with the `-path` argument to rename `c:\Program Files\MyCustomSoftware\ConfigArchive\ConfigFile.txt` using the `-newname` argument to `c:\Program Files\MyCustomSoftware\ConfigArchive\Old_ConfigFile.txt`. You follow this command with the `-force` argument to force the renaming of the file. At the end of this script, you will have successfully renamed a folder, moved a file into that renamed folder, and renamed a file in the newly created folder.

In the instance that you want to rename a registry key, do the following action:

```
New-item -path "HKCU:\Software\MyCustomSoftware\" -name CInfo -force |
out-null

Rename-item -path "HKCU:\Software\MyCustomSoftware\CInfo" -newname
ConnectionInformation -force
```

The output of this is shown in the following screenshot:

PS C:\> New-item -path "HKCU:\Software\MyCustomSoftware\" -name CInfo -force | out-null
PS C:\> Rename-item -path "HKCU:\Software\MyCustomSoftware\CInfo" -newname ConnectionInformation -force

After renaming the subkey, the registry will look like the following screenshot:

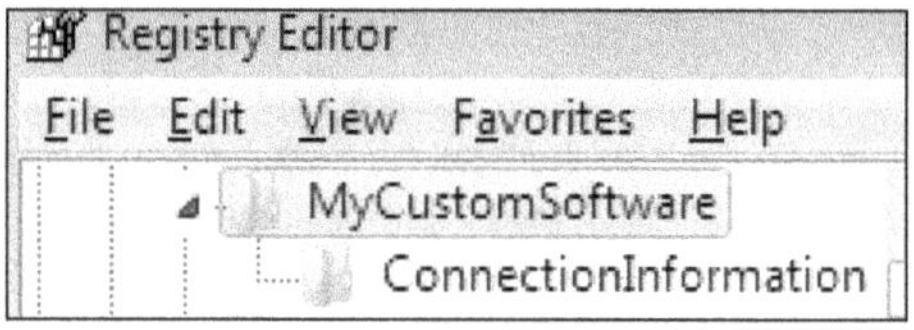
Registry Editor
File Edit View Favorites Help
MyCustomSoftware
ConnectionInformation

This example displays how to create a new subkey and rename it. You first start by using the `new-item` cmdlet to create a new sub key with the `-path` argument of the `HKCU:\Software\MyCustomSoftware\` key and the `-name` argument set to `CInfo`. You then pipe that line to out-null in order to suppress the standard output from the script. You proceed to execute the `rename-item` cmdlet with the `-path` argument set to `HKCU:\Software\MyCustomSoftware\CInfo` and the `-newname` argument set to `ConnectionInformation`. You then use the `-force` argument to force the renaming in instances when the subkey is restricted by UAC. After executing this command, you will see that the `CInfo` subkey located in `HKCU:\Software\MyCustomSoftware\` is now renamed to `ConnectionInformation`.

When you want to update named values in the registry, you will not be able to use the `rename-item` cmdlet. This is due to the named values being properties of the keys themselves. Instead, PowerShell provides the `rename-itemproperty` cmdlet to rename the named values in the key. The proper syntax for this cmdlet is calling `rename-itemproperty` by using the `-path` argument, followed by the path to the key that contains the named value. You then issue the `-name` argument to specify the named value you want to rename. Finally, you specify the `-newname` argument and the name you want the named value to be renamed to.

To rename the registry named value, do the following action:

```
$regpath = "HKCU:\Software\MyCustomSoftware\ConnectionInformation"
$regname = "DBServer"
$regvalue = "mySQLserver.mydomain.local"
New-itemproperty -path $regpath -name $regname -PropertyType String -
value $regvalue | Out-null
Rename-itemproperty -path $regpath -name DBServer -newname DatabaseServer
```

The output of this is shown in the following screenshot:

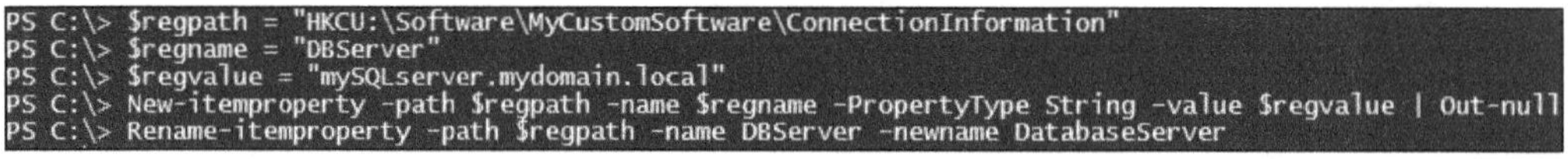
PS C:\> $regpath = "HKCU:\Software\MyCustomSoftware\ConnectionInformation"
PS C:\> $regname = "DBServer"
PS C:\> $regvalue = "mySQLserver.mydomain.local"
PS C:\> New-itemproperty -path $regpath -name $regname -PropertyType String -value $regvalue | Out-null
PS C:\> Rename-itemproperty -path $regpath -name DBServer -newname DatabaseServer

After updating the named value, the registry will reflect this change, and so should look like the following screenshot:

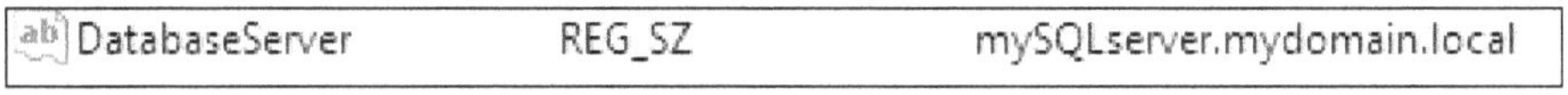

The preceding script displays how to create a new named value and rename it to a different named value. You first start by defining the variables to be used with the `new-itemproperty` cmdlet. You define the location of the registry subkey in the `$regpath` variable and set it to `HKCU:\Software\MyCustomSoftware\ConnectionInformation`. You then specify the named value name of `DBServer` and store it in the `$regname` variable. Finally, you define the `$regvalue` variable and store the value of `mySQLserver.mydomain.local`.

To create the new named value, leverage `new-itemproperty`, specify the `-path` argument with the `$regpath` variable, use the `-name` argument with the `$regname` variable, and use the `-value` argument with the `$regvalue` variable. You then pipe this command to `out-null` in order to suppress the default output of the command. This command will create the new named value of `DBServer` with the value of `mySQLserver.mydomain.local` in the `HKCU:\Software\MyCustomSoftware\ConnectionInformation` subkey.

The last step in the script is renaming the `DBServer` named value to `DatabaseServer`. You first start by calling the `rename-itemproperty` cmdlet and then using the `-path` argument and specifying the `$regpath` variable which contains the `HKCU:\Software\MyCustomSoftware\ConnectionInformation` subkey; you then proceed by calling the `-name` argument and specifying `DBServer` and finally calling the `-newname` argument with the new value of `DatabaseServer`. After executing this command, you will see that the `HKCU:\Software\MyCustomSoftware\ConnectionInformation` key has a new named value of `DatabaseServer` containing the same value of `mySQLserver.mydomain.local`.

Deleting files, folders, registry keys, and named values

When you are creating scripts, there are instances when you need to delete items from a computer. PowerShell has the `remove-item` cmdlet that enables the removal of objects from a computer. The syntax of this cmdlet starts by calling the `remove-item` cmdlet and proceeds with specifying the `-path` argument with a file, folder, or registry key to delete.

The `remove-item` cmdlet has several useful arguments that can be leveraged. The `-force` argument is available to delete files, folders, and registry keys that are read-only, hidden, or restricted by UAC. The `-recurse` argument is available to enable recursive deletion of files, folders, and registry keys on a system. The `-include` argument enables you to delete specific files, folders, and registry keys. The `-include` argument allows you to use the wildcard character of an asterisk (`*`) to search for specific values in an object name or a specific object type. The `-exclude` argument will exclude specific files, folders, and registry keys on a system. It also accepts the wildcard character of an asterisk (`*`) to search for specific values in an object name or a specific object type.

The named values in the registry are properties of the key that they are contained in. As a result, you cannot use the `remove-item` cmdlet to remove them. Instead, PowerShell offers the `remove-itemproperty` cmdlet to enable the removal of the named values. The `remove-itemproperty` cmdlet has arguments similar to those of the `remove-item` cmdlet. It is important to note, however, that the `-filter`, `-include`, and `-exclude` arguments will not work with named values in the registry. They only work with item paths such as registry keys.

To set up the system for the deletion example, you need to process the following script:

```
# Create New Directory
new-item -path "c:\program files\MyCustomSoftware\Graphics\" -ItemType
Directory | Out-null
# Create Files for This Example
new-item -path "c:\program files\MyCustomSoftware\Graphics\" -name
FirstGraphic.bmp -ItemType File | Out-Null
new-item -path "c:\program files\MyCustomSoftware\Graphics\" -name
FirstGraphic.png -ItemType File | Out-Null
new-item -path "c:\program files\MyCustomSoftware\Graphics\" -name
SecondGraphic.bmp -ItemType File | Out-Null
new-item -path "c:\program files\MyCustomSoftware\Graphics\" -name
SecondGraphic.png -ItemType File | Out-Null
new-item -path "c:\program files\MyCustomSoftware\Logs\" -name
201301010101LogFile.txt -ItemType File | Out-Null
new-item -path "c:\program files\MyCustomSoftware\Logs\" -name
201302010101LogFile.txt -ItemType File | Out-Null
new-item -path "c:\program files\MyCustomSoftware\Logs\" -name
201303010101LogFile.txt -ItemType File | Out-Null
# Create New Registry Keys and Named Values
```

```
New-item -path "HKCU:\Software\MyCustomSoftware\AppSettings" | Out-null

New-item -path "HKCU:\Software\MyCustomSoftware\ApplicationSettings" |
Out-null

New-itemproperty -path "HKCU:\Software\MyCustomSoftware\
ApplicationSettings" -name AlwaysOn -PropertyType String -value True |
Out-null

New-itemproperty -path "HKCU:\Software\MyCustomSoftware\
ApplicationSettings" -name AutoDeleteLogs -PropertyType String -value
True | Out-null
```

The output of this is shown in the following screenshot:

PS C:\> # Create New Directory
PS C:\> new-item -path "c:\program files\MyCustomSoftware\Graphics\" -ItemType Directory | Out-null
PS C:\> # Create Files for This Example
PS C:\> new-item -path "c:\program files\MyCustomSoftware\Graphics\" -name FirstGraphic.bmp -ItemType File | Out-Null
PS C:\> new-item -path "c:\program files\MyCustomSoftware\Graphics\" -name FirstGraphic.png -ItemType File | Out-Null
PS C:\> new-item -path "c:\program files\MyCustomSoftware\Graphics\" -name SecondGraphic.bmp -ItemType File | Out-Null
PS C:\> new-item -path "c:\program files\MyCustomSoftware\Graphics\" -name SecondGraphic.png -ItemType File | Out-Null
PS C:\> new-item -path "c:\program files\MyCustomSoftware\Logs\" -name 201301010101LogFile.txt -ItemType File | Out-Null
PS C:\> new-item -path "c:\program files\MyCustomSoftware\Logs\" -name 201302010101LogFile.txt -ItemType File | Out-Null
PS C:\> new-item -path "c:\program files\MyCustomSoftware\Logs\" -name 201303010101LogFile.txt -ItemType File | Out-Null
PS C:\> # Create New Registry Keys and Named Values
PS C:\> New-item -path "HKCU:\Software\MyCustomSoftware\AppSettings" | Out-null
PS C:\> New-item -path "HKCU:\Software\MyCustomSoftware\ApplicationSettings" | Out-null
PS C:\> New-itemproperty -path "HKCU:\Software\MyCustomSoftware\ApplicationSettings" -name AlwaysOn -PropertyType String
-value True | Out-null
PS C:\> New-itemproperty -path "HKCU:\Software\MyCustomSoftware\ApplicationSettings" -name AutoDeleteLogs -PropertyType
String -value True | Out-null

The preceding example is designed to set up the file structure for the following example. You first use the `new-item` cmdlet to create a new directory called `Graphics` in `c:\program files\MyCustomSoftware\`. You then use the `new-item` cmdlet to create new files named `FirstGraphic.bmp`, `FirstGraphic.png`, `SecondGraphic.bmp`, and `SecondGraphic.png` in the `c:\Program Files\MyCustomSoftware\Graphics\` directory. You then use the `new-item` cmdlet to create new log files in `c:\Program Files\MyCustomSoftware\Logs` named `201301010101LogFile.txt`, `201302010101LogFile.txt`, and `201303010101LogFile.txt`. After creating the files, you create two new registry keys located at `HKCU:\Software\MyCustomSoftware\AppSettings` and `HKCU:\Software\MyCustomSoftware\ApplicationSettings`. You then populate the `HKCU:\Software\MyCustomSoftware\ApplicationSettings` key with a named value of `AlwaysOn` set to `True` and a named value of `AutoDeleteLogs` set to `True`.

To remove files, folders, and registry items from a system, do the following action:

```
# Get Current year
$currentyear = get-date -f yyyy
# Build the Exclude String
$exclude = "*" + $currentyear + "*"
```

```
# Remove Items from System

Remove-item -path "c:\Program Files\MyCustomSoftware\Graphics\" -include
*.bmp -force -recurse

Remove-item -path "c:\Program Files\MyCustomSoftware\Logs\" -exclude
$exclude -force -recurse

Remove-itemproperty -path "HKCU:\Software\MyCustomSoftware\
ApplicationSettings" -Name AutoDeleteLogs

Remove-item -path "HKCU:\Software\MyCustomSoftware\ApplicationSettings"
```

The output of this is shown in the following screenshot:

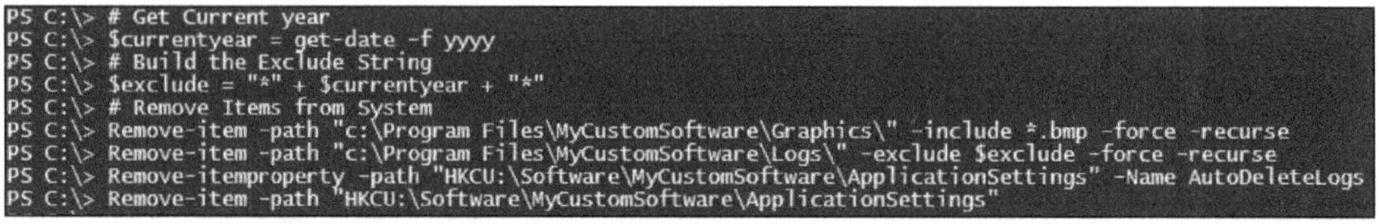
PS C:\> # Get Current year
PS C:\> $currentyear = get-date -f yyyy
PS C:\> # Build the Exclude String
PS C:\> $exclude = "*" + $currentyear + "*"
PS C:\> # Remove Items from System
PS C:\> Remove-item -path "c:\Program Files\MyCustomSoftware\Graphics\" -include *.bmp -force -recurse
PS C:\> Remove-item -path "c:\Program Files\MyCustomSoftware\Logs\" -exclude $exclude -force -recurse
PS C:\> Remove-itemproperty -path "HKCU:\Software\MyCustomSoftware\ApplicationSettings" -Name AutoDeleteLogs
PS C:\> Remove-item -path "HKCU:\Software\MyCustomSoftware\ApplicationSettings"

This script displays how you can leverage PowerShell to clean up files and folders with the `remove-item` cmdlet and the `-exclude` and `-include` arguments. You first start by building the exclusion string for the `remove-item` cmdlet. You retrieve the current year by using the `get-date` cmdlet with the `-f` parameter set to `yyyy`. You save the output into the `$currentyear` variable. You then create a `$exclude` variable that appends asterisks on each end of the `$currentyear` variable, which contains the current date. This will allow the exclusion filter to find the year anywhere in the file or folder names.

The first command is that you use the `remove-item` cmdlet and call the `-path` argument with the path of `c:\Program Files\MyCustomSoftware\Graphics\`. You then specify the `-include` argument with the value of `*.bmp`. This tells the `remove-item` cmdlet to delete all files that end in `.bmp`. You then specify `-force` to force the deletion of the files and `-recurse` to search the entire `Graphics` directory to delete the files that meet the `*.bmp` inclusion criteria but leaves the other files you created with the `*.png` extension.

The second command leverages the `remove-item` cmdlet with the `-path` argument set to `c:\Program Files\MyCustomSoftware\Logs\`. You use the `-exclude` argument with the value of `$exclude` to exclude files that contain the current year. You then specify `-force` to force the deletion of the files and `-recurse` to search the entire logs directory to delete the files and folders that do not meet the exclusion criteria.

The third command leverages the `remove-itemproperty` cmdlet with the `-path` argument set to `HKCU:\Software\MyCustomSoftware\ApplicationSettings` and the `-name` argument set to `AutoDeleteLogs`. After execution, the `AutoDeleteLogs` named path is deleted from the registry.

The last command leverages the `remote-item` cmdlet with the `-path` argument set to `HKCU:\Software\MyCustomSoftware\ApplicationSettings`. After running this last command, the entire subkey of `ApplicationSettings` is removed from `HKCU:\Software\MyCustomSoftware\`.

After executing this script, you will see that the script deletes the `.BMP` files in the `c:\Program Files\MyCustomSoftware\Graphics` directory, but it leaves the `.PNG` files. You will also see that the script deletes all of the log files except the ones that had the current year contained in them. Last, you will see that the `ApplicationSettings` sub key that was created in the previous step is successfully deleted from `HKCU:\Software\MyCustomSoftware\`.

> When you use the `remove-item` and `-recurse` parameters together, it is important to note that if `remote-item` cmdlet deletes all the files and folders in a directory, the `-recurse` parameter will also delete the empty folder and subfolders that contained those files. This is only true when there are no remaining files in the folders in a particular directory. This may create undesirable results on your system, and so you should use caution while performing this combination.

Summary

This chapter thoroughly explained the interaction of PowerShell with the files, folders, and registry objects. It began by displaying how to create a folder and a registry key by leveraging the `new-item` cmdlet. It also displayed the additional arguments that can be used with the `new-item` cmdlet to create a log file with the date time integrated in the filename. The chapter proceeded to display how to create and view a registry key property using the `get-itemproperty` and `new-itemproperty` cmdlets

This chapter then moved to verification of files, folder, and registry items through the `test-path` cmdlet. By using this cmdlet, you can test to see if the object exists prior to interacting with it. You also learned how to interact with copying and moving files and folders by leveraging the `copy-item` and `move-item` cmdlets. You also learned how to rename files, folders, registry keys and registry properties with the use of the `rename-item` and `rename-itemproperty` cmdlets. This chapter ends with learning how to delete files, folders, and registry items by leveraging the `remove-item` and `remove-itemproperty` cmdlets. In the next chapter, you'll learn about file, folder, and registry attributes, access control lists, and properties. You'll learn how to fully modify these items with the use of PowerShell cmdlets.

9

File, Folder, and Registry Attributes, ACLs, and Properties

In the previous chapter, you learned how to create, manage, and test the existence of files, folders, and registry items. You also learned how to rename these items and even copy and move the items to a new location. You ended the chapter by learning how to delete these items from a system.

This chapter extends what you learned in the previous chapter by providing an in-depth view into the attributes, properties, and **access control lists** (**ACL**) for files, folders, and registry items.

In this chapter, you will learn the following techniques:

- Retrieving attributes and properties for file, folder, and registry items
- Viewing file and folder extended attributes
- Setting mode and extended file and folder attributes
- Managing file, folder, and registry permissions
- Copying access control lists
- Adding and removing access control list rules

> The examples in this chapter require you to run PowerShell as administrator. You will not be able to successfully execute the examples if you don't run the PowerShell console as administrator.

This chapter uses script examples that build on the previous chapter. If you have not executed all the steps in the previous chapter, you can run the following script to set up the files, folders, and registry for this chapter:

```
# If the files, folders, and registry items don't exist, create them.
if (!(test-path "HKCU:\Software\MyCustomSoftware\ConnectionInformation"))
{ New-item -path "HKCU:\Software\MyCustomSoftware\ConnectionInformation"
-force | out-null }
if (!(test-path "HKCU:\Software\MyCustomSoftware\AppSettings")) { New-
item -path "HKCU:\Software\MyCustomSoftware\AppSettings" -force | out-
null  }
if (!(test-path "c:\Program Files\MyCustomSoftware\Graphics\")){ New-
item -path "c:\Program Files\MyCustomSoftware\" -name Graphics -ItemType
Directory | out-null }
if (!(test-path "c:\Program Files\MyCustomSoftware\Logs\")){ New-item -
path "c:\Program Files\MyCustomSoftware\" -name Logs -ItemType Directory
| out-null }
if (!(test-path "c:\Program Files\MyCustomSoftware\Graphics\FirstGraphic.
png")) { New-item -path "c:\Program Files\MyCustomSoftware\Graphics\"
-name "FirstGraphic.png" -ItemType File | out-null }
if (!(test-path "c:\Program Files\MyCustomSoftware\Graphics\
SecondGraphic.png")) { New-item -path "c:\Program Files\MyCustomSoftware\
Graphics\" -name "SecondGraphic.png" -ItemType File | out-null }
```

The output of this script is shown in the following screenshot:

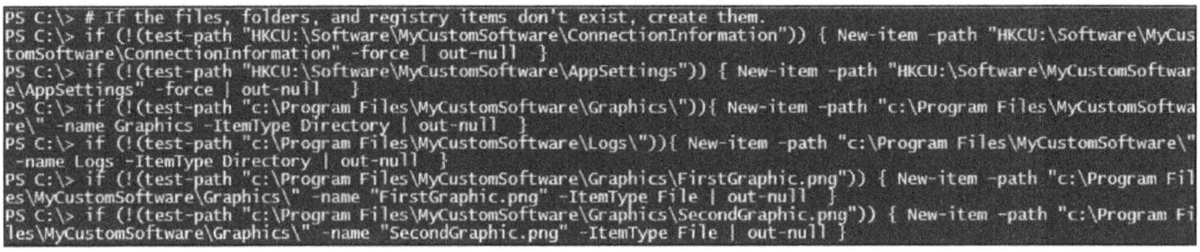
PS C:\> # If the files, folders, and registry items don't exist, create them.
PS C:\> if (!(test-path "HKCU:\Software\MyCustomSoftware\ConnectionInformation")) { New-item -path "HKCU:\Software\MyCus
tomSoftware\ConnectionInformation" -force | out-null }
PS C:\> if (!(test-path "HKCU:\Software\MyCustomSoftware\AppSettings")) { New-item -path "HKCU:\Software\MyCustomSoftwar
e\AppSettings" -force | out-null }
PS C:\> if (!(test-path "c:\Program Files\MyCustomSoftware\Graphics\")){ New-item -path "c:\Program Files\MyCustomSoftwa
re\" -name Graphics -ItemType Directory | out-null }
PS C:\> if (!(test-path "c:\Program Files\MyCustomSoftware\Logs\")){ New-item -path "c:\Program Files\MyCustomSoftware\"
-name Logs -ItemType Directory | out-null }
PS C:\> if (!(test-path "c:\Program Files\MyCustomSoftware\Graphics\FirstGraphic.png")) { New-item -path "c:\Program Fil
es\MyCustomSoftware\Graphics\" -name "FirstGraphic.png" -ItemType File | out-null }
PS C:\> if (!(test-path "c:\Program Files\MyCustomSoftware\Graphics\SecondGraphic.png")) { New-item -path "c:\Program Fi
les\MyCustomSoftware\Graphics\" -name "SecondGraphic.png" -ItemType File | out-null }

Retrieving attributes and properties

PowerShell provides the ability to view a structure of files, folders, and registry keys. This is performed by leveraging the `get-item` cmdlet. The proper syntax for using this cmdlet is calling `get-item`, followed by the `-path` trigger and the path to the file, folder, or registry location you want to look at. The result of the command will display the folders and files or the keys and subkeys for the registry.

When you use the `get-item` cmdlet, it evaluates only the actual object you are referencing. This means that if you reference `c:\windows` as your `-path` trigger, it will only return the properties of the folder itself. Likewise if you are attempting to view the properties of the registry key `HKLM:\Software\Microsoft\Windows\CurrentVersion\`, it will only display the named values and properties in that key and not the subkeys contained in that key.

To view the objects that are contained in a folder or registry key, you can use the `get-childitem` cmdlet. The proper syntax for this cmdlet starts by calling `get-childitem` and then proceeds with using the `-path` trigger and specifying a folder or registry key. After executing this command, you can interact with the child objects that are contained with in that folder and registry key.

When you are interacting with files and folders using the `get-item` and `get-childitem` cmdlets, you will have the ability to see the file and folder mode attributes. These mode attributes provide the operating system-specific instructions on how to interact with the file and folder objects.

The available mode attributes for this include:

- `d----`: This directory attribute specifies that the object is a directory and can contain subdirectories and files.
- `-a---`: This archive attribute is used in backup scenarios to inform the back software if the file has changed since the last backup. When the archive attribute is present, the backup software will back up that file and clear the attribute.
- `--r–`: This read-only attribute specifies that the file or folder can only be read and the contents of that file or folder cannot be modified.
- `---h-`: This hidden attribute specifies that the file or folder objects are hidden from view while exploring the filesystem. In order to see these items, you need to select **Show Hidden Files, Folders, or Drives** in the folder options, given that you've proper permissions to do so.
- `----s`: This system attribute is much like the hidden attribute where it will hide the file or folder from view while exploring the filesystem. This also indicates that the file or folder is integral to the functionality of the operating system and should not be changed or modified.

To view the properties of registry and folder items, you can perform the following action:

```
$regItem = get-item -path "HKCU:\Software\MyCustomSoftware\"
$regItem
```

```
$regChildItem = get-childitem -path "HKCU:\Software\MyCustomSoftware\"
$regChildItem
$dirItem = get-item -path "c:\Program Files\MyCustomSoftware\Graphics\"
$dirItem
$dirChildItem = get-childitem -path "c:\Program Files\MyCustomSoftware\
Graphics\"
$dirChildItem
```

The output of this script is shown in the following screenshot:

PS C:\> $regItem
Hive: HKEY_CURRENT_USER\Software
Name Property
MyCustomSoftware
PS C:\> $regChildItem = get-childitem -path "HKCU:\Software\MyCustomSoftware\"
PS C:\> $regChildItem
Hive: HKEY_CURRENT_USER\Software\MyCustomSoftware
Name Property
AppSettings
ConnectionInformation
PS C:\> $dirItem = get-item -path "c:\Program Files\MyCustomSoftware\Graphics\"
PS C:\> $dirItem
Directory: C:\Program Files\MyCustomSoftware
Mode LastWriteTime Length Name
d---- 03/18/2015 9:47 AM Graphics
PS C:\> $dirChildItem = get-childitem -path "c:\Program Files\MyCustomSoftware\Graphics\"
PS C:\> $dirChildItem
Directory: C:\Program Files\MyCustomSoftware\Graphics
Mode LastWriteTime Length Name
-a--- 03/18/2015 9:47 AM 0 FirstGraphic.png
-a--- 03/18/2015 9:47 AM 0 SecondGraphic.png

The preceding example displays how to properly view the attributes and properties of files, folders, and registry keys. It also displays how to view the attributes and properties of the child items of files, folders, and registry keys. You first start by declaring the variable of `$regitem` and then call the `get-item` cmdlet, with the `-path` trigger referencing the registry path of `HKCU:\Software\MyCustomSoftware\`. You then call `$regitem` which displays only the properties of the `MyCustomSoftware` subkey.

You then proceed to declare the `$regChildItem` variable with the `get-childitem` cmdlet and supply the `-path` trigger referencing the registry path of `HKCU:\Software\MyCustomSoftware\`. You then call the `$regChildItem` variable, which will then display the child items of `MyCustomSoftware` including its subkeys and properties.

You continue the script by declaring the `$dirItem` variable, followed by the `get-item` cmdlet and the `-path` trigger pointing to `c:\Program Files\MyCustomSoftware\Graphics\`. You then call the `$diritem` variable which will display the attributes and properties of the `Graphics` directory. You will see that the `Mode` attribute is set to `d----`, which indicates that `Graphics` is a directory. You will also see the `LastWriteTime` attribute, which is the last time that an item was written or deleted in that directory.

Finally, you declare the `$dirChildItem` variable, followed by the `get-childitem` cmdlet. You reference the `-path` trigger and set the path to `c:\Program Files\MyCustomSoftware\Graphics\`. You then call the `$dirChildItem` variable, which will contain the child items of the `Graphics` directory. You will also see the properties of these child items with the `Mode` attribute of `-a---`, which indicates that these files have changed since the last backup of the system. You will also see the `LastWriteTime` attribute, which is the last time when those files were modified.

Viewing file and folder extended attributes

When you use the standard `get-item` and `get-childitem` cmdlets, you are able to see the default `mode` attributes for the files and folders that are available with FAT32 file systems. With the introduction of **New Technology File System** (**NTFS**), however, Microsoft extended the file and folder attributes to a much larger set. This was done to support additional features and technologies surrounding NTFS such as encryption and compression.

The list of new attributes includes:

- `Compressed`: This attribute designates that the filesystem applied compression to the files or folders.
- `Encrypted`: This attribute designates that the filesystem applied encryption to the files or folders.
- `Normal`: This attribute, when assigned, clears the other attributes to make the files to have only the `NotContentIndexed` attribute and folders to have the `NotContentIndexed` and `Directory` attributes.
- `NotContentIndexed`: This attribute designates that the filesystem should include the file or folder as part of the routine indexing of the operating system so that searching can be expedited.
- `ReparsePoint`: A reparse point is a sector in the filesystem which designates user data for an application. A reparse point may also be a mounted volume designated by a folder.
- `SparseFile`: This attribute designates a large file that is made up of empty bit values. This could be a fixed size database or a virtual disk that is preprovisioned to be of a fixed size. While the file is reserving space contagiously, it may not be filled with data.
- `Temporary`: This attribute designates the files or folders to be temporary, and the operating system will parse the file or folders in memory while in use. This is designated for files and folders which have a very short lifetime on a system like the software installation source.

In order to expose all of the attributes, methods, and properties available to an object, you can leverage the `get-member` cmdlet. The `get-member` cmdlet is typically used in a piped scenario where you first reference an object using the `get-item` or `get-childitem` cmdlets with a file and then pipe the object to `get-member`. The `get-member` cmdlet will then display the `Attributes`, `Properties`, `Methods`, and other `Extended Properties` about that file.

To view the attributes, properties, methods, and extended properties of a file, do the following action:

```
get-item -path "c:\Program Files\MyCustomSoftware\Graphics\FirstGraphic.
png" | get-member
```

The truncated output of this script is shown in the following screenshot:

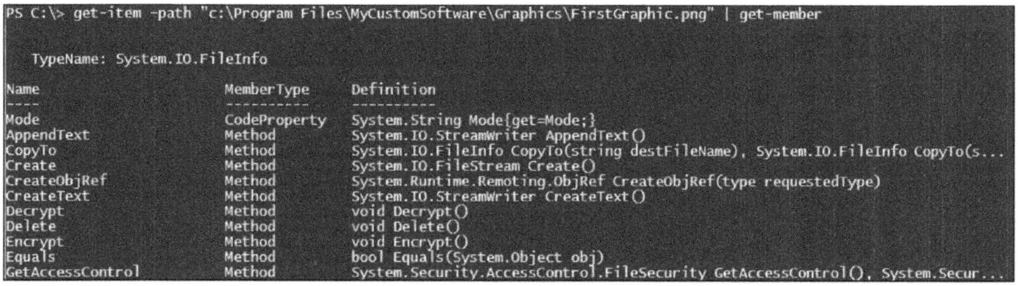

```
PS C:\> get-item -path "c:\Program Files\MyCustomSoftware\Graphics\FirstGraphic.png" | get-member

   TypeName: System.IO.FileInfo

Name             MemberType     Definition
----             ----------     ----------
Mode             CodeProperty   System.String Mode{get=Mode;}
AppendText       Method         System.IO.StreamWriter AppendText()
CopyTo           Method         System.IO.FileInfo CopyTo(string destFileName), System.IO.FileInfo CopyTo(s...
Create           Method         System.IO.FileStream Create()
CreateObjRef     Method         System.Runtime.Remoting.ObjRef CreateObjRef(type requestedType)
CreateText       Method         System.IO.StreamWriter CreateText()
Decrypt          Method         void Decrypt()
Delete           Method         void Delete()
Encrypt          Method         void Encrypt()
Equals           Method         bool Equals(System.Object obj)
GetAccessControl Method         System.Security.AccessControl.FileSecurity GetAccessControl(), System.Secur...
```

The preceding script shows how you display the `Attributes`, `Properties`, `Methods`, and other `Extended Properties` about a file. You first start by using the `get-item` cmdlet, with `the -path` trigger set to `c:\Program Files\MyCustomSoftware\Graphics\FirstGraphic.png`. You then pipe that result to the `get-member` cmdlet. The result of this command is printing to the console a list of `48` different `Attributes`, `Properties`, `Methods`, and other `Extended Properties`. Some of the more notable attributes are the `Attributes` property, the `Mode` property, the `CodeProperty` property, the `LastAccessTime` property, the `LasteWriteTime` property, the `Delete` method, the `Encrypt` method, the `Decrypt` method, and the `Open` method. Each of these items describes an action or information pertaining to the file located at `c:\Program Files\MyCustomSoftware\Graphics\FirstGraphic.png`.

Setting the mode and extended file and folder attributes

When you want to change the mode and the extended attributes of a file or folder, you need to access the extended property named `Attributes`. The `Attributes` property allows you to read and write to itself. This means that if you want to replace all of the file or folder attributes, you can just declare the new `Attributes` and set them to the `Attributes` property. Likewise, if you want to maintain the existing `Attributes` but want to add new `Attributes`, you declare a variable and call the existing `Attributes` property; then you add the new `Attributes` using a comma separator. You then set that new variable to the `Attributes` property of a file or folder.

To view and add a new extended file attribute, do the following action:

```
# Get file attributes
$file = get-item -path "c:\Program Files\MyCustomSoftware\Graphics\
FirstGraphic.png"
```

```
$attributes = $file.attributes
$attributes
# Append ReadOnly attribute to existing attributes
$newattributes = "$attributes, ReadOnly"
# Write over existing attributes with new attributes
$file.attributes = $newattributes
$file.attributes
```

The output of this script is shown in the following screenshot:

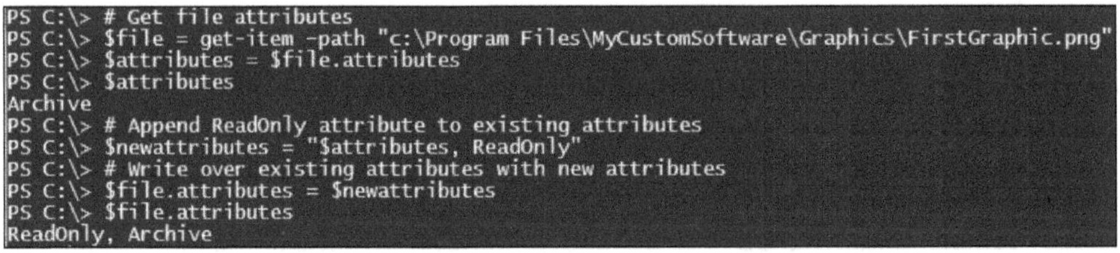
PS C:\> # Get file attributes
PS C:\> $file = get-item -path "c:\Program Files\MyCustomSoftware\Graphics\FirstGraphic.png"
PS C:\> $attributes = $file.attributes
PS C:\> $attributes
Archive
PS C:\> # Append ReadOnly attribute to existing attributes
PS C:\> $newattributes = "$attributes, ReadOnly"
PS C:\> # Write over existing attributes with new attributes
PS C:\> $file.attributes = $newattributes
PS C:\> $file.attributes
ReadOnly, Archive

After executing the preceding script, the `FirstGraphic.png` file will have properties as shown in the following screenshot:

Attributes:
Read-only
Hidden

This script displays how to retrieve the existing `Attributes` of a file, how to add the `ReadOnly Attribute`, and how to write the attribute back to the file. You first start by declaring the `$file` variable. You then call the `get-item` cmdlet with the `-path` trigger set to `c:\Program Files\MyCustomSoftware\Graphics\FirstGraphic.png`. This will set the `FirstGraphic.png` file object to the variable. You then declare the `$attributes` variable and set that equal to the `Attributes` property by calling `$file.Attributes`. After that, you call the `$attributes` property to display the attributes to the console which reads `Archive, NotContentIndexed`.

You proceed to declare the `$newattributes` variable by setting it equal to the existing attributes of `$attributes` and by adding the comma separator and the `Attribute` of `ReadOnly`. You then set the `$file.attributes` property of `c:\Program Files\MyCustomSoftware\Graphics\FirstGraphic.png` equal to `$newattributes`. You verify that the new attributes are set by calling the `$file.attributes` property again. After executing this script, you have successfully added the `ReadOnly` attribute to `c:\Program Files\MyCustomSoftware\Graphics\FirstGraphic.png`.

When you want to remove attributes from files and folders, you typically want to preserve the existing attributes that have already been assigned to those items. This means that you cannot simply overwrite the file and folder attributes with the desired ones because each individual file and folder may have different attributes. The best way to handle this is to retrieve the attributes of a file or folder, place them into an array, loop through the attributes in the array, and rebuild a new array with only the attributes you want to use. You then set the attributes in that new array to the file or folder effectively removing the attributes you no longer want on a file.

To parse file attributes and remove them, you can perform the following action:

```
# Get File Attributes
$file = get-item -path "c:\Program Files\MyCustomSoftware\Graphics\
FirstGraphic.png"
$attributes = $file.attributes
# Convert attributes to string
$attributes = $attributes.tostring()
# Split individual attributes into array
$attributes = $attributes.split(",")
# Read through the individual attributes
Foreach ($attribute in $attributes) {
  # If read Only, skip
  if ($attribute -like "*ReadOnly*") {
      write-host "Skipping Attribute: $attribute"
    }
    # Else add attribute to attribute list
  else {
      $newattribute += "$attribute,"
      Write-Host "Attribute Added: $attribute"
    }
}
# Remove the trailing comma
$newattribute = $newattribute.trimend(",")
# Write over existing attributes with new attributes
$file.attributes = $newattribute
Write-host "New File attributes are: " $file.attributes
```

The output of this script is shown in the following screenshot:

```
PS C:\> # Get File Attributes
PS C:\> $file = get-item -path "c:\Program Files\MyCustomSoftware\Graphics\FirstGraphic.png"
PS C:\> $attributes = $file.attributes
PS C:\> # Convert attributes to string
PS C:\> $attributes = $attributes.tostring()
PS C:\> # Split individual attributes into array
PS C:\> $attributes = $attributes.split(",")
PS C:\> # Read through the individual attributes
PS C:\> Foreach ($attribute in $attributes) {
>> # If read Only, skip
>> if ($attribute -like "*ReadOnly*") {
>> write-host "Skipping Attribute: $attribute"
>> }
>> # Else add attribute to attribute list
>> else {
>> $newattribute += "$attribute,"
>> Write-Host "Attribute Added: $attribute"
>> }
>> }
>> # Remove the trailing comma
>> $newattribute = $newattribute.trimend(",")
>> # Write over existing attributes with new attributes
>> $file.attributes = $newattribute
>> Write-host "New File attributes are: " $file.attributes
>>
Skipping Attribute: ReadOnly
Attribute Added:  Archive
New File attributes are:  Archive
```

After executing the preceding script, the `FirstGraphic.png` file will have properties, as shown in the following screenshot:

The preceding script displays how to properly read the attributes of a file, store the attributes in a variable, identify the attribute to be removed, create a new variable with the attributes to be set, and set the attributes back on the file. To start, you first use the `get-item` cmdlet, with the `-path` trigger pointing to `c:\Program Files\MyCustomSoftware\Graphics\FirstGraphic.png` and then save the object to `$file`. You then create the `$attributes` variable and populate the file's attributes by issuing `$file.attributes`. As the `Attributes` property is an object, you have to convert that property to text to parse the individual values. You then convert the object to a string by re-declaring the `$attributes` variable and using the `.tostring()` method on that variable. The result will have all of the attributes listed in a string format.

After converting the value to string, you have to use the `split()` method to place the individual `Attributes` as separate array items. You re-declare the `$attribute` variable and issue the `$attributes.split(",")` method to split the individual values into `$attributes` variables. From here you need to read through the individual attributes and create a `foreach` loop structure to evaluate each `$attribute` in the `$attributes` variable. You create an `IF` statement to evaluate if the current `$attribute` is `-like "*ReadOnly*"`. If it is so, you write to the console `Skipping Attribute: $atttribute`. If the value does not match `*ReadOnly*`, then you add the existing `$attribute` being evaluated, followed by a comma to the `$newattribute` variable. You also write `Attribute Added: $attribute` to the console.

The `Attributes` property is very specific regarding the format of the `Attributes` property being passed into a file or a folder. As a result, you cannot have a trailing comma at the end of the `$newattribute` variable because the `Attribute` property will be looking for another `Attribute` value after that comma. To trim any trailing commas from the `$newattribute` variable, you execute the `$newattribute.trimend(",")` method, which removes the comma at the end of the variable. Finally, you set the `$file.attributes` property to the `$newattribute` variable and write `New File Attributes are: $file.attributes` to the console. After executing this script, you will see that `c:\Program Files\MyCustomSoftware\Graphics\FirstGraphic.png` no longer has the `ReadOnly` attribute.

> If a file or a folder has the `Hidden` attribute, you will not be able to interact with the file or folder using cmdlets. The workaround for this is to leverage the `-force` trigger in order to bypass the `Hidden` attribute. You will then be able to modify the hidden files and folders using the script described in this section.

Managing file, folder, and registry permissions

PowerShell provides the ability to manage file, folder, and registry permissions. To update security permissions, you have to interact with the access control list. The ACL contains access rules that permit or deny specific actions on a file, folder, or registry item. The most common security permissions that can be set on files and folders are shown here:

- **Full control**: This allows writing, reading, changing, and deleting objects.
- **Modify**: This allows writing, reading, and deleting objects. It does not permit taking ownership of objects.

- **Read and execute**: This allows reading, listing objects in a directory, and executing objects.
- **List folder contents**: This allows listing of objects in a directory and executing them.
- **Read**: This allows viewing and listing files and directories.
- **Write**: This allows the addition of new files and directories.

> Executing and reading files are two different actions. Reading is much like opening a PowerShell `.PS1` file in ISE. You have the ability to view the code inside the file itself. Executing is like running a `.PS1` file as a script within PowerShell. If you have read permissions but not executed them, Windows will block the execution of this script. It will, however, allow you to view the code in the script.

Copying access control lists

The process of copying the access control lists is for scenarios where you already have defined files, folders, and registry items, and you need to ensure that the additional objects have the same permissions as the other files, folders, and registry items. The method of copying access control lists leverages the `get-acl` and `set-acl` cmdlets. The `get-acl` cmdlet is responsible for reading the access control list on a file, folder, or registry item. The proper syntax of this cmdlet is defining a variable, calling the `get-acl` cmdlet, and using the `-path` trigger to specify the location of an object. The variable will then contain the access control list of the object that you defined. When you want to change the ACL of a file or folder, you need to use the `set-acl` cmdlet with the variable that you defined to overlay the permissions on a different object. The proper syntax of this cmdlet includes calling the `set-acl` cmdlet, referencing the `-path` trigger with the path of the object who's ACL you want to change, followed by the `-aclobject` with the variable that contains the ACL. After executing these two cmdlets, you will have effectively copied permissions from one object to another.

To copy an access control list from one item to another, you can perform the following action:

```
# Get the existing ACL on the FirstGraphic.png file
$fileACL = get-acl -path "c:\Program Files\MyCustomSoftware\Graphics\FirstGraphic.png"
# Set the ACL from FirstGraphic.png on SecondGraphic.png
Set-acl -path "c:\Program Files\MyCustomSoftware\Graphics\SecondGraphic.png" -aclobject $fileACL
```

```
# Get the existing ACL on the Logs directory
$dirACL = get-acl -path "c:\Program Files\MyCustomSoftware\Logs"
# Set the ACL from the Logs directory on the Graphics directory
Set-acl -path "c:\Program Files\MyCustomSoftware\Graphics" -aclobject
$dirACL
# Get the existing ACL from the ConnectionInformation key
$regACL = get-acl -path "HKCU:\Software\MyCustomSoftware\
ConnectionInformation"
# Set the ACL from ConnectionInformation on the AppSettings key
Set-acl -path "HKCU:\Software\MyCustomSoftware\AppSettings" -aclobject
$regACL
```

The output of this is shown in the following screenshot:

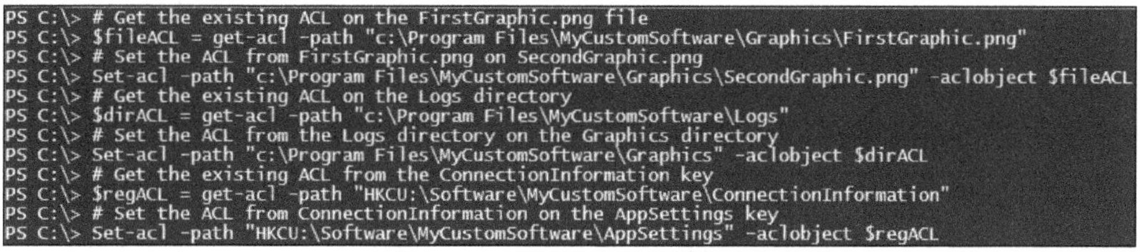
PS C:\> # Get the existing ACL on the FirstGraphic.png file
PS C:\> $fileACL = get-acl -path "c:\Program Files\MyCustomSoftware\Graphics\FirstGraphic.png"
PS C:\> # Set the ACL from FirstGraphic.png on SecondGraphic.png
PS C:\> Set-acl -path "c:\Program Files\MyCustomSoftware\Graphics\SecondGraphic.png" -aclobject $fileACL
PS C:\> # Get the existing ACL on the Logs directory
PS C:\> $dirACL = get-acl -path "c:\Program Files\MyCustomSoftware\Logs"
PS C:\> # Set the ACL from the Logs directory on the Graphics directory
PS C:\> Set-acl -path "c:\Program Files\MyCustomSoftware\Graphics" -aclobject $dirACL
PS C:\> # Get the existing ACL from the ConnectionInformation key
PS C:\> $regACL = get-acl -path "HKCU:\Software\MyCustomSoftware\ConnectionInformation"
PS C:\> # Set the ACL from ConnectionInformation on the AppSettings key
PS C:\> Set-acl -path "HKCU:\Software\MyCustomSoftware\AppSettings" -aclobject $regACL

This example displays how to properly copy an ACL from a file, folder, and registry key and apply these permissions to a different file, folder, and registry key. You start by declaring the `$fileACL` variable and then use the `get-acl` cmdet and call the `-path` trigger pointing at the `c:\Program Files\MyCustomSoftware\Graphics\FirstGraphic.png` file. This copies the ACL from the file to the `$fileACL` variable. You then leverage the `set-acl` cmdlet and use the `-path` trigger pointing at the `c:\Program Files\MyCustomSoftware\Graphics\SecondGraphic.png` file; then you call `-aclobject` with the `$fileACL` variable. After executing these lines of code, the security permissions defined in the ACL of the `FirstGraphic.png` file have been copied over the permissions of the `SecondGraphic.png` file.

You then declare the `$dirACL` variable and use the `get-acl` cmdlet, followed by calling the `-path` trigger pointing at the `c:\Program Files\MyCustomSoftware\Logs` directory. This copies the ACL of that directory to the `$dirACL` variable. You then leverage the `set-acl` cmdlet and use the `-path` trigger pointing at the `c:\Program Files\MyCustomSoftware\Graphics\` directory, followed by calling `-aclobject` with the `$dirACL` variable. After executing this portion of the script, the security permissions defined in the ACL of the directory `Logs` are successfully copied over the permissions of the directory `Graphics`.

Finally, you set the permissions on the registry key. You first declare the `$regACL` variable, use the `get-acl` cmdlet, and call the `-path` trigger pointing at the `HKCU:\Software\MyCustomSoftware\ConnectionInformation` registry key. This copies the ACL of that key to the `$regACL` variable. You then leverage the `set-acl` cmdlet and use the `-path` trigger pointing at the `HKCU:\Software\MyCustomSoftware\AppSettings` registry key, followed by calling `-aclobject` with the `$regACL` variable. After executing this portion of the script, the security permissions defined in the ACL of the `ConnectionInformation` registry key are successfully copied over the permissions of the `AppSettings` registry key.

Adding and removing ACL rules

PowerShell provides the ability to reference .NET classes in order to be able to perform advanced programming operations within scripts. While Microsoft has done a great job in expanding cmdlets to modify a large portion of the operating system, PowerShell doesn't provide the direct ability to add and remove individual access control list rules. This means that there isn't a direct method to add or remove a user or a group to a file, folder, or registry object.

The adding and removing ACL process flow is represented in the following diagram:

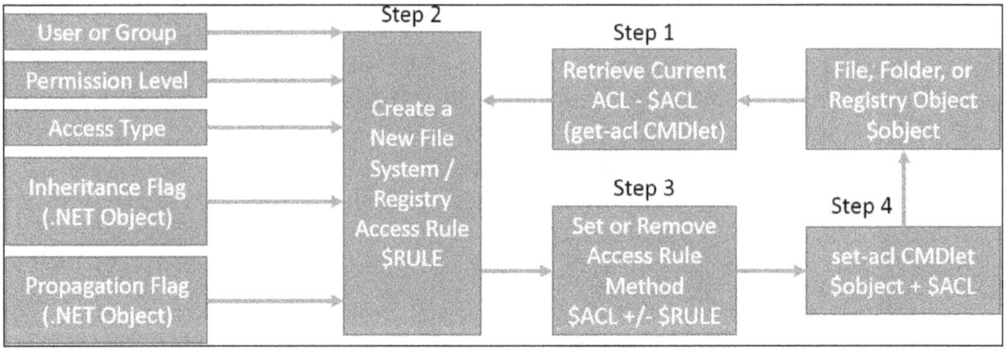

When you want to change an ACL, you are required to create a new access rule. An access rule defines permissions that are to be set or removed on a file, folder, or registry item. This is done by leveraging `system.security.accesscontrol.filesystemaccessrule` and the `system.security.accesscontrol.registryaccessrule` .NET class. This class is used in conjunction with the `get-acl` and `set-acl` cmdlets to create and set access rules on particular objects.

To create a new access rule, you first have to obtain an ACL from a particular file, folder, or registry object. You will need to define a variable like `$ACL` to contain the ACL of an object. You will then set the `$ACL` variable equal to the `get-acl` cmdlet with the `-path` trigger pointing to a specific object.

The second step in the process is to create the access rule itself. Access rules require several components, which need to be declared for the rule to be properly set on an operating system. These requirements include the following objects:

- **User or group**: This is the user or group that you wanted to be added or removed from a file, folder, or registry object.
- **Inheritance flag**: This specifies that any new objects created in that directory have the permissions defined by the new access control rule. This will not apply to the existing objects in the directory. The inheritance flag must be set as a variable calling the `[system.security.accesscontrol.InheritanceFlags]` .NET class with the `ContainerInherit` and `ObjectInherit` arguments. This will ensure that the directories and subsequent objects will inherit the values(which are not required for registry access rules).
- **Propagation flag**: This specifies that the operating system should apply this permission to the subdirectories and subobjects recursively. This means that any file or folder below the object you are setting the new access control rule on will receive the new access rule. The propagation flag must be set as a variable calling the `[system.security.accesscontrol.PropagationFlags]` .NET class with the `none` argument. (This is not required for registry access rules.)
- **Permission level**: This specifies the permission level that you want to define for the user or group.
- **Access type**: This specifies whether you want the permission specified to be `Allow` or `Deny`.

The second step requires that you create a variable for the `$inherit` requirement, which contains the `[system.security.accesscontrol.InheritanceFlags]"ContainerInherit, ObjectInherit"` object. This will set the inheritance flag properly for use with the new access control rule. You also need to create a variable for the `$propagation` requirement which contains the object `[system.security.accesscontrol.PropagationFlags]"None"`. This will set the propagation flag properly for use with the new access control rule.

To complete the second step, you have to create the access rule. To do this, you start by declaring a variable like `$rule` to contain the new access rule. You then need to create a new object with the `new-object` cmdlet and reference the `system.security.accesscontrol.filesystemaccessrule` or the `system.security.accesscontrol.registryaccessrule` .NET class. For file system permissions, you will provide the arguments required for the rule, which are these: `(User/Group, PermissionLevel, $inherit, $propagation, AccessType)`. For registry permissions, you will provide the arguments required for the rule, which are these: `(User/Group, PermissionLevel, AccessType)`. Upon successful entry of the required access rule items, the access rule will be stored in the `$rule` variable.

The third step in the process is updating ACL variable with the new access rule. In the instances where you want to add or modify existing rules, you will use the `$ACL.setaccessrule($Rule)` method to modify the `$ACL` variable to have the new `Allow` or `Deny` permissions. If you want to remove permissions, you will use the `$ACL.removeAccessRuleAll($Rule)` method to modify the `$ACL` variable to not contain the items in the access rule.

The fourth and final step is leveraging the `set-acl` cmdlet with the `-path` trigger pointing to the file, folder, or registry item you want to modify. You also need to specify the `-aclobject` trigger with the `$ACL` variable of which you want the new permissions to be. Upon execution of this portion of the script, the permissions will be added, modified, or removed from the file, folder, or registry item you specified.

To modify the access control list on a folder, you can perform the following action:

```
# Get the ACL from the Graphics directory
$ACL = Get-Acl "c:\program files\MyCustomSoftware\Graphics"
# Search the updated ACL for the Everyone group
$ACL.access | where { $_.IdentityReference -contains "Everyone" }
# Populate group variable for permissions
$group = "Everyone"
# Populate the permissions variable for setting permissions
$permission = "FullControl, Synchronize"
# Designate the inheritance information for permissions
$inherit = [system.security.accesscontrol.InheritanceFlags]"ContainerInhe
rit, ObjectInherit"
# Designate the propagation information for permission propagation
$propagation = [system.security.accesscontrol.PropagationFlags]"None"
# Set to Allow Permissions
$accesstype = "Allow"
```

```
# Create the New Access Control list Rule
$Rule = New-Object system.security.accesscontrol.filesystemaccessrule($gr
oup,$permission,$inherit,$propagation,$accesstype)
# Merge new permissions with the existing ACL object
$ACL.SetAccessRule($RULE)
# Set the ACL on folder
Set-Acl -path "c:\program files\MyCustomSoftware\Graphics" -aclobject
$Acl
# Get Updated ACL on folder
$ACL = Get-Acl "c:\program files\MyCustomSoftware\Graphics"
# Search the updated ACL for the Everyone group
$ACL.access | where { $_.IdentityReference -contains "Everyone" }
```

The output of this script is shown in the following screenshot:

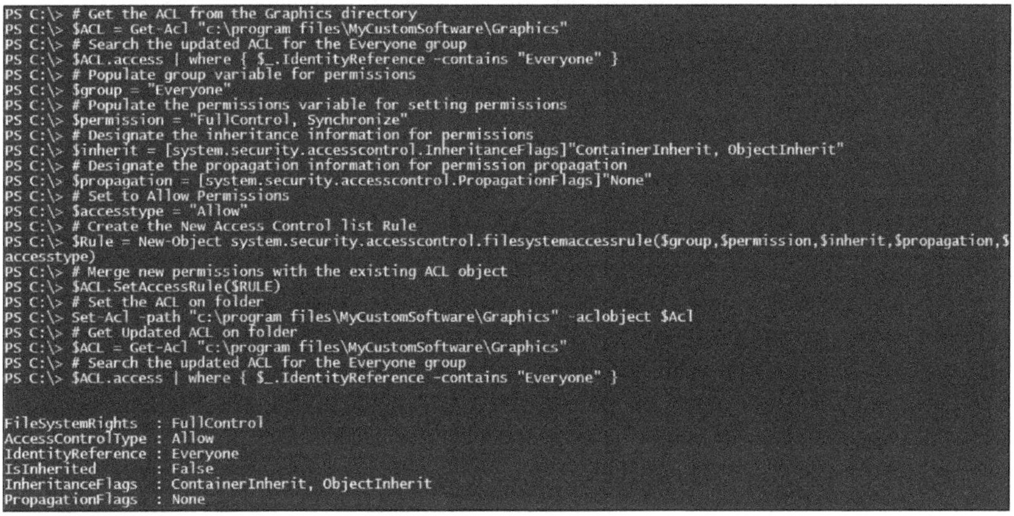

PS C:\> # Get the ACL from the Graphics directory
PS C:\> $ACL = Get-Acl "c:\program files\MyCustomSoftware\Graphics"
PS C:\> # Search the updated ACL for the Everyone group
PS C:\> $ACL.access | where { $_.IdentityReference -contains "Everyone" }
PS C:\> # Populate group variable for permissions
PS C:\> $group = "Everyone"
PS C:\> # Populate the permissions variable for setting permissions
PS C:\> $permission = "FullControl, Synchronize"
PS C:\> # Designate the inheritance information for permissions
PS C:\> $inherit = [system.security.accesscontrol.InheritanceFlags]"ContainerInherit, ObjectInherit"
PS C:\> # Designate the propagation information for permission propagation
PS C:\> $propagation = [system.security.accesscontrol.PropagationFlags]"None"
PS C:\> # Set to Allow Permissions
PS C:\> $accesstype = "Allow"
PS C:\> # Create the New Access Control list Rule
PS C:\> $Rule = New-Object system.security.accesscontrol.filesystemaccessrule($group,$permission,$inherit,$propagation,$accesstype)
PS C:\> # Merge new permissions with the existing ACL object
PS C:\> $ACL.SetAccessRule($RULE)
PS C:\> # Set the ACL on folder
PS C:\> Set-Acl -path "c:\program files\MyCustomSoftware\Graphics" -aclobject $Acl
PS C:\> # Get Updated ACL on folder
PS C:\> $ACL = Get-Acl "c:\program files\MyCustomSoftware\Graphics"
PS C:\> # Search the updated ACL for the Everyone group
PS C:\> $ACL.access | where { $_.IdentityReference -contains "Everyone" }
FileSystemRights : FullControl
AccessControlType : Allow
IdentityReference : Everyone
IsInherited : False
InheritanceFlags : ContainerInherit, ObjectInherit
PropagationFlags : None

This script displays how to obtain an existing ACL of a folder, how to create an access rule, how to apply the access rule to an existing ACL, and how to set the updated ACL back on the folder. This will successfully update permissions on the folder specified. You begin by obtaining the ACL of `c:\program files\MyCustomSoftware\Graphics` using the `get-acl` cmdlet and then proceed to storing the value in the `$ACL` variable. You then search the `$ACL.access` property to the `Graphics` folder and pipe that where there is an `IdentityReference` that matches the group named `Everyone`. Since the `Everyone` group is not currently assigned permissions on the folder, it will return nothing.

You then start building the prerequisites for the access rule by defining the group of `Everyone` to the `$group` variable and the permissions of `FullControl, Synchronize` in the `$permission` variable. You then create a new variable named `$inherit` and specify the .NET class `[system.security.accesscontrol.InheritanceFlags]` with the `"ContainerInherit, ObjectInherit"` properties on the inheritance flag. This ensures that objects and other directories inherit the permissions as they are being created or moved to that location. You create a new variable named `$propagation` and specify the .NET class `[system.security.accesscontrol.PropagationFlags]` with the `None` properties on the propagation flag. This will ensure that the operating system will not propagate the permissions to the subdirectory or subobjects in that directory. You then create a variable of `$accesstype` and set the access type property to `Allow`. Finally, you create the new access rule in the `$rule` variable with the `new-object` cmdlet, referencing the .NET class `system.security.accesscontrol.filesystemaccessrule` and the arguments of `($group,$permission,$inherit,$propagation,$accesstype)`.

After creating the access rule, you apply the access rule to the `$ACL` variable using the `setaccessrule` method with the `($Rule)` argument. The `$Rule` object will then apply to `$ACL`, and the new permissions will be contained in the `$ACL` variable. You then set the new ACL back on the `c:\program files\MyCustomSoftware\Graphics` folder with the `set-acl` cmdlet, the `-path` trigger to the folder location, and the `-aclobject` trigger pointing to the updated ACL in the `$ACL` variable.

After applying the new ACL you then verify that the permissions were set properly by defining the `$ACL` variable by using the `get-acl` cmdlet pointing at the `c:\program files\MyCustomSoftware\Graphics` folder. You then search the updated `$ACL.access` property to the `Graphics` folder and pipe `Where` there is an `IdentityReference` that matches the group named `Everyone`. As the `Everyone` is now assigned permissions on the folder, the search will return with the `Everyone` group having `FullControl, Synchronize` permissions on the `c:\program files\MyCustomSoftware\Graphics` directory.

To modify the access control list of a registry key, you can perform the following action:

```
# Get the ACL from the ConnectionInformation registry key
$ACL = Get-Acl "HKCU:\Software\MyCustomSoftware\ConnectionInformation"
# Search the updated ACL for the Everyone group
$ACL.access | where { $_.IdentityReference -contains "Everyone" }
# Populate group variable for permissions
$group = "Everyone"
# Populate the permissions variable for setting permissions
```

```
$permission = "FullControl"
# Set to Allow Permissions
$accesstype = "Allow"
# Create the New Access Control list Rule
$Rule = New-Object system.security.accesscontrol.RegistryAccessrule($grou
p,$permission,$accesstype)
# Merge new permissions with the existing ACL object
$ACL.SetAccessRule($RULE)
# Set the ACL on registry key
Set-Acl -path "HKCU:\Software\MyCustomSoftware\ConnectionInformation"
-aclobject $Acl
# Get Updated ACL on registry key
$ACL = Get-Acl "HKCU:\Software\MyCustomSoftware\ConnectionInformation"
# Search the updated ACL for the Everyone group
$ACL.access | where { $_.IdentityReference -contains "Everyone" }
```

The output of this script is shown in the following screenshot:

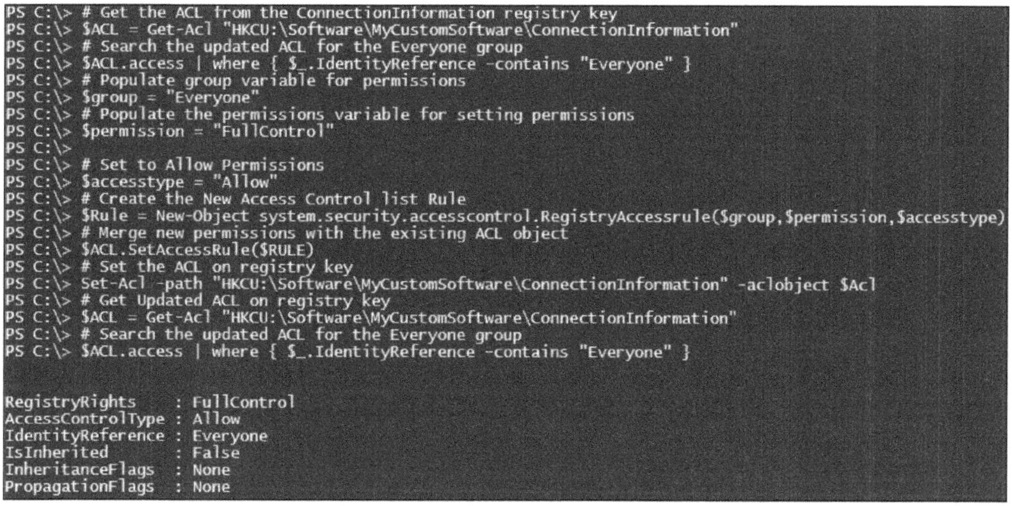
PS C:\> # Get the ACL from the ConnectionInformation registry key
PS C:\> $ACL = Get-Acl "HKCU:\Software\MyCustomSoftware\ConnectionInformation"
PS C:\> # Search the updated ACL for the Everyone group
PS C:\> $ACL.access | where { $_.IdentityReference -contains "Everyone" }
PS C:\> # Populate group variable for permissions
PS C:\> $group = "Everyone"
PS C:\> # Populate the permissions variable for setting permissions
PS C:\> $permission = "FullControl"
PS C:\>
PS C:\> # Set to Allow Permissions
PS C:\> $accesstype = "Allow"
PS C:\> # Create the New Access Control list Rule
PS C:\> $Rule = New-Object system.security.accesscontrol.RegistryAccessrule($group,$permission,$accesstype)
PS C:\> # Merge new permissions with the existing ACL object
PS C:\> $ACL.SetAccessRule($RULE)
PS C:\> # Set the ACL on registry key
PS C:\> Set-Acl -path "HKCU:\Software\MyCustomSoftware\ConnectionInformation" -aclobject $Acl
PS C:\> # Get Updated ACL on registry key
PS C:\> $ACL = Get-Acl "HKCU:\Software\MyCustomSoftware\ConnectionInformation"
PS C:\> # Search the updated ACL for the Everyone group
PS C:\> $ACL.access | where { $_.IdentityReference -contains "Everyone" }
RegistryRights : FullControl
AccessControlType : Allow
IdentityReference : Everyone
IsInherited : False
InheritanceFlags : None
PropagationFlags : None

This script displays how to obtain an existing ACL of a registry key, how to create an access rule and apply it to an existing ACL, and how to set the updated ACL back on the registry key. This will successfully update permissions on the registry key specified. You begin by obtaining the ACL of `HKCU:\Software\MyCustomSoftware\ConnectionInformation` using the `get-acl` cmdlet, and then you store the value in the `$ACL` variable. You then search the `$ACL.access` property to the `ConnectionInformation` registry key and pipe that `where` there is `IdentityReference` that matches the group named `Everyone`. As the `Everyone` group is not currently assigned permissions on the registry key, it will return nothing.

You then start building the prerequisites for the access rule by defining the group of `Everyone` to the `$group` variable and the permissions of `FullControl` in the `$permission` variable. You then create a variable of `$accesstype` and set the access type property to `Allow`. Finally, you create the new access rule in the `$rule` variable with the `new-object` cmdlet, referencing the `system.security.accesscontrol.registryaccessrule` .NET class and the arguments of `($group,$permission,$accesstype)`.

After creating the access rule, you apply the access rule to the `$ACL` variable using the `setaccessrule` method with the `($Rule)` argument. The `$Rule` object will then apply to `$ACL`, and the new permissions will be contained in the `$ACL` variable. You then set the new ACL back on the `HKCU:\Software\MyCustomSoftware\ConnectionInformation` registry key with the `set-acl` cmdlet, the `-path` trigger to the registry key location, and the `-aclobject` trigger pointing to the updated ACL in the `$ACL` variable.

After applying the new ACL, you verify that the permissions were set properly by defining the `$ACL` variable using the `get-acl` cmdlet pointing at the `HKCU:\Software\MyCustomSoftware\ConnectionInformation` registry key. You then search the updated `$ACL.access` property to the `ConnectionInformation` registry key and pipe that `where` there is an `IdentityReference` that matches the group named `Everyone`. Since `Everyone` is now assigned permissions on the registry key, the search will return with the `Everyone` group having `FullControl` permissions on the `HKCU:\Software\MyCustomSoftware\ConnectionInformation` registry key.

Summary

This chapter thoroughly explained the interaction of PowerShell with the files, folders, and registry attributes and access control lists. It began by explaining how to use the `get-item` and `get-childitem` cmdlets to obtain the file, folder, and registry attributes. You also learned that these cmdlets are used to browse the subitems of the files, folders, and registry items. You then learned how to use the `get-item` cmdlet with the `get-member` cmdlet to list all of the available properties and methods available for a specific object type. You then proceeded to configure file attributes through the use of the built-in `Attribute` property of files. You learned how to remove attributes by converting the attribute's property to a string, splitting the values by the comma separator, creating a `foreach` loop to read through the individual attributes, and replacing the `Attributes` property of a file with the new attributes.

You also explored the `get-acl` and the `set-acl` cmdlets to copy permissions from one file, folder, or registry item to another. You learned that if you want to set permissions on a file or a folder, you need to follow four steps. First, you need to use the `get-acl` cmdlet to retrieve an existing access control list of the file, folder, or registry item you are trying to set permissions on. The second item is to create a filesystem or registry access rule. This rule is comprised of a user or a group, permission level, access type, and the inheritance and propagation flags for files and folders. The third step is to use the `setaccessrule()` or `removeaccessruleall()` methods to apply the new rule to the copied access control list. This will add, change, or remove the items specified in the access control list. You finally use the `set-acl` cmdlet to apply the new access control list to the file, folder, or registry item. You learned that in order to set permissions, you need to use the `system.security.accesscontrol.filesystemaccessrule` or `system.security.accesscontrol.registryaccessrule` .NET classes to properly set permissions. Now, at the end of this chapter, you may be fully proficient in modifications of file, folders, and registry objects. In the next chapter, you'll explore **Windows Management Instrumentation** (**WMI**). You'll learn how to leverage WMI and CIM cmdlets to view different classes and facilitate better management of systems.

10

Windows Management Instrumentation

Windows Management Instrumentation (**WMI**) was created by Microsoft as a management engine for Windows-based operating systems. It provides the ability to view detailed information about a system's hardware and the operating system. WMI also provides the ability to perform actions on a computer, such as opening a program.

In this chapter, you will learn the following:

- WMI structure
- Using WMI objects
- Searching WMI classes
- Creating, modifying, and removing WMI object property instances
- Invoking WMI class methods

WMI structure

WMI is made up of three components. These three components include the **WMI consumers**, the **WMI infrastructure**, and the **WMI providers**. When you are using PowerShell, you will leverage all three of these components to interact with the hardware and operating system.

WMI structure is shown as follows:

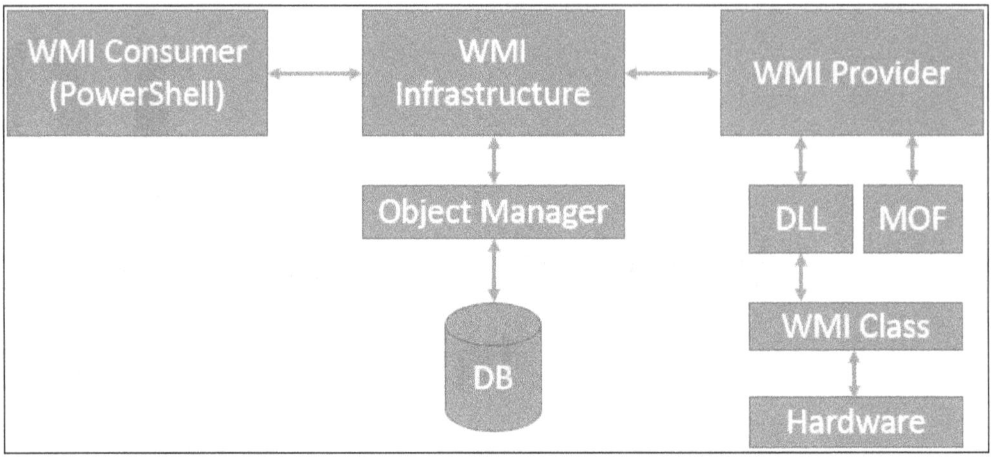

WMI consumers are applications that can query and interact with the WMI. This may include PowerShell, .NET, C, C++, and other scripting and programming languages. Consumers communicate with the WMI infrastructure to obtain information about a system. WMI consumers do not, however, interact directly with the hardware or operating system through WMI.

The WMI infrastructure consists of an object manager and a WMI repository. The object manager keeps track of the used WMI instances on a system. The WMI repository is like a database, which keeps inventory of all the available WMI objects to interact with. These objects are imported into the **CIM Object Manager** (**CIMOM**), via **Managed Object Format** (**MOF**) files. The MOF files provide the WMI infrastructure with a set of instructions on how the WMI consumers may interact with the hardware or the operating system. This can include fields that can be read, or actions that can be invoked on the hardware itself.

The WMI infrastructure, by default, places everything into a location, within the object manager, referred to as a **namespace**. The majority of the WMI objects that you will query will be created in the default namespace of `root\CIMv2`. Occasionally, applications may request the WMI infrastructure to create a new namespace to place the information into. **System Center Configuration Manager** (**SCCM**), for example, creates a new namespace of `root\CCM` when you install its client on a system. This namespace then maintains information collected about a system, software settings, and even methods that can be invoked by the SCCM.

The WMI provider is the actual driver that interacts with the operating system or hardware component. The WMI provider consists of a DLL and an MOF File. These provide information on what data is accessible by the WMI calls. They also provide information on the methods that can control the operating system or hardware components. The **drivers** (**DLL**) consist of classes which interact with the hardware and the operating system. When the WMI infrastructure interacts with the WMI provider, it is able to interact only with the items made available by the driver, and those specified in the MOF file.

Using WMI objects

When you leverage PowerShell to interact with WMI, you are interacting with WMI *namespaces* and WMI *classes*. WMI namespaces are collections of classes that represent management of a particular system. The Windows operating system, for example, uses the default `root\cimv2` namespace, and that collection contains over a thousand classes. Classes have multiple attributes such as properties and methods. Class properties represent information about that particular class, which is typically represented by a string or a numeric format. Methods are more like *actions*, which allow you to interact with that object, or other objects on a system.

The two primary cmdlets that allow you to retrieve a WMI object on a system are `get-wmiobject` and `get-ciminstance`. The `get-wmiobject` cmdlet is primarily used for querying a local system's WMI providers. You can leverage the `get-wmiobject` cmdlet by calling `get-wmiobject`, optionally defining a namespace with the `-namespace` parameter, and referencing a class name with the `-class` parameter. If you omit the `-namespace` parameter, the cmdlet assumes the default window's namespace of `root\cimv2`.

To properly leverage `get-wmiobject` cmdlet and retrieve a class, do the following:

```
get-wmiobject -namespace root\cimv2 -class win32_computersystem
```

This command gives the output as shown in the following screenshot:

```
PS C:\> get-wmiobject -namespace root\cimv2 -class win32_computersystem


Domain              : corp.cdw.com
Manufacturer        : LENOVO
Model               : 20BE0085US
Name                : LT-A0032132
PrimaryOwnerName    : CDW
TotalPhysicalMemory : 16849174528
```

The preceding example displays how to retrieve a class using the `get-wmiobject` cmdlet. You first start by calling the `get-wmiobject` cmdlet. You then specify the `-namespace` parameter with the `root\cimv2` argument. Now you specify the `-class` parameter with the `win32_computersystem` class name argument. On executing the script, you will see the default properties from the `win32_computersystem` class.

The `get-ciminstance` cmdlet is very similar to the `get-wmiobject` cmdlet, though it has several differences. The `get-ciminstance` cmdlet has the ability to run on remote systems over a CIM session, whereas the `get-wmiobject` only permits local execution. By leveraging the `-cimsession` parameter, you can specify a CIM session to query a remote WMI instance. The `get-ciminstance` cmdlet also returns the same data in a different format. This is due to the `get-ciminstance` cmdlet being newer than the `get-wmiobject` cmdlet. This newer cmdlet follows the latest management specifications from the **Distributed Management Task Force** (**DMTF**), and will display the results from commands according to the latest standards.

You can leverage the `get-ciminstance` cmdlet by calling `get-ciminstance`, optionally defining a namespace with the `-namespace` parameter, and referencing a class name with the `-class` parameter. If you omit the `-namespace` parameter, the cmdlet assumes the default window's namespace of `root\cimv2`.

To properly leverage the `get-ciminstance` cmdlet, and retrieve a class, do the following:

```
get-ciminstance -namespace root\cimv2 -class win32_computersystem
```

The output of this command is shown in the following screenshot:

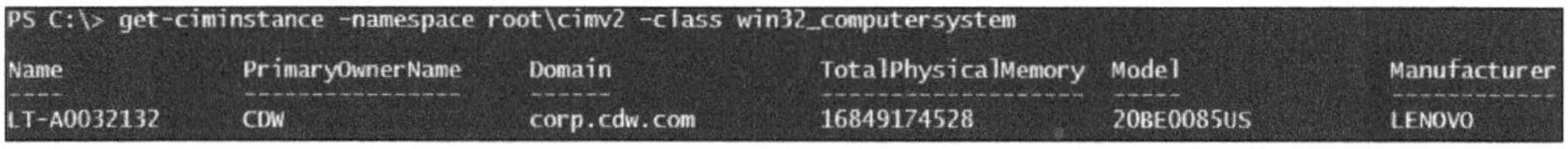

PS C:\> get-ciminstance -namespace root\cimv2 -class win32_computersystem
Name PrimaryOwnerName Domain TotalPhysicalMemory Model Manufacturer
LT-A0032132 CDW corp.cdw.com 16849174528 20BE0085US LENOVO

The preceding example displays how to retrieve a class using the `get-ciminstance` cmdlet. You first start by calling the `get-ciminstance` cmdlet. Then you specify the `-namespace` parameter with the `root\cimv2` argument. Now you specify the `-class` parameter with the `win32_computersystem` class name argument. On executing the script, you will see the default properties from the `win32_computersystem` class.

Both, the `get-wmiobject` and the `get-ciminstance` cmdlets, list the default properties for classes when you leverage them. In most cases, additional properties and methods are contained in the class itself. If you want to dig deeper into the class, you can pipe the results to `get-member`, and it will display the full listing of all the attributes of that class.

To retrieve all the attributes of the `win32_computersystem` class, do the following:

```
get-wmiobject -class win32_computersystem | get-member
```

The following screenshot displays the output of this command:

```
PS C:\> get-wmiobject -class win32_computersystem | get-member

   TypeName: System.Management.ManagementObject#root\cimv2\Win32_ComputerSystem

Name                      MemberType    Definition
----                      ----------    ----------
PSComputerName            AliasProperty PSComputerName = __SERVER
JoinDomainOrWorkgroup     Method        System.Management.ManagementBaseObject JoinDomainOrWorkgroup(System.String...
Rename                    Method        System.Management.ManagementBaseObject Rename(System.String Name, System.S...
SetPowerState             Method        System.Management.ManagementBaseObject SetPowerState(System.UInt16 PowerSt...
UnjoinDomainOrWorkgroup   Method        System.Management.ManagementBaseObject UnjoinDomainOrWorkgroup(System.Stri...
AdminPasswordStatus       Property      uint16 AdminPasswordStatus {get;set;}
AutomaticManagedPagefile  Property      bool AutomaticManagedPagefile {get;set;}
AutomaticResetBootOption  Property      bool AutomaticResetBootOption {get;set;}
AutomaticResetCapability  Property      bool AutomaticResetCapability {get;set;}
BootOptionOnLimit         Property      uint16 BootOptionOnLimit {get;set;}
```

The preceding example displays how to retrieve all the class attributes using the `get-wmiobject` cmdlet and the `get-member` cmdlet. You first start by calling the `get-wmiobject` cmdlet. You then specify the `-namespace` parameter with the `root\cimv2` argument. Now you specify the `-class` parameter with the `win32_computersystem` class name argument. Finally, you pipe the results to the `get-member` cmdlet, and you will see all the attributes of the `win32_computersystem` class.

Searching for WMI classes

There are instances when you may want to search for different WMI classes on a system. The two primary cmdlets that enable you to search WMI are `get-wmiobject`, and `get-cimclass`. You can simply leverage the `get-wmiobject` cmdlet with the `-list` argument to list all the classes in a particular namespace. You can further narrow down the list by piping the command to the statement `where {$_.Name -like "*Search*"}`. This will search the `Name` property of the classes that match a specific criterion.

An example of using the `get-wmiobject` cmdlet to find classes with a specific value would look like:

```
get-wmiobject -list | where{$_.Name -like "*Time*"}
```

The output of this command is shown in the following screenshot:

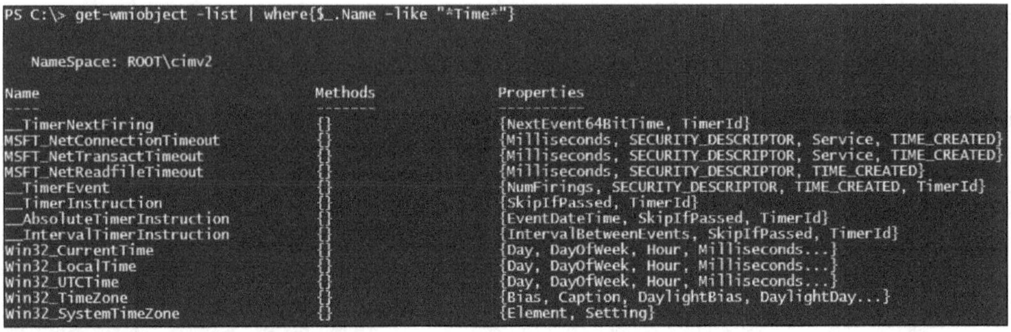
PS C:\> get-wmiobject -list | where{$_.Name -like "*Time*"}
NameSpace: ROOT\cimv2
Name
Methods
Properties
__TimerNextFiring {} {NextEvent64BitTime, TimerId}
MSFT_NetConnectionTimeout {} {Milliseconds, SECURITY_DESCRIPTOR, Service, TIME_CREATED}
MSFT_NetTransactTimeout {} {Milliseconds, SECURITY_DESCRIPTOR, Service, TIME_CREATED}
MSFT_NetReadfileTimeout {} {Milliseconds, SECURITY_DESCRIPTOR, TIME_CREATED}
__TimerEvent {} {NumFirings, SECURITY_DESCRIPTOR, TIME_CREATED, TimerId}
__TimerInstruction {} {SkipIfPassed, TimerId}
__AbsoluteTimerInstruction {} {EventDateTime, SkipIfPassed, TimerId}
__IntervalTimerInstruction {} {IntervalBetweenEvents, SkipIfPassed, TimerId}
Win32_CurrentTime {} {Day, DayOfWeek, Hour, Milliseconds...}
Win32_LocalTime {} {Day, DayOfWeek, Hour, Milliseconds...}
Win32_UTCTime {} {Day, DayOfWeek, Hour, Milliseconds...}
Win32_TimeZone {} {Bias, Caption, DaylightBias, DaylightDay...}
Win32_SystemTimeZone {} {Element, Setting}

The preceding example displays how to properly leverage the `get-wmiobject` cmdlet to search for WMI classes. You first start by declaring the `get-wmiobject` cmdlet with the `-list` parameter. You then leverage where the pipeline property of `Name` is like the word `Time`. After executing this script, you will see all the class names that have the word `Time` in them.

> It is important to remember that when you are searching the full list of classes, it may take a few seconds to return results. This is due to the large number of classes available on the system, and having to evaluate the individual properties of these classes.

You may also choose the `get-cimclass` cmdlet to search for WMI classes. Like the other CIM-based cmdlets, the `get-cimclass` cmdlet supports sessions and allows you to query remote systems. You can simply leverage the `get-cimclass` cmdlet alone to return a full list of classes. You can further narrow down the list by piping the command to the statement `where {$_.CIMClassName -like "*Search*"}`. This will search the `CimClassName` property of the classes that match a specific criterion. You may also choose to use the `-cimsession` parameter and specify a CIM session to query the WMI on a remote system.

An example of using the `get-cimclass` cmdlet to find classes with a specific value would look like this:

```
get-cimclass | where{$_.CimClassName -like "*Time*"}
```

The output of this command is shown in the following screenshot:

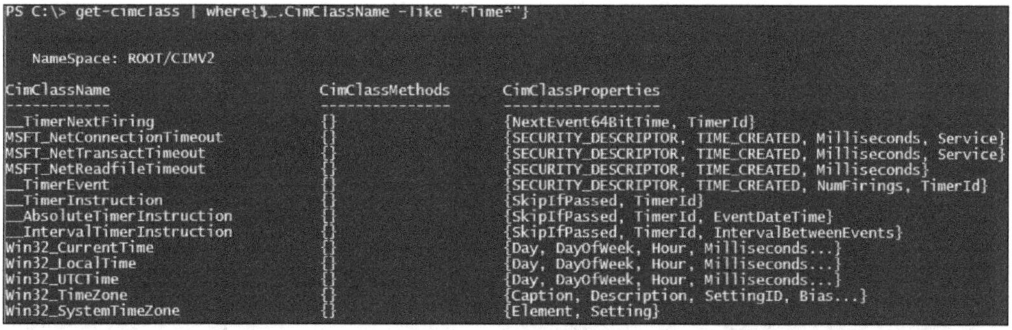
PS C:\> get-cimclass | where{$_.CimClassName -like "*Time*"}
NameSpace: ROOT/CIMV2
CimClassName CimClassMethods CimClassProperties
__TimerNextFiring {} {NextEvent64BitTime, TimerId}
MSFT_NetConnectionTimeout {} {SECURITY_DESCRIPTOR, TIME_CREATED, Milliseconds, Service}
MSFT_NetTransactTimeout {} {SECURITY_DESCRIPTOR, TIME_CREATED, Milliseconds, Service}
MSFT_NetReadfileTimeout {} {SECURITY_DESCRIPTOR, TIME_CREATED, Milliseconds}
__TimerEvent {} {SECURITY_DESCRIPTOR, TIME_CREATED, NumFirings, TimerId}
__TimerInstruction {} {SkipIfPassed, TimerId}
__AbsoluteTimerInstruction {} {SkipIfPassed, TimerId, EventDateTime}
__IntervalTimerInstruction {} {SkipIfPassed, TimerId, IntervalBetweenEvents}
Win32_CurrentTime {} {Day, DayOfWeek, Hour, Milliseconds...}
Win32_LocalTime {} {Day, DayOfWeek, Hour, Milliseconds...}
Win32_UTCTime {} {Day, DayOfWeek, Hour, Milliseconds...}
Win32_TimeZone {} {Caption, Description, SettingID, Bias...}
Win32_SystemTimeZone {} {Element, Setting}

The preceding example displays how to properly leverage the `get-cimclass` cmdlet to search for WMI classes. You first start by declaring the `get-cimclass` cmdlet. You then leverage where the pipeline property of `CimClassName` is like the word `Time`. After executing this script, you will be left with all the class names that have the word `Time` in them.

You may also choose to leverage the `get-cimclass` cmdlets to query the class attributes. To start, you can use the `-class` parameter and declare a class name. Embracing the prior statement in parentheses, you can then leverage the dot notation to call either the `.CimClassProperties`, or `.CimClassMethods` attributes. This will list all the respective class properties or class methods.

To leverage the `get-cimclass` cmdlet to view the class properties, do the following:

```
$classProperties = (get-cimclass -class win32_Printer).CimClassProperties
$classProperties.count
```

This set of commands gives the output as shown in the following screenshot:

PS C:\> $classProperties = (get-cimclass -class win32_Printer).CimClassProperties
PS C:\> $classProperties.count
86

This example displays the proper syntax for retrieving the `CimClassProperties` property of `win32_printer` class and counting the number of properties available for use. You first start by declaring the `$classproperties` variable and setting it to a parenthetically enclosed `get-cimclass` properties with the `-class` parameter value set to `win32_printer`. You then leverage the dot notation to view the `CimClassProperties` of that item. Finally, you retrieve the property count of that class by leveraging the `.count` property on the `$classProperties` variable. On executing this script, you will have something similar to the number `86` printed to the screen, which is the number of properties for `win32_printer`.

To leverage the `get-cimclass` cmdlet to view the class methods, do the following:

```
(get-cimclass -class win32_Printer).CimClassMethods
```

The output of this command is shown in the following screenshot:

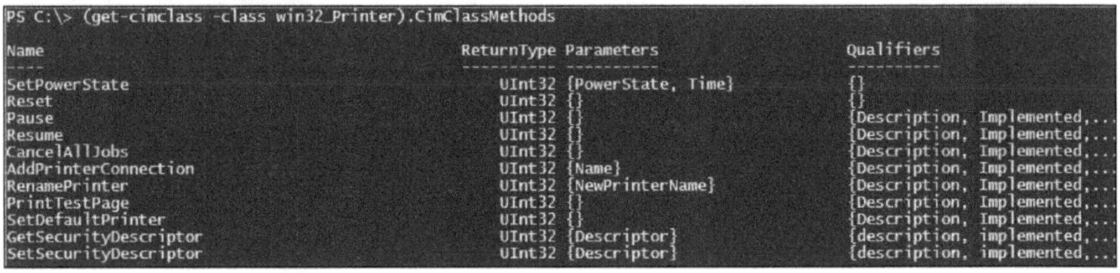

PS C:\> (get-cimclass -class win32_Printer).CimClassMethods
Name ReturnType Parameters Qualifiers
SetPowerState UInt32 {PowerState, Time} {}
Reset UInt32 {} {}
Pause UInt32 {} {Description, Implemented,...
Resume UInt32 {} {Description, Implemented,...
CancelAllJobs UInt32 {} {Description, Implemented,...
AddPrinterConnection UInt32 {Name} {Description, Implemented,...
RenamePrinter UInt32 {NewPrinterName} {Description, Implemented,...
PrintTestPage UInt32 {} {Description, Implemented,...
SetDefaultPrinter UInt32 {} {Description, Implemented,...
GetSecurityDescriptor UInt32 {Descriptor} {description, implemented,...
SetSecurityDescriptor UInt32 {Descriptor} {description, implemented,...

This example displays the proper syntax for retrieving the `CimClassMethods` property of the `win32_printer` class. You first enclose the command in parentheses, and call `get-cimclass` with the `-class` parameter pointing to `win32_printer`. Then, leverage the dot notation to call the `CimClassMethods` property of that item. After executing the command, you will see all the methods, or actions that you can perform on that class.

> An alternative method to write this code is leveraging the pipe command and not using the dot notation. The PowerShell code would look similar to `$method = get-cimclass -class win32_Printer | foreach-object CimClassMethods`. You may also pipe the output to the selection criteria of `select -ExpandProperty CimClassMethods`. The PowerShell code would look similar to `$method = get-cimclass -class win32_Printer | select -ExpandProperty CimClassMethods`.

To search for method qualifiers using the `get-cimclass` cmdlet, you can perform the following:

```
$method = (get-cimclass -class win32_Printer).CimClassMethods | where
{$_.name -eq "SetDefaultPrinter"}
$method
$method.qualifiers
```

The output of this set of commands is shown in the following screenshot:

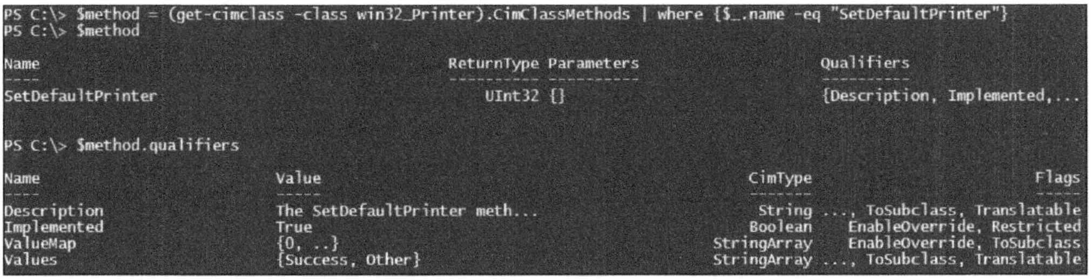

PS C:\> $method = (get-cimclass -class win32_Printer).CimClassMethods | where {$_.name -eq "SetDefaultPrinter"}
PS C:\> $method
Name ReturnType Parameters Qualifiers
SetDefaultPrinter UInt32 {} {Description, Implemented,...
PS C:\> $method.qualifiers
Name Value CimType Flags
Description The SetDefaultPrinter meth... String ..., ToSubclass, Translatable
Implemented True Boolean EnableOverride, Restricted
ValueMap {0, ..} StringArray EnableOverride, ToSubclass
Values {Success, Other} StringArray ..., ToSubclass, Translatable

The example we just saw displays how you can dig deeper into the `win32_printer` class on a system. You first start by declaring the variable of `$method` and set it equal to the output from the next command. Next, you enclose the `get-cimclass` cmdlet with the `-class` parameter pointing to `win32_printer`. Then you use the dot notation to call the `CimClassMethods` for that item. From the previous example, you know that one of the `Method` properties of `win32_printer` is the value `Name`. You also know that one of the items is `SetDefaultPrinter`. To view more details about the method, you then pipe the output of that command to the evaluation statement of `where {$_.Name -eq "SetDefaultPrinter"}`. On executing the first line, you print to screen the `SetDefaultPrinter` information by calling the variable, `$method`. You then discover one of the properties of the `SetDefaultPrinter` method as `Qualifiers`. You leverage the dot notation to view the `Qualifiers` property by calling `$method.qualifiers`. After executing this command, the properties of that property will print to the screen.

Creating, modifying, and removing WMI property instances

PowerShell provides the ability to create, modify, and remove new properties in WMI classes. If you want to modify an instance of a property, you have to determine if the property has writeable attributes using the `get-cimclass` cmdlet. To do this, you select a WMI class by calling the `get-cimclass` cmdlet and referencing the class you want to evaluate. You then gather the expanded properties of the class by piping the `get-cimclass` output to the selection criteria of `Select -ExpandedProperty CimClassProperties`.

After gathering the expanded properties, the results need to be piped to the selection criteria of `where {$_.Qualifiers -match "write"}`. On entering this command, you will see all the properties that permit writing and removing properties. Subsequently, if you want to see the properties that are read-only, you can change the selection criteria of `where {$_.Qualifiers -notmatch "write"}`. This will display just the read-only properties.

To determine the writeable properties for the `win32_environment` class, do the following:

```
Get-cimclass win32_Environment | select -ExpandProperty
CimClassProperties | where {$_.Qualifiers -match "write"}
```

The output of these commands is shown in the following screenshot:

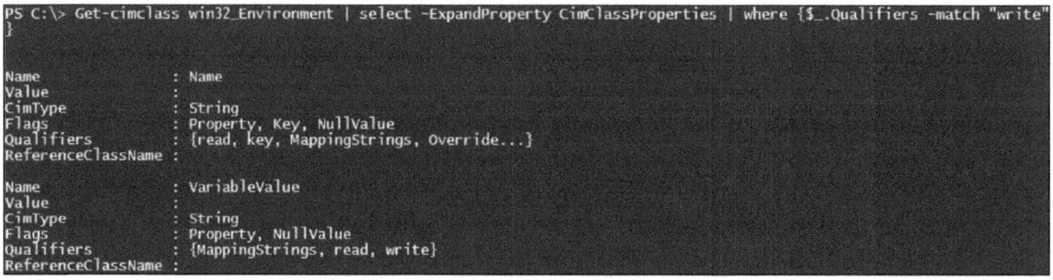

```
PS C:\> Get-cimclass win32_Environment | select -ExpandProperty CimClassProperties | where {$_.Qualifiers -match "write"
}


Name                : Name
Value               :
CimType             : String
Flags               : Property, Key, NullValue
Qualifiers          : {read, key, MappingStrings, Override...}
ReferenceClassName  :

Name                : VariableValue
Value               :
CimType             : String
Flags               : Property, NullValue
Qualifiers          : {MappingStrings, read, write}
ReferenceClassName  :
```

This example displays how to use the `get-cimclass` cmdlet and the selection criteria to determine what properties in a class have the 'write' qualifier. You first start by calling the `get-cimclass` cmdlet referencing the `win32_environment` class. Next, you pipe those results to the selection criteria of `select -ExpandProperty CimClassProperties`. These results are finally piped to the selection criteria of `where {$_.Qualifiers -match "Write"}`. This will output to the console all the properties that have the 'write' qualifier.

To determine the non-writeable properties for the `win32_environment` class, do the following:

```
Get-cimclass win32_Environment | select -ExpandProperty
CimClassProperties | where {$_.Qualifiers -notmatch "write"} | select -
ExpandProperty Name
```

The following screenshot displays the output of these commands:

PS C:\> Get-cimclass win32_Environment | select -ExpandProperty CimClassProperties | where {$_.Qualifiers -notmatch "wri
te"} | select -ExpandProperty Name
Caption
Description
InstallDate
Name
Status
SystemVariable
UserName
VariableValue

This example displays how to use the `get-cimclass` cmdlet, and the selection criteria to determine the properties in a class that do not have the 'write' qualifier. You first start by calling the `get-cimclass` cmdlet referencing the `win32_environment` class. Then, you pipe those results to the selection criteria of `select -ExpandProperty CimClassProperties`. These results are piped to the selection criteria of `where {$_.Qualifiers -notmatch "Write"}`. You finally pipe those results to the selection criteria of `select -ExpandProperty Name`. The final pipe that you follow in the sequence is to truncate the list of items. If you didn't select only the `Name` property, all the properties of `CimClassProperties` would print to the screen. After executing the command, the `Name` property of `Qualifiers` which do not have the 'write' property will be printed to the console.

Once you find a class that has writeable properties, you need to determine what property values are required for that particular class. You can do this by using the `get-ciminstance` cmdlet, and declaring a class name to find the required fields.

To use the `get-ciminstance` cmdlet with the `win32_environment` class, do the following:

```
get-ciminstance win32_environment
```

The output of this command is shown in the following screenshot:

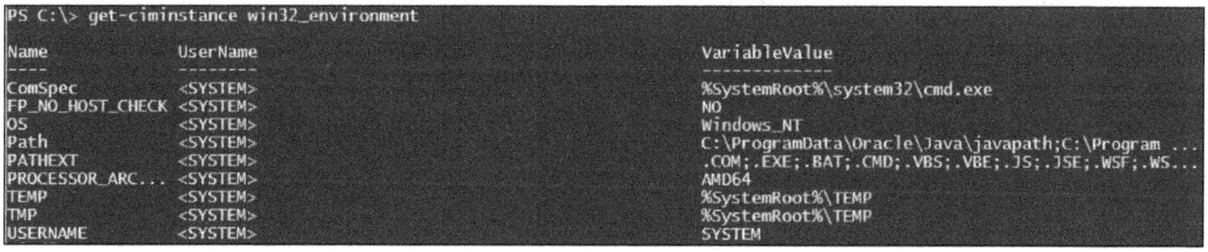
PS C:\> get-ciminstance win32_environment
Name UserName VariableValue
ComSpec <SYSTEM> %SystemRoot%\system32\cmd.exe
FP_NO_HOST_CHECK <SYSTEM> NO
OS <SYSTEM> Windows_NT
Path <SYSTEM> C:\ProgramData\Oracle\Java\javapath;C:\Program ...
PATHEXT <SYSTEM> .COM;.EXE;.BAT;.CMD;.VBS;.VBE;.JS;.JSE;.WSF;.WS...
PROCESSOR_ARC... <SYSTEM> AMD64
TEMP <SYSTEM> %SystemRoot%\TEMP
TMP <SYSTEM> %SystemRoot%\TEMP
USERNAME <SYSTEM> SYSTEM

This example displays how to use the `get-ciminstance` cmdlet to determine the properties that need to be created for new properties in the `Win32_Environment` class. You first start by running the `get-ciminstance` cmdlet, pointing to `Win32_Environment`. After running this script, you will see that there are three properties for each property. These properties include `Name`, `UserName`, and `VariableValue`. In the instance that you want to create a new instance property in the `win32_environment` class, the properties of `Name`, `UserName`, and `VariableValue` would be required.

Creating property instances

To create a new instance of a class property, you can leverage the `new-ciminstance` cmdlet. The proper syntax of using this cmdlet is calling `new-ciminstance`, and referencing the class that you want to create a new property in. You will then leverage the `-property` parameter and create a hash table of items that are required for the new property. This is done by creating a hash table similar to `@{Property="SomeValueName";Property="Value You Want To Set The property To"}`. When you create a property, WMI validates the input of these values prior to setting it in the WMI infrastructure. If you are missing properties or they don't meet a certain criteria, the command will fail.

> The `UserName` property in the `Win32_Environment` class is validated against the **Security Account Manager** (**SAM**) of a Windows system. If the username specified in the `UserName` property isn't a valid user on the computer, this script will fail.

In the instance where you want to add a new property to the `win32_environment` class, do the following:

```
# Update the Domain\Username with valid credentials
New-CimInstance Win32_Environment -Property @{Name="PurchasedDate";VariableValue="10/17/2015"; UserName="DOMAIN\USERNAME"}
Get-Ciminstance Win32_Environment | Where {$_.name -match "PurchasedDate"}
```

The output of this set of commands is shown in the following screenshot:

```
PS C:\> # Update the Domain\Username with valid credentials
PS C:\> New-CimInstance Win32_Environment -Property @{Name="PurchasedDate";VariableValue="10/17/2015"; UserName="DOMAIN\
USERNAME"};

Name            UserName                                  VariableValue
----            --------                                  -------------
PurchasedDate   DOMAIN\USERNAME                           10/17/2015

PS C:\> Get-Ciminstance Win32_Environment | Where {$_.name -match "PurchasedDate"}

Name            UserName                                  VariableValue
----            --------                                  -------------
PurchasedDate   DOMAIN\USERNAME                           10/17/2015
```

This example displays how to successfully create a new property with three properties in the `Win32_Environment` class. After running the previous example, you learned that the three required properties for the `Win32_Environment` class are `Name`, `UserName`, and `VariableName`. You first start by leveraging the `new-ciminstance` cmdlet pointing to the `Win32_Environment` class, and the `-property` parameter pointing to a hash table of objects. The hash table you build is `@{Name="PurchasedDate";VariableValue="10/17/2015"; UserName="DOMAIN\USERNAME"}`. After executing this script, there will be a new property in `Win32_Environment` with the property of `Name` set to the value of `PurchasedDate`, the property of `UserName` set to the value of `DOMAIN\USERNAME`, and the property of `VariableValue` set to the value of `10/17/2015`.

After creating the new property, you then leverage the `get-ciminstance` cmdlet pointing to the `Win32_Environment` class to validate the creation. You pipe the output to the selection criteria of `where {$_.name -match "PurchasedDate"}`. After submitting this command, the console will print the property with all its properties.

Modifying property instances

If you want to modify instances of properties, you need to use both the `get-ciminstance` and the `set-ciminstance` cmdlets. This is due to you needing to place the WMI object into a variable to modify it and set it back into the WMI infrastructure. To start, you first have to declare a variable for the WMI instance and set it equal to the `get-ciminstance` cmdlet with the `-class` parameter pointing to a class. This will access an instance of the class and store it in the variable that you declared. You then will use the `set-ciminstance` cmdlet to modify the property. To do this, you will call `set-ciminstance` with the `-ciminstance` parameter pointing to the variable you defined earlier. You then declare the `-Property` parameter and build a hash table of what you want to set it to. The hash table will look similar to `@{Name="SomePropertyName";VariableValue="Value You Want To Set It To"}`. When you modify a property, WMI validates the input of these values prior to setting it in the WMI infrastructure. After validating all of the properties, you will have successfully updated that property with the `set-ciminstance` cmdlet.

To modify a property in the `win32_environment` class, do the following:

```
$instance = Get-Ciminstance Win32_Environment | Where {$_.name -match
"PurchasedDate"}
Set-ciminstance -ciminstance $instance -property @{Name="PurchasedDate";V
ariableValue="October 17, 2015";}
Get-Ciminstance win32_Environment | Where {$_.name -match
"PurchasedDate"}
```

The output of these commands is shown in the following screenshot:

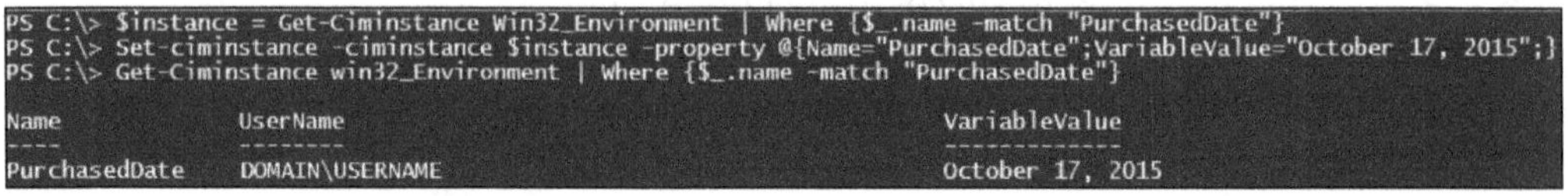
PS C:\> $instance = Get-Ciminstance Win32_Environment | Where {$_.name -match "PurchasedDate"}
PS C:\> Set-ciminstance -ciminstance $instance -property @{Name="PurchasedDate";VariableValue="October 17, 2015";}
PS C:\> Get-Ciminstance win32_Environment | Where {$_.name -match "PurchasedDate"}
Name UserName VariableValue
PurchasedDate DOMAIN\USERNAME October 17, 2015

This example displays how you can use the `set-ciminstance` cmdlet to change properties of a WMI property. You first start by using the `get-ciminstance` cmdlet with the `Win32_Environment` class piped to the selection criteria of `where {$_.name -match "PurchasedDate"}`. You then store this WMI property object in a variable named `$instance`. You then continue to use the `set-ciminstance` cmdlet with the `-ciminstance` parameter pointing to the `$instance` variable, and the `-property` parameter with a new hash table of objects. The hash table you specify is `@{Name="PurchasedDate";VariableValue="October 17, 2015";}`, which updates the property with the `Name` of `PurchasedDate` and property the `VariableValue` to reflect `October 17, 2015`. You then use the `get-ciminstance` cmdlet pointing to the `Win32_Enviroment` class with the selection criteria of where `{$._name -match "PurchasedDate"}`. After executing this command, the console will print the updated property of the `Win32_Environment` class for the `Name` value of `PurchasedDate`. You will see that the `VariableValue` property has been updated to `October 17, 2015`.

> In this example, the `UserName` property is a read-only property. If you attempt to update or use this value, you will receive an error message. In this example, you will only call the `Name` and `VariableValue` properties in the array you are building, to successfully update that WMI property.

There are properties, however, which, after creation, become `Read-Only`. Even though you were able to define them during the creation process, the class may prevent these properties from undergoing future modification. The only way to change these properties would be to remove the property, and recreate it with different properties. To determine if a class has 'write' properties, you can leverage the `get-cimclass` cmdlet to evaluate the `Quantifier` properties that permit writing.

Removing property instances

If you want to remove instances of properties, you need to use both the `get-ciminstance` and the `remove-ciminstance` cmdlets. To start with, you have to declare a variable for the instance and set it equal to the `get-ciminstance` cmdlet, with the `-class` parameter pointing to a class. You then need to pipe it to the selection criteria of `where {$_.name -like "PropertyName"}`. This will access an instance of the property and store it in the variable that you declared. The second step is to remove the property by using the `remove-ciminstance` cmdlet. The proper syntax of using this cmdlet is calling `remove-ciminstance`, and the `-ciminstance` parameter pointing to the variable you defined earlier. After executing this step, the property will be removed from the system.

To remove an instance of a property in the `win32_environment` class, do the following:

```
$instance = Get-Ciminstance win32_environment | Where {$_.name -match
"PurchasedDate"}
Remove-ciminstance -ciminstance $instance
Get-Ciminstance win32_environment | Where {$_.name -match
"PurchasedDate"}
```

This set of commands gives the output as shown in the following screenshot:

PS C:\> $instance = Get-Ciminstance win32_environment | Where {$_.name -match "PurchasedDate"}
PS C:\> Remove-ciminstance -ciminstance $instance
PS C:\> Get-Ciminstance win32_environment | Where {$_.name -match "PurchasedDate"}

This example displays how to delete a WMI property leveraging the `remove-ciminstance` cmdlet. You first start by using the `get-ciminstance` cmdlet, with the `Win32_Environment` class piped to the selection criteria of `where {$_.name -match "PurchasedDate"}`. You then store this WMI property object in a variable named `$instance`. Next, you continue to use the `remove-ciminstance` cmdlet with the `-ciminstance` parameter pointing to the `$instance` variable. On executing this command, the WMI property is deleted from the system. You verify this by using the `get-ciminstance` cmdlet pointing to the `Win32_Enviroment` class with the selection criteria of `where {$._name -match "PurchasedDate"}`. You will not receive any results from this, implying, therefore, that the instance of the property has been removed.

Invoking WMI class methods

WMI methods enable you to execute different activities on a system. PowerShell provides the ability to hook onto these methods to perform different actions using the `invoke-cimmethod` cmdlet. In order to determine what methods are available for use in a WMI class, you can leverage the `get-cimclass` cmdlet, with the optional `-class` parameter pointing to a WMI class. You then can pipe those results to the selection criteria of `| select -ExpandProperty CimClassMethods`. This will display all the methods and properties for those methods in that WMI class. This will help you expose what methods are available for a particular class.

To leverage the `get-cimclass` cmdlet to see the methods in the `win32_process` class, you can do the following:

```
get-cimclass win32_process | select -ExpandProperty CimClassMethods
```

The output of this command is shown in the following screenshot:

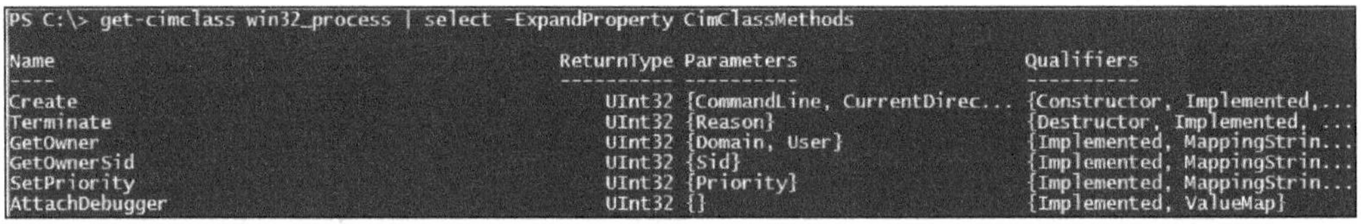

PS C:\> get-cimclass win32_process | select -ExpandProperty CimClassMethods
Name ReturnType Parameters Qualifiers
Create UInt32 {CommandLine, CurrentDirec... {Constructor, Implemented,...
Terminate UInt32 {Reason} {Destructor, Implemented, ...
GetOwner UInt32 {Domain, User} {Implemented, MappingStrin...
GetOwnerSid UInt32 {Sid} {Implemented, MappingStrin...
SetPriority UInt32 {Priority} {Implemented, MappingStrin...
AttachDebugger UInt32 {} {Implemented, ValueMap}

There are two popular ways to utilize the `invoke-cimmethod` cmdlet. The first is to use the `-MethodName` parameter referencing a method name, along with the `-arguments` parameter with a hash table of options. The hash table for the arguments would look similar to `@{Property="ActionItem"}`.

To leverage the `invoke-cimmethod` cmdlet with `-arguments` parameter, do the following:

```
Invoke-CimMethod Win32_Process -MethodName "Create" -Arguments @{
CommandLine = 'mspaint.exe'}
```

The output of this command is shown in the following screenshot:

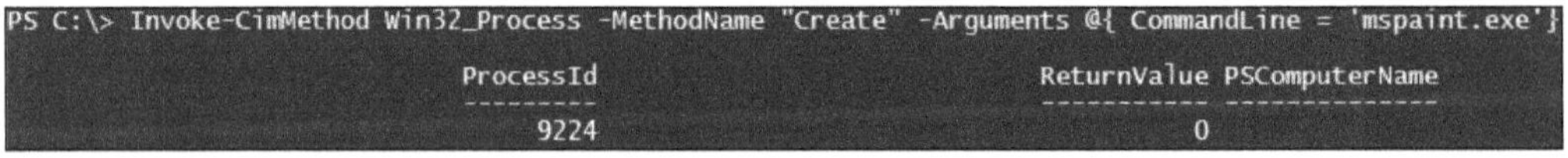

This example displays how to use the `invoke-cimmethod` cmdlet with the -`arguments` parameter to start a new process for Microsoft Paint, using the `win32_process` class. You first start by leveraging the `invoke-cimmethod` cmdlet calling the `win32_process` class. You then use the `-MethodName` parameter with the `Create` parameter, and the `-arguments` parameter with the array of `@{ CommandLine = 'mspaint.exe'}`. On executing this command, the method will create a new `ProcessId` and launch the `mspaint.exe` application.

The second method to use the `invoke-cimmethod` cmdlet is through using a query parameter. The proper syntax of using the query parameter is calling `invoke-cimmethod` referencing a class name, then the `-MethodName` parameter referencing the method you want to invoke , and finally the `-query` parameter with a **WMI Query Language** (**WQL**) query to run against that method name.

To leverage the `invoke-cimmethod` cmdlet with the `-query` parameter, do the following:

```
Invoke-CimMethod -Query 'select * from Win32_Process where name like
"mspaint.exe"' -MethodName "Terminate"
```

The output of this command is shown in the following screenshot:

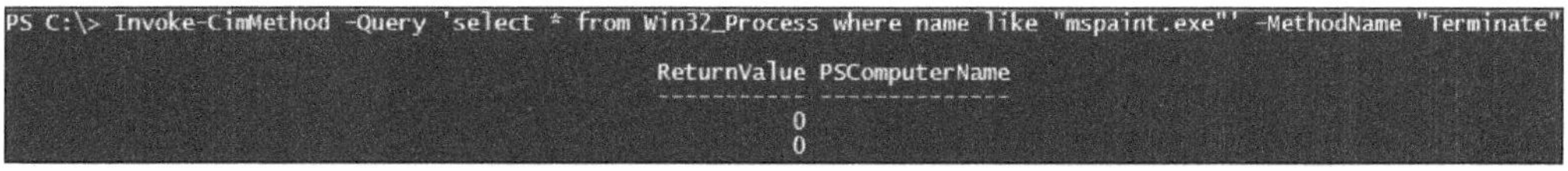

This example displays how to use the `invoke-cimmethod` cmdlet with the `-query` parameter to terminate the Microsoft Paint process using the `win32_process` class. You first start by leveraging the `invoke-cimmethod` cmdlet calling the `win32_process` class. You then use the `-query` parameter with the WQL query of `'select * from Win32_Process where name like "mspaint.exe"'`, and the -`MethodName` parameter with the `Terminate` parameter. On executing this command, the method will terminate all processes that have the "`name`" property similar to `mspaint.exe`. After executing this you will see `ReturnValue` is `0`, which means that it has been successful. If you attempt to run this command a second time, there will be no return, due to the application already being terminated.

Summary

This chapter explained how to use PowerShell to interact with WMI. It showed you the components that make up the WMI, namely consumers, infrastructure, and providers. It also explained how these WMI components are used while interacting with the WMI and PowerShell.

You learned a variety of cmdlets that allow you to navigate the WMI structure. You explored how to search different WMI classes for their attributes, which include methods and properties. You then worked through creating, modifying, and removing WMI object property instances. At the end of the chapter, you learned how to invoke WMI class methods in a variety of ways. In the next chapter you will dive into the XML structure and learn how to leverage PowerShell to read and manipulate XML based items.

11
XML Manipulation

When you are working with Microsoft-based systems, there is a high probability that you are leveraging **eXtensible Markup Language** (**XML**) for data and communications. XML was created by the **World Wide Web Consortium** (**W3C**) to standardize the encoding of documents to make them both legible to humans and usable by computer systems. XML's format is very similar to that of **Hypertext Markup Language** (**HTML**). If you know the basics of HTML, you should be able to pick up XML pretty quickly. While the syntax is very similar between HTML and XML, the purposes of these languages are very different. HTML is used by web browsers to render objects and text on a website. XML is used to encapsulate data to be stored on a system, or passed between systems.

In this chapter, we will learn about:

- The XML file structure
- Reading XML files
- Adding XML content
- Modifying XML content
- Removing XML content

XML file structure

When PowerShell interacts with XML, it leverages an XML reading engine known as an **XML parser**. Much like how PowerShell parses PS1 scripts, the XML parser will read line by line and interpret the contents of the XML file. When the PowerShell XML parser reads the file, it has all of the encoding logic built in, so that it can read the different parts of the XML file. After the XML parser reads the file, it will make the contents available for use within your PowerShell scripts.

For an XML parser to know the file is an XML file, you have to make an XML declaration at the beginning of the file. The following graphic represents a properly created XML declaration:

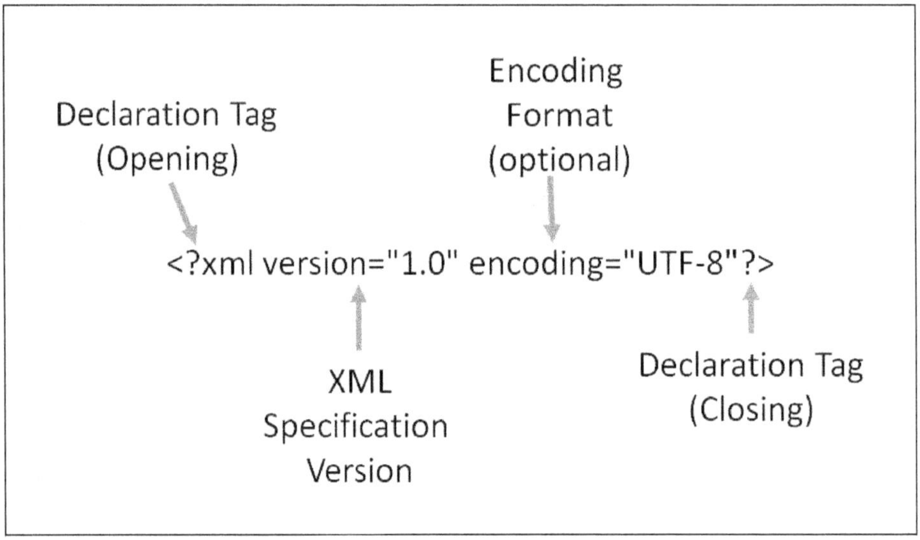

The XML declaration is a mandatory line at the very beginning of the XML document itself. There are several parts of the XML declaration that are mandatory. The declaration tag of XML starts by leveraging the code `<?xml` and is required to tell the XML parser that the version and encoding items may be following. You must then specify the mandatory attribute of `version`, equal to an XML standardization version number. You can then specify the optional `encoding` attribute, where you have the ability to define what format of `encoding` the XML file has been prepared in. To close the declaration section of the code, you use the `?>` closing tag. The preceding example is declaring that an XML file will be XML version `1` with the encoding format set to `UTF-8`.

> UTF-8 and UTF-16 are the two common XML encoding types used with PowerShell. **Universal Characters Set Transformation Format 8-bit/16-bit (UTF-8/16)** is the default Unicode character set that can be used in the XML file. UTF-8 is the most used encoding on the World Wide Web.

After you specify the encoding, you can start defining the data inside the XML file itself. This data is represented as XML tags, which can contain elements (`innerXML`), attributes, and attribute values. The following graphic represents a properly created XML tag:

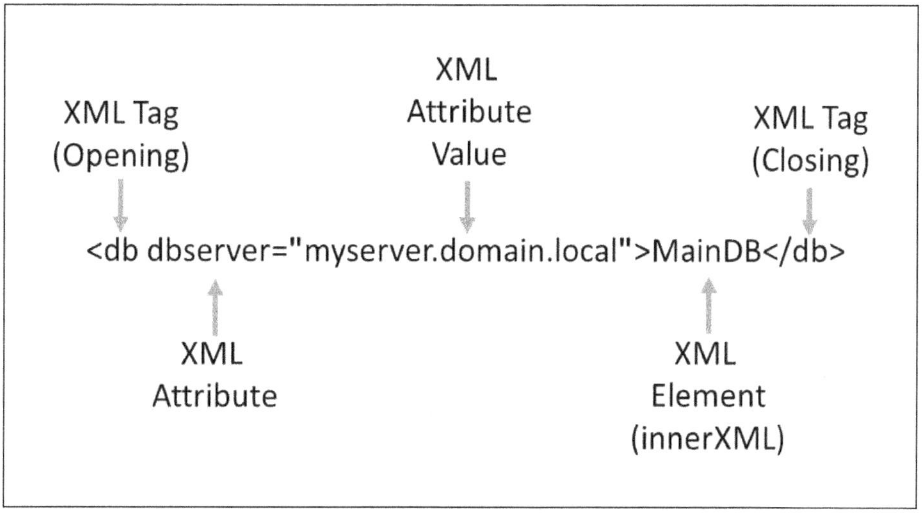

When you define an XML tag, you are declaring an object that contains the related data about that tag. There are two methods to define the data about the individual XML tag. The first method is leveraging attributes and attribute values. An attribute is a unique name that describes an item related to the XML tag. The attribute value is whatever data you want to store for that attribute's value. In the preceding example, the XML tag is for a database or `db`. The attribute refers to a database server name or `dbserver`, and the value is the actual server name of `myserver.domain.local`. You can define multiple attributes and attribute values per tag, which can be helpful in linking similar data together.

The second method is to leverage the elements or the `innerXML` data. This is the data that is also associated with the tag. When the XML parser calls a tag in a script, the element is returned for use. In the preceding example, the XML element is `MainDB`, which is the database name correlated to the `db` tag. Elements can only store one value per tag. This is why many developers skip using the elements and only leverage the attributes, as they provide multiple corresponding data points per tag.

The alternative to multiple attributes is to provide multiple XML tags, and process each individual tag gathering the elements. There are no official rules defined by W3C that specify which you should use per XML file. It is recommended, however, to only use one format syntax per file.

In instances where you want to make notes about the XML tags, attributes, or elements, you may want to leverage the use of comments. The following graphic represents a properly created XML comment:

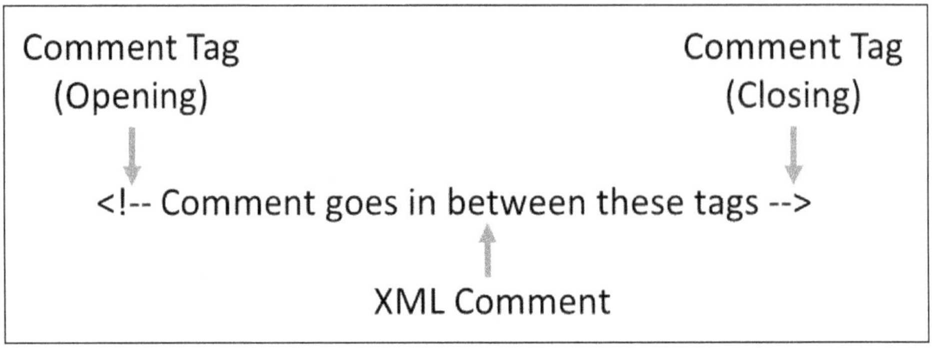

Comments are data that are just like comments in PowerShell. They provide developers with information on each of the sections or individual items in an XML file. The comments have the special opening comment tag of <!--. To close the comment, you can leverage the closing comment tag of -->. Any text or XML data in between these two comment tags are ignored by the XML parser on a system.

As you are building multiple tags in your XML files, you will need to follow the XML W3C **Document Object Model** (**DOM**) tree structure. In simple terms, the XML DOM tree structure consists of a parent, child, and siblings. The parent is a grouping tag that groups the child tags. If there are multiple child tags in the parent tag, the individual child tags are siblings.

An XML file with parents, children, and siblings may look like this:

```
<?xml version="1.0" encoding="UTF-8"?>
<settings> <!--Parent Tag-->
   <db dbserver="myserver.domain.local">MainDB</db> <!--Child Tag-->
</settings>
<access> <!-- Parent Tag -->
   <user>user1</user> <!-- Child and Sibling Tag -->
   <user>user2</user> <!-- Child and Sibling Tag -->
   <group>Group1</group> <!-- Child and Sibling Tag -->
</access>
```

The XML structure is a hierarchy of components within each other. The preceding example displays the contents of an XML file with multiple parent, child, and sibling tags. Each tag can have child tags which can be named the same, like the <user> tags, to represent a grouping of similar child elements. You also define a child tag like <group>, which specifies a child and a sibling tag that has different elements.

Reading XML files

PowerShell has the ability to natively read and parse the data in XML files. This is done by loading an XML file into an XML document object leveraging the `get-content` cmdlet. You start by defining a variable like `$xmlfile` with the data type set to `[xml]`. You then call the `get-content` cmdlet with the `-path` argument set to the location of an XML file. If you omit the `[xml]` data type while defining the variable, it will interpret the file as a text file. This means that you will not be able to leverage any of the built-in XML support.

The following graphic represents the required XML file to complete the remaining examples in this chapter:

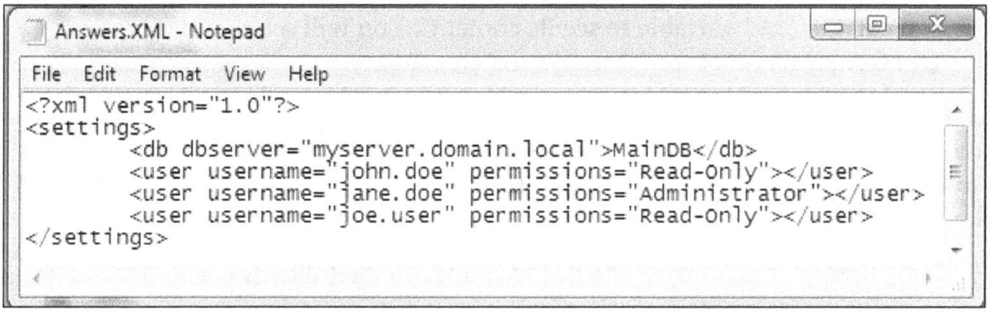

To complete the examples in this chapter, you will need to create a new XML file named `Answers.xml` in the location of `c:\Program Files\MyCustomSoftware2\`. Leveraging the text editor of your choice, insert the preceding data inside the `Answers.xml` file. The examples also build on each other, so you will want to execute this chapter sequentially to have all of the code samples work appropriately.

> You may also refer to this chapter's code file to quickly create the described content.

After creating the example (XML file), you can load the `Answers.xml` file into a variable:

```
$xmlfile = "c:\Program Files\MyCustomSoftware2\Answers.xml"
$xml = [xml] (get-content $xmlfile)
$xml
```

The output of this script is shown in the following screenshot:

```
PS C:\> $xmlfile = "c:\Program Files\MyCustomSoftware2\Answers.xml"
PS C:\> $xml = [xml] (get-content $xmlfile)
PS C:\> $xml

xml                                                      settings
---                                                      --------
version="1.0"                                            settings
```

The preceding example displays how to properly load an XML document into an XML document object by leveraging the `get-content` cmdlet. You start by defining the `$xmlfile` variable and setting it equal to `c:\Program Files\MyCustomSoftware2\Answers.xml`. You then define the `$xml` variable, leverage the `get-content` cmdlet pointing to the `$xmlfile` and defining a data type of `[XML]`. You then call the `$xml` variable to see its contents. You will see that the contents are the DOM tree structure of the XML file you created.

After you load the contents of an XML file into memory, you can interact with the data, using different methods. One method to navigate the XML document object is to leverage the dot notation. By using the dot notation, you can retrieve all of the parent, child, and sibling tags simply by calling the tag names.

To use the dot notation to navigate the XML file, do the following action:

```
$xml.xml
$xml.settings
$xml.settings.db
$xml.settings.user
```

The output of this script is shown in the following screenshot:

```
PS C:\> $xml.xml
version="1.0"
PS C:\> $xml.settings

db                                               user
--                                               ----
db                                               {user, user, user}


PS C:\> $xml.settings.db

dbserver                                         #text
--------                                         -----
myserver.domain.local                            MainDB


PS C:\> $xml.settings.user

username                                         permissions
--------                                         -----------
john.doe                                         Read-Only
jane.doe                                         Administrator
joe.user                                         Read-Only
```

This example displays how to navigate the XML file by using the dot notation. You start by referencing the XML declaration tag by typing `$xml.xml`. You will see the version attribute printed to the screen. You then view the parent tag by typing `$xml.settings`. The output of this command displays the two child objects of `db` and `user`. You then use the dot notation to view the `db` child object by typing `$xml.settings.db`. You will see the attributes and elements of the child object `db`. Last, you view the multiple siblings of the tag `user` by typing `$xml.settings.user`. The siblings and their attributes print to the console after executing the command.

Another approach to navigating an XML file is through the use of XML methods. The `.GetElementsByTagName()` method enables you to search the XML file for tags named as specific values. This will return the attributes and elements of an XML tag. In the instance when there are tags that are named the same, the method will return all values that are equal to the tag value specified in the method. This method provides data in a format where you can leverage the dot notation to obtain the attributes and elements of the tag. This is done by calling `$XMLVariable.GetElementsByTagName("Tag").AttributeName` for an attribute and `$XMLVariable.GetElementsByTagName("Tag"."#text")` for the element data.

To retrieve attributes leveraging the `.GetElementsByTagName()` method, do the following operation:

```
$xml.GetElementsByTagName("db")
$xml.GetElementsByTagName("db").dbserver
```

The output of this script is shown in the following screenshot:

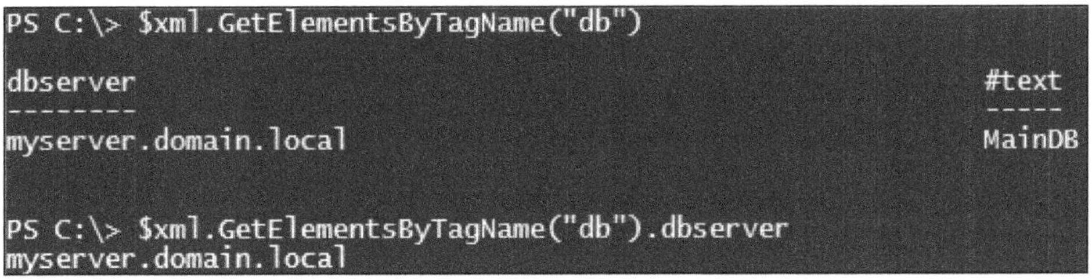
PS C:\> $xml.GetElementsByTagName("db")
dbserver
#text

-----
myserver.domain.local
MainDB
PS C:\> $xml.GetElementsByTagName("db").dbserver
myserver.domain.local

This example displays how to read the `dbserver` attribute of the `db` tag by using the `.GetElementsByTagName()` method and dot notation. You start by viewing the `db` tag by leveraging the `GetElementsByTagName` method with the value of `db`. You see that `db` has two properties the `dbserver` attribute and the `#text` node type. You then use the dot notation to view the attribute value inside the `dbserver` attribute by calling `$xml.GetElementsByTagName("db").dbserver`. The console will print to the screen `myserver.domain.local`, which is the attribute value for `dbserver` in the `db` tag.

To retrieve the elements leveraging the `.GetElementsByTagName()` method, do the following operation:

```
$xml.GetElementsByTagName("db")
$xml.GetElementsByTagName("db")."#text"
```

The output of this command is shown in the following screenshot:

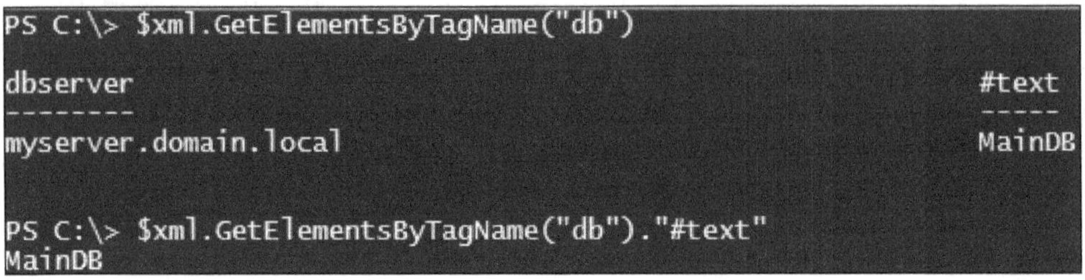
PS C:\> $xml.GetElementsByTagName("db")
dbserver
#text

-----
myserver.domain.local
MainDB
PS C:\> $xml.GetElementsByTagName("db")."#text"
MainDB

This example displays how to read the text element in the `db` tag. You start viewing the `db` tag by leveraging the `GetElementsByTagName` method with the value of `db`. You see that `db` has two properties, the `dbserver` attribute and the `#text` node type. You then use the dot notation to view the attribute value inside the `#text` node type by calling `$xml.GetElementsByTagName("db")."#text"`. The console will print to the screen `MainDB`, which is the element in the `db` tag.

To view the individual sibling `user` tags and print their attribute values to the console, do the following action:

```
$users = $xml.GetElementsByTagName("user")
Foreach ($user in $users) {
  Write-host "Username: " $user.username
  Write-host "Permission: " $user.permissions
  Write-host ""
}
```

The output of this script is shown in the following screenshot:

```
PS C:\> $users = $xml.GetElementsByTagName("user")
PS C:\> Foreach ($user in $users) {
>> Write-host "Username: " $user.username
>> Write-host "Permission: " $user.permissions
>> Write-host ""
>> }
>>
Username:  john.doe
Permission:  Read-Only

Username:  jane.doe
Permission:  Administrator

Username:  joe.user
Permission:  Read-Only
```

This example displays how to process XML files with tags that are the same. To start, you retrieve the `user` tag data from the XML variable and set it to the `$users` variable. To do this, you create the `$users` variable and set it equal to the result from `$xml.GetElementsByTagName("user")`. All of the tags that have the name of `user` are now stored in an array in the `$users` variable. You then create a `Foreach` loop to loop through each `$user` in the variable `$users`. You then use the dot notation to write to the console the word `Username:` with the `$user.username` attribute value. You also write to the console the word `Permission:` with the `$user.permissions` attribute values. After executing this script, you will see three users and three permissions that match the values of the XML file.

Adding XML content

When you are working with XML files, there may be instances where you need to add, modify, and remove content from the XML file. PowerShell's integration with XML provides many methods that you can use to manipulate the XML data.

The following example displays how you can add different types of data into an XML file:

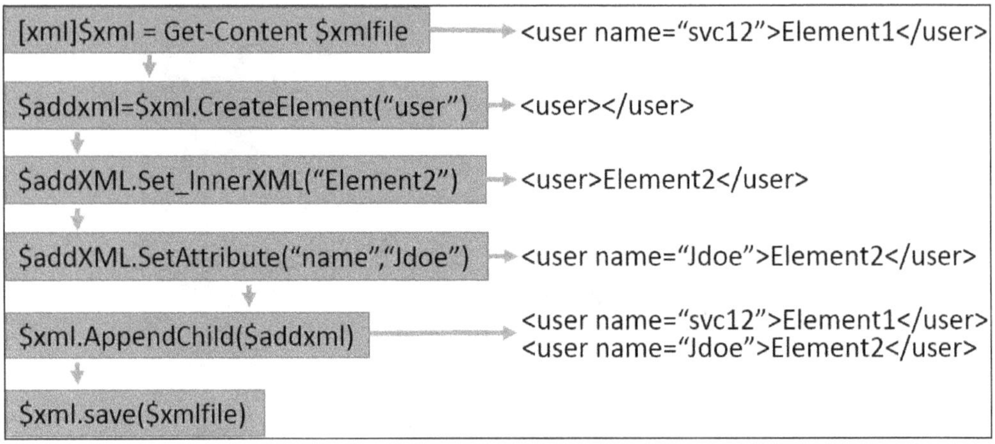

Adding XML data to an existing XML structure is a multistep process. This can be done through the following steps:

1. **Retrieving the XML file and place in memory**: As shown in the preceding example, you first have to retrieve the XML document and place it into a variable.
2. **Creating a new variable containing the new tag object**: You need to create the new user tag object by leveraging `.CreateElement` referencing a new or existing tag name and set the output to a variable. This will create a new instance of the tag to modify the element and attributes.
3. **Appending elements (if needed)**: To set an element to the `user` tag, you can leverage `.Set_innerXML` with the element data you want to add to the XML file.
4. **Appending attributes and attribute values (if needed)**: If you want to add attributes to the `user` tag, you can use `.SetAttribute` with the attribute name and attribute value.
5. **Merging the new tag, elements, and attributes into the XML content in memory**: At this point, you only created a new `user` tag object in memory, and you need to merge it into the XML document object you have in memory by using `.AppendChild()`, referencing the variable containing the new XML tag.

6. **Saving updated XML content in memory over the existing XML file**: When you are done merging the new tag into the XML content in memory, you can save the changes over the existing XML file. When you are ready to save the XML variable back to the file, you can leverage the `.Save()` method, pointing to the XML file path location.

To create a new `user` tag in an existing XML file with elements and attributes, do the following action:

```
$xmlfile = "c:\Program Files\MyCustomSoftware2\Answers.xml"
[xml]$xml = get-content $xmlfile
$addxml = $xml.CreateElement("user")
$addxml.SetAttribute("username","john.smith")
$addxml.SetAttribute("permissions","Administrator")
$xml.Settings.AppendChild($addxml)
$xml.save($xmlfile)
```

The output of this script is shown in the following screenshot:

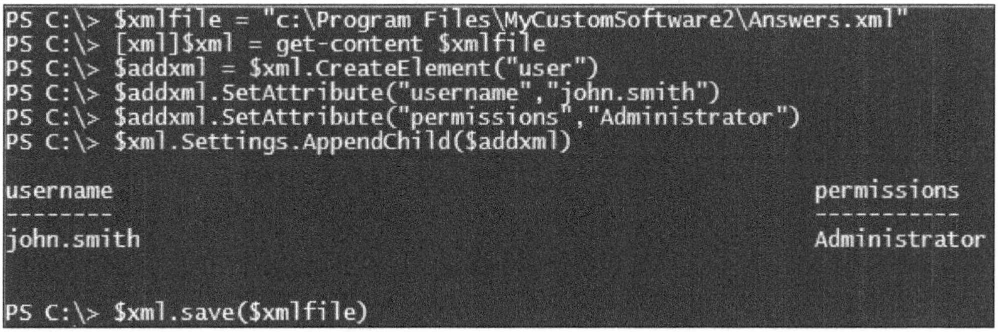
PS C:\> $xmlfile = "c:\Program Files\MyCustomSoftware2\Answers.xml"
PS C:\> [xml]$xml = get-content $xmlfile
PS C:\> $addxml = $xml.CreateElement("user")
PS C:\> $addxml.SetAttribute("username","john.smith")
PS C:\> $addxml.SetAttribute("permissions","Administrator")
PS C:\> $xml.Settings.AppendChild($addxml)
username
permissions

----
john.smith
Administrator
PS C:\> $xml.save($xmlfile)

This example displays how to create a new tag with attributes and append them to an XML file. You start by declaring the XML file variable of `$xmlfile` set to the location of the XML file which is `c:\Program Files\MyCustomSoftware2\Answers.xml`. You then declare an `[xml]` variable type by calling `[xml]$xml` and setting the contents from `get-content $xmlfile` to this variable. You then create a new tag of user by calling the `$xml.CreateElement("user")` method and placing it in the `$addxml` variable. This allows you to modify the new object through the `$addxml` variable. You then apply the `username` attribute with the `john.smith` attribute data to that new element by using the `$addxml.SetAttribute("username","john.smith")` method. You can also apply the `permissions` attribute with `Administrator` to the element by using the `$addxml.SetAttribute("permissions", "administrator")` method.

Finally, you leverage the `.appendchild($addxml)` method to the `$xml` variable and save the contents in the `$xml` variable over the XML file using `$xml.Save($xmlfile)`. After executing this command, you will have created a new user tag, with the `username` attribute containing `john.smith`, the `permissions` attribute containing `Administrator`, and a blank XML element.

To create an entire XML tag with an element, do the following action:

```
$xmlfile = "c:\Program Files\MyCustomSoftware2\Answers.xml"
[xml]$xml = get-content $xmlfile
$addxml = $xml.CreateElement("webserver")
$addxml.set_InnerXML("MyWebServer.domain.local")
$xml.Settings.AppendChild($addxml)
$xml.save($xmlfile)
```

The output of this script is shown in the following screenshot:

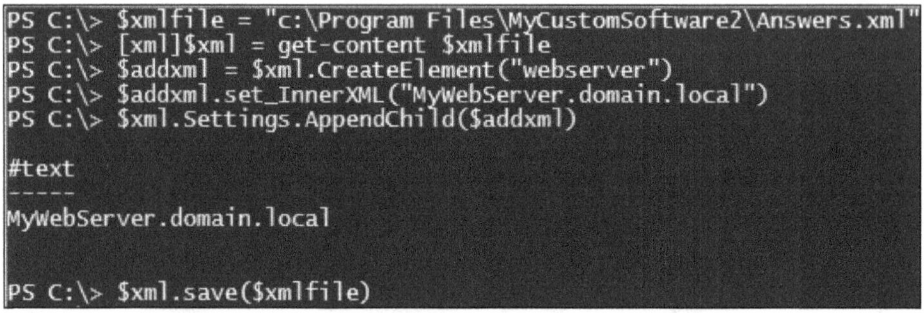
PS C:\> $xmlfile = "c:\Program Files\MyCustomSoftware2\Answers.xml"
PS C:\> [xml]$xml = get-content $xmlfile
PS C:\> $addxml = $xml.CreateElement("webserver")
PS C:\> $addxml.set_InnerXML("MyWebServer.domain.local")
PS C:\> $xml.Settings.AppendChild($addxml)
#text

MyWebServer.domain.local
PS C:\> $xml.save($xmlfile)

This example displays how to create a new XML tag with elements and append them to an XML file. You start by declaring the XML file variable of `$xmlfile` set to the location of the XML file which is `c:\Program Files\MyCustomSoftware2\Answers.xml`. You then declare an `[xml]` variable type by calling `[xml]$xml` and setting the contents from `get-content $xmlfile` to this variable. You then create a new tag of webserver by calling the `$xml.CreateElement("webserver")` method and placing it in the `$addxml` variable. This allows you to modify the new object through the `$addxml` variable. You then create the new inner XML element for the webserver tag by declaring `$addxml.set_innerxml("MyWebServer.domain.local")`. You append this new child tag and element in the `$xml` variable by declaring `$xml.Settings.AppendChild($addxml)`. Finally, you save the updated content of the `$XML` variable to the XML file using the `$xml.save($xmlfile)`. After executing this script, `c:\Program Files\MyCustomSoftware2\Answers.xml` will contain a new child tag in the settings tag named webserver with the element of `MyWebServer.Domain.Local`.

Modifying XML content

There may be instances where you need to update content in an XML file. The following graphic displays how you can modify content in an XML file:

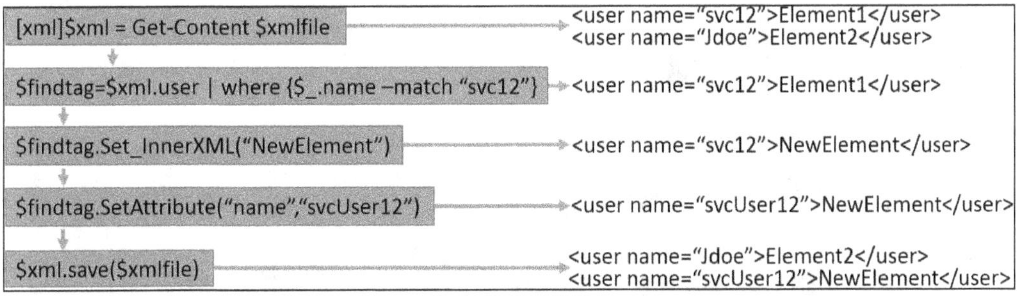

The process to modify existing XML tags is similar to adding new XML tags. The main difference is that instead of creating a new element, you search for an existing tag to modify it. To start, you need to use the `get-content` cmdlet to place the contents of the XML file into a variable, named `$XML`. You then declare a variable, like `$findtag` and leverage the dot notation to find the tag you want to modify. If there are multiple tags for the item you are referencing, you can pipe the tag results to the selection criteria to find an attribute value or element value. In this example, you search for the `name` attribute and use the selection criteria of `where {$_.name -match "svc12"}`.

After obtaining the tag that you want to modify, you can now leverage the `.set_innerXML()` and `.SetAttribute()` methods to modify the tag attributes and elements. After modifying the file, the final step is to leverage the `.Save()` method to append the modified data back into the original XML file.

To search for an attribute and modify the contents and then save it back to a file, do the following action:

```
$xmlfile = "c:\Program Files\MyCustomSoftware2\Answers.xml"
[xml]$xml = get-content $xmlfile
$findtag = $xml.settings.user | where {$_.username -match "jane.doe"}
$findtag
$findtag.SetAttribute("permissions","Read-Only")
$findtag
$xml.save($xmlfile)
```

The output of this script is shown in the following screenshot:

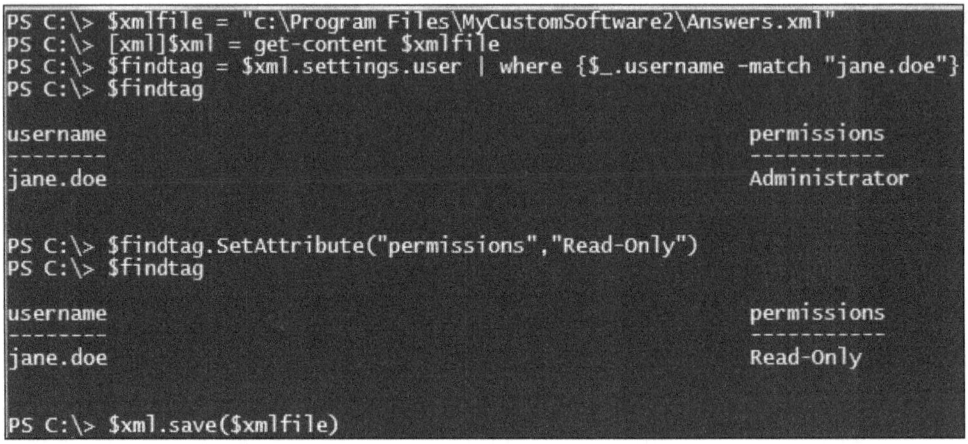

```
PS C:\> $xmlfile = "c:\Program Files\MyCustomSoftware2\Answers.xml"
PS C:\> [xml]$xml = get-content $xmlfile
PS C:\> $findtag = $xml.settings.user | where {$_.username -match "jane.doe"}
PS C:\> $findtag

username                                                     permissions
--------                                                     -----------
jane.doe                                                     Administrator


PS C:\> $findtag.SetAttribute("permissions","Read-Only")
PS C:\> $findtag

username                                                     permissions
--------                                                     -----------
jane.doe                                                     Read-Only


PS C:\> $xml.save($xmlfile)
```

This example displays how to find a tag, modify attributes, and save it back to an XML file. You start by declaring the XML file variable of `$xmlfile` set to the location of the XML file, which is `c:\Program Files\MyCustomSoftware2\Answers.xml`. You then declare an `[xml]` variable type by calling `[xml]$xml` and setting the contents from `get-content $xmlfile` to this variable. You then declare a variable for the tag you want to update, named `$findtag`, and search the `$xml` variable by using dot notation to view the `$xml.settings.user` tags in the XML file. You then pipe those results to a further selection criteria of `where {$_.username -match "jane.doe"}` to search the `username` attribute for the value of `jane.doe`. You then print to screen the result contained in `$findtag`, which displays the `username` attribute value of `jane.doe` and `permissions` attribute value of `Administrator`. To modify the permissions attribute, you leverage `$findtag.SetAttribute("permissions","Read-Only")` to update the tag found in the `$findtag` variable. You then print to screen the updated values of `$findtag`, where you see that the `username` attribute value is still `jane.doe`, but the `permissions` attribute is now updated to `Read-Only`. Finally, you save the updated `$xml` with the updated tag by leveraging the `$xml.save($xmlfile)` method. After executing this script, the user tag with the `username` attribute value set to `jane.doe` will have the `permissions` attribute value set to `Read-Only`.

To search for an element and modify the contents and then save it back to a file, do the following action:

```
$xmlfile = "c:\Program Files\MyCustomSoftware2\Answers.xml"
[xml]$xml = get-content $xmlfile
$findtag = $xml.settings.db | where {$_."#text" -match "MainDB"}
```

```
$findtag
$findtag.set_InnerXML("MainDatabase")
$findtag
$xml.save($xmlfile)
```

The output of this command is shown in the following screenshot:

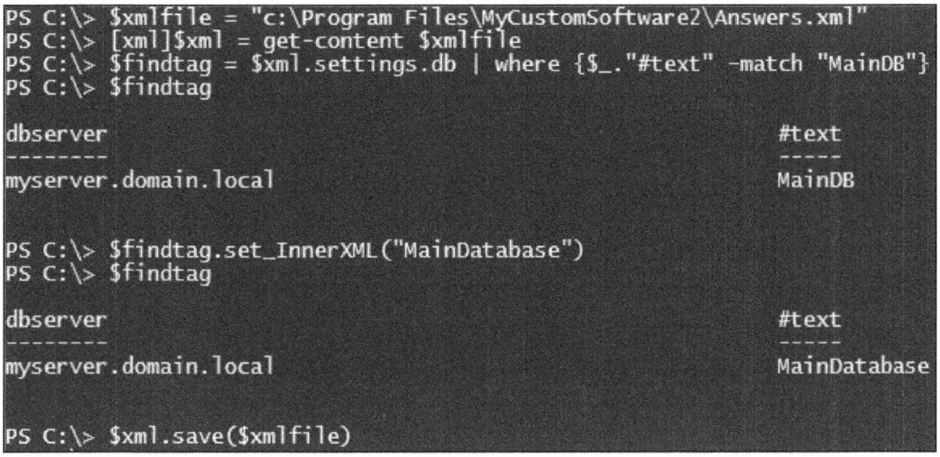

```
PS C:\> $xmlfile = "c:\Program Files\MyCustomSoftware2\Answers.xml"
PS C:\> [xml]$xml = get-content $xmlfile
PS C:\> $findtag = $xml.settings.db | where {$_."#text" -match "MainDB"}
PS C:\> $findtag

dbserver                                                   #text
--------                                                   -----
myserver.domain.local                                      MainDB


PS C:\> $findtag.set_InnerXML("MainDatabase")
PS C:\> $findtag

dbserver                                                   #text
--------                                                   -----
myserver.domain.local                                      MainDatabase


PS C:\> $xml.save($xmlfile)
```

This example shows how to find a tag, modify inner XML, and save it back to an XML file. You start by declaring the XML file variable of `$xmlfile` set to the location of the XML file, which is `c:\Program Files\MyCustomSoftware2\Answers.xml`. You then declare an `[xml]` variable type by calling `[xml]$xml` and setting the contents from `get-content $xmlfile` to this variable. You then declare a variable for the tag you want to update, named `$findtag`, and search the `$xml` variable using dot notation to view the `$xml.settings.db` tags in the XML file. You then pipe those results to a further selection criteria of `where {$_."#text" -match "MainDB"}` to search the element for the value of `MainDB`. You then print to screen the result contained in `$findtag`, which displays the `dbserver` attribute value of `myserver.domain.local` and the element value `#text` of `MainDB`. To modify the element of the `db` tag, you then leverage `$findtag.Set_InnerXML("MainDatabase")` to update the tag found in the `$findtag` variable. You then print to screen the updated values of `$findtag`, where you see that the element value is updated to `MainDatabase`, but the `dbserver` attribute remains `myserver.domain.local`. Finally, you save the updated `$xml` with the updated tag by leveraging the `$xml.save($xmlfile)` method. After executing this script, the `db` tag with the `dbserver` attribute value of `myserver.domain.local` has an updated element of `MainDatabase`.

Removing XML content

There may be instances where you need to remove content from an XML file. The following graphic displays how you can remove content from an XML file:

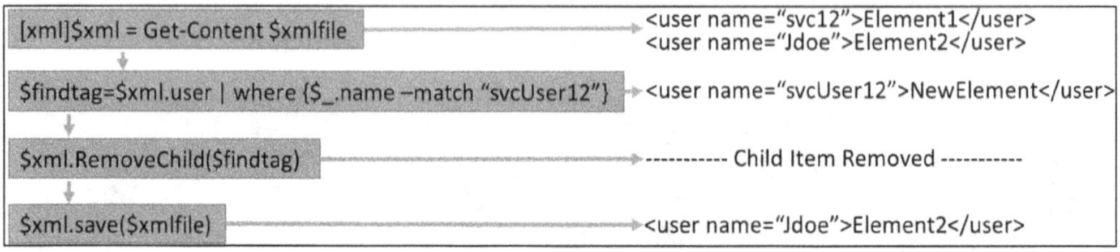

When you want to remove XML tags, you can follow a syntax similar to modifying an XML tag. To start, you need to use the `get-content` cmdlet to place the contents of the XML file into a variable named `$XML`. You then declare a variable like `$findtag` and leverage the dot notation to find the tag you want to remove. If there are multiple tags for the item you are referencing, you can pipe the tag results to the selection criteria to find an attribute value or element value. In this example, you search for the name attribute and use the selection criteria of `where {$_.name -match "svcUser12"}`.

After obtaining the tag that you want to remove, you can now leverage the `.RemoveChild()` methods to remove the tag. After removing the tag from the `$xml` variable, the final step is to leverage the `.Save()` method to append the changes back into the original XML file.

To remove a child item from an XML file, you can perform the following action:

```
$xmlfile = "c:\Program Files\MyCustomSoftware2\Answers.xml"
[xml]$xml = get-content $xmlfile
$findtag = $xml.settings.user | where {$_.username -match "john.doe"}
$xml.settings.RemoveChild($findtag)
$xml.save($xmlfile)
```

The output of this command is shown in the following screenshot:

```
PS C:\> $xmlfile = "c:\Program Files\MyCustomSoftware2\Answers.xml"
PS C:\> [xml]$xml = get-content $xmlfile
PS C:\> $findtag = $xml.settings.user | where {$_.username -match "john.doe"}
PS C:\> $xml.settings.RemoveChild($findtag)

username                                                     permissions
--------                                                     -----------
john.doe                                                     Read-Only


PS C:\> $xml.save($xmlfile)
```

This example displays how to find a tag, remove the tag, and save updates to an XML file. You start by declaring the XML file variable of `$xmlfile` set to the location of the XML file, which is `c:\Program Files\MyCustomSoftware2\Answers.xml`. You then declare an `[xml]` variable type by calling `[xml]$xml` and setting the contents from `get-content $xmlfile` to this variable. You then declare a variable for the tag you want to update, named `$findtag`, and search `the $xml` variable using dot notation to view the `$xml.settings.user` tags in the XML file. You then pipe those results to more selection criteria of `where {$_.username -match "john-doe"}` to search the `username` attribute for the value of `jane.doe`. To remove the user tag with the username attribute value set to `john.doe`, you leverage the `$xml.settings.RemoveChild($findtag)` method. PowerShell will print to the screen the tag that has been removed from the `$xml` variable. Finally, you save the updated `$xml` with the removed tag by leveraging the `$xml.save($xmlfile)` method. After executing this script, the user tag with the `username` attribute value set to `john.doe` will be removed from `c:\Program Files\MyCustomSoftware2\Answers.xml`.

Summary

This chapter explained how you can leverage PowerShell to manipulate XML files. To start, you learned the core make up of an XML structure. You continued to learn about the DOM tree structure and how parents, children, and siblings relate to each other in an XML file. You also to learned how to read XML files and navigate their structure. You learned that you can also use dot notation to navigate an XML structure in PowerShell. Finally, you saw the steps to add, modify, and remove content from an XML file. In the next chapter, you will learn different methods to manage Microsoft systems using PowerShell. You will learn items such as local user and group management, interacting with Window services, and working with Windows processes.

12
Managing Microsoft Systems with PowerShell

This chapter explores many facets of managing Microsoft systems. You will start by learning about the **active directory services interface** (**ADSI**) adapter, and how it interacts with local objects on a system. You will learn to create and delete users and groups on a local system, and also how to add and remove users from the groups you created. You then learn how to verify that users or groups exist on a system. You will then proceed to learn how to start, stop, and modify Windows services and processes on a system. This chapter ends by explaining how to get information about installed and available Windows features and how to install and remove these features from the system.

> This chapter explains interaction with local users and groups. For more information on Active Directory cmdlets, please refer to `https://technet.microsoft.com/en-us/library/ee617195.aspx`.
>
> To properly follow the examples in this chapter, you will need to sequentially execute the examples. Each example builds on the previous examples, and some of them may not function properly if you do not execute the previous steps.

Managing local users and groups

When you are working with building new systems, there may be instances where you need to create new users and groups on a system. While you may be familiar with the `net` commands to manipulate the local users and groups, PowerShell provides other options for communicating with the local system. This section displays how to leverage ADSI calls to interact with local users and groups.

The first step in leveraging ADSI to communicate with a local or remote system is to set up the connection string. This is done by calling the string `[ADSI]"WinNT://SystemName"` and storing the call in a variable such as `$ADSI`. After the connection is made, you can execute different methods and interact with local objects of that system.

Managing local users

To create a user leveraging the ADSI connection, you first have to declare the connection by calling `[ADSI]"WinNT://SystemName"` and setting it to the `$ADSI` variable. You then leverage the `.create()` method of the connection variable `$ADSI`. Next, you define a new variable for the user, such as `$username`, and set it equal to the object output of the `.create()` method with the arguments of `("User","User Name")`. You then need to define a password for the user, specifying the `.setpassword()` method on `$username` with `("Password")` as the argument. Finally, you can commit the user to the **Security Account Manager** (**SAM**) by calling `$username` with the `.setinfo()` method. After creating the security account, you can add a description for the user by using the `$username.description` method and setting it equal to the description you desire. You then have to call the `$username.setinfo()` method to commit the change to the SAM.

To create new local users, do the following:

```
$computername = [system.net.dns]::GetHostName()
Function create-user { param($Computer, $username, $password)
    $ADSI = [ADSI]"WinNT://$Computer"
    $user = $ADSI.Create("User", $username)
    $user.setpassword("$Password")
    $user.setinfo()
}
create-user $computername "svcLocalAccount" "P@ssw0rd"
create-user $computername "remLocalAccount" "P@ssw0rd"
```

The output of this is shown in the following screenshot:

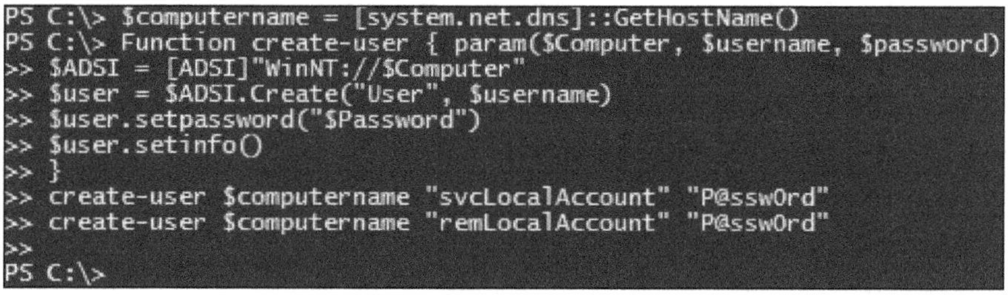
PS C:\> $computername = [system.net.dns]::GetHostName()
PS C:\> Function create-user { param($Computer, $username, $password)
>> $ADSI = [ADSI]"WinNT://$Computer"
>> $user = $ADSI.Create("User", $username)
>> $user.setpassword("$Password")
>> $user.setinfo()
>> }
>> create-user $computername "svcLocalAccount" "P@ssw0rd"
>> create-user $computername "remLocalAccount" "P@ssw0rd"
>>
PS C:\>

This script displays how to create a function to create local users on a system. You start by defining the computer name by leveraging the `[system.net.dns]` .NET assembly, using its `GetHostName()` method, and saving the name to the `$computername` variable. You then create a function named `create-user` with the `param` arguments of `$computer`, `$username`, and `$password`. Thereafter, you create the ADSI connection string into the computer by calling `[ADSI]"WinNT://$computer"` and setting it to the variable `$ADSI`. Then, you invoke the `$ADSI.Create()` method with the arguments of `user` and `$username` to create the object type of `User` with the name of `$username`, and set it to the `$user` variable. Next, you call the `$user.setpassword()` method and specify the password variable of `$password`. To complete the function, you call the `$user.setinfo()` method to set the information into the SAM. You complete the script by calling the `create-user` function with the `$computername` variable, the `svcLocalAccount` username, and the `P@ssword` password. This creates a new user named `svcLocalAccount` with the password of `P@ssword`. You then call the `create-user` function again, with the `$computername` variable, `remLocalAccount username`, and the `P@ssword` password. This creates a new user named `remLocalAccount` with the password of `P@ssword`.

To delete a user, you leverage a similar methodology as creating a user. You first have to declare the connection by calling `[ADSI]"WinNT://SystemName"` and setting it to the `$ADSI` variable. You then leverage the `.Delete()` method of the connection variable `$ADSI` and reference the arguments of `("User","User Name")`. After running the `$ADSI.Delete("User","User Name")` method, the `User` will be deleted from the system.

To delete a local user, do the following:

```
$computername = [system.net.dns]::GetHostName()
Function delete-user { param($Computer, $username)
    $ADSI = [ADSI]"WinNT://$Computer"
    $ADSI.Delete("user", "$username")
}
delete-user $computername "remLocalAccount"
```

The output of this is shown in the following screenshot:

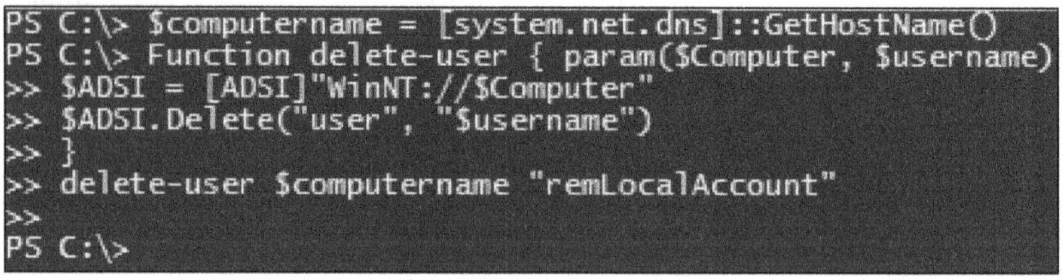
PS C:\> $computername = [system.net.dns]::GetHostName()
PS C:\> Function delete-user { param($Computer, $username)
>> $ADSI = [ADSI]"WinNT://$Computer"
>> $ADSI.Delete("user", "$username")
>> }
>> delete-user $computername "remLocalAccount"
>>
PS C:\>

This script displays how to create a function to delete local users from a system. You first define the computer name by leveraging the `[system.net.dns]` .NET assembly, using its `GetHostName()` method, and saving the name to the `$computername` variable. You then create a function named `delete-user` with the `param` arguments of `$computer` and `$username`. Next, you create the ADSI connection string into the computer by calling `[ADSI] "WinNT://$computer"` and setting it to the variable `$ADSI`. You then invoke the `$ADSI.Delete()` method with the arguments of `user` and `$username` to delete the object type of `User` with the name of `$username`. You finally complete the script by calling the `delete-user` function with `$computername` and `remLocalAccount`. This deletes the user `remLocalAccount`.

Managing local groups

To create a group leveraging the ADSI connection, you first have to declare the connection by calling `[ADSI]"WinNT://SystemName"` and setting it to the `$ADSI` variable. You then leverage the `.create()` method of the connection variable `$ADSI`. Thereafter, you define a new variable for the group, such as `$group`, and set it equal to the object output of the `.create()` method with the arguments of `("Group","Group Name")`. Finally, you can commit the group to the SAM by declaring `$group` with the `.setinfo()` method. After creating the security account, you can add a description for the group by using the `$group.description` method and setting it equal to the description you desire. You would then have to call the `$group.setinfo()` method to commit the change to the SAM.

To create local groups, do the following:

```
Function create-group{ param($computer, $groupname, $description)
    $ADSI = [ADSI]"WinNT://$Computer"
    $Group = $ADSI.Create("Group", $groupname)
    $Group.setinfo()
    $Group.Description = "$description"
    $Group.setinfo()
}
# Create the MyLocalGroup
create-group $computername "MyLocalGroup" "This is a test local group"
# Create the remLocalGroup
create-group $computername "remLocalGroup" "This is a test local group"
```

The output of this is shown in the following screenshot:

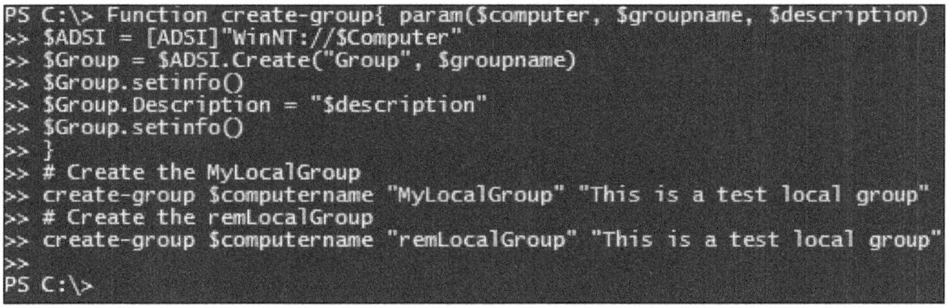
PS C:\> Function create-group{ param($computer, $groupname, $description)
>> $ADSI = [ADSI]"WinNT://$Computer"
>> $Group = $ADSI.Create("Group", $groupname)
>> $Group.setinfo()
>> $Group.Description = "$description"
>> $Group.setinfo()
>> }
>> # Create the MyLocalGroup
>> create-group $computername "MyLocalGroup" "This is a test local group"
>> # Create the remLocalGroup
>> create-group $computername "remLocalGroup" "This is a test local group"
>>
PS C:\>

This script displays how to create functions to create local groups on a system. You start by defining the computer name by leveraging the `[system.net.dns]` .NET assembly, using its `GetHostName()` method, and saving the name to the `$computername` variable. You then create a function named `create-group` with the `param` arguments of `$computer`, `$groupname`, and `$description`. Next, you create the ADSI connection string into the computer by calling `[ADSI]"WinNT://$computer"` and setting it to the variable `$ADSI`. Following this, you invoke the `$ADSI.Create()` method with the arguments of `Group` and `$groupname` to create the object type of `Group` with the name of `$groupname`, and set it to the `$group` variable. You then call the `$Group.setinfo()` method to set the information into the SAM. Finally, the function creates a description by calling the `$Group.description` method and setting it equal to the `$description` variable.

You commit the description changes by calling the `$Group.setinfo()` method to set the description information into the SAM. The script is completed by calling the `create-group` function with the `$computername` variable, the `MyLocalGroup` group name, and the `This is a test local group` description. This creates a new group named `MyLocalGroup` with the description of `This is a test local group`. You then call the `create-group` function again with the `$computername` variable, the `remLocalGroup` group name, and the `This is a test local group` description. This creates a new group named `remLocalGroup` with the description of `This is a test local group`.

To delete a group, you leverage a similar methodology as creating a group. You first have to declare the connection by calling `[ADSI] "WinNT://SystemName"` and setting it to the `$ADSI` variable. You then leverage the `.Delete()` method of the connection variable `$ADSI` and reference the arguments of `("Group","Group Name")`. After running the `$ADSI.Delete("Group","Group Name")` method, the group will be deleted from the system.

To delete a local group, do the following:

```
$computername = [system.net.dns]::GetHostName()
Function delete-group { param($computer, $groupname)
    $ADSI = [ADSI]"WinNT://$Computer"
    $ADSI.Delete("Group", $groupname)
}
# Delete the local group remLocalGroup
delete-group $computername "remLocalGroup"
```

The output of this is shown in the following screenshot:

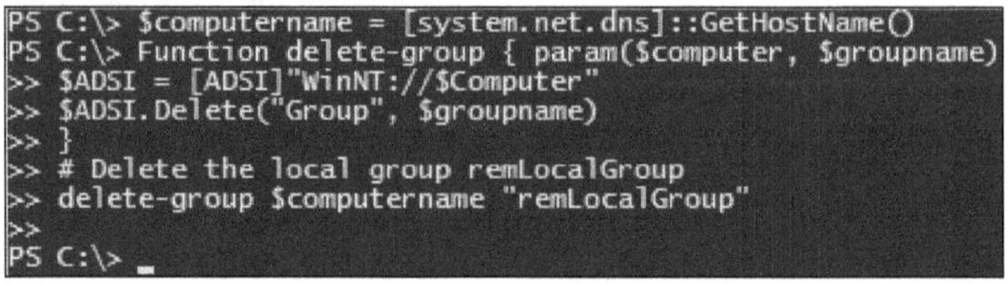
PS C:\> $computername = [system.net.dns]::GetHostName()
PS C:\> Function delete-group { param($computer, $groupname)
>> $ADSI = [ADSI]"WinNT://$Computer"
>> $ADSI.Delete("Group", $groupname)
>> }
>> # Delete the local group remLocalGroup
>> delete-group $computername "remLocalGroup"
>>
PS C:\>

This script displays how to create functions to remove local groups from a system. You start by defining the computer name by leveraging the `[system.net.dns]` .NET assembly, using its `GetHostName()` method, and saving the name to the `$computername` variable. You then create a function named `delete-group` with the `param` arguments of `$computer` and `$groupname`. You then create the ADSI connection string into the computer by calling `[ADSI]"WinNT://$computer"` and setting it to the variable `$ADSI`. Next, you invoke the `$ADSI.Delete()` method with the arguments of `Group` and `$Groupname` to delete the object type of `User` with the name of `$username`. Finally, you call the `delete-group` function with `$computername` and `remLocalGroup`. This deletes the group `remLocalGroup`. After execution of the whole script, you will have the `MyLocalGroup` group created on the system.

There may be instances where you want to add users to a local group. To add members to a group, you first have to define where the user object exists on the system using ADSI, and store the user object in a variable. This is done through defining a variable and setting it equal to an ADSI path like `[ADSI]"WinNT://SystemName/User"`. You then need to define a variable for the destination group object using an ADSI path. This is done through defining a variable and setting it equal to an ADSI path like `[ADSI]"WinNT://SystemName/MyGroup, Group"`. The `,Group` argument tells the ADSI provider that you aren't looking for a user named `MyGroup`, but rather for a group named `MyGroup`.

The last step to adding a user to a group is to leverage the group object method of `.Add()`. As an argument to the method, you specify the user object you want to add to that group. After executing this, the user will be added to the group.

To create a function to add a user to a group, do the following:

```
$computername = [system.net.dns]::GetHostName()
Function add-groupmember { param($computer, $user, $groupname)
    $userADSI = ([ADSI]"WinNT://$computer/$user").path
    $group = [ADSI]"WinNT://$computer/$groupname, group"
    $group.Add($userADSI)
}
add-groupmember $computername "svcLocalAccount" "MyLocalGroup"
add-groupmember $computername "svcLocalAccount" "Administrators"
```

The output of this is shown in the following screenshot:

```
PS C:\> $computername = [system.net.dns]::GetHostName()
PS C:\> Function add-groupmember { param($computer, $user, $groupname)
>> $userADSI = ([ADSI]"WinNT://$computer/$user").path
>> $group = [ADSI]"WinNT://$computer/$groupname, group"
>> $group.Add($userADSI)
>> }
>> add-groupmember $computername "svcLocalAccount" "MyLocalGroup"
>> add-groupmember $computername "svcLocalAccount" "Administrators"
>>
PS C:\>
```

This script displays how to create functions to add local users to local groups. You start by defining the computer name by leveraging the `[system.net.dns]` .NET assembly, using its `GetHostName()` method, and saving the name to the `$computername` variable. You then create a function named `add-groupmember` with the `param` arguments of `$computer`, `$user`, and `$groupname`. After this, you retrieve the ADSI connection string for the user by calling `([ADSI]"WinNT://$computer/$user").path` and setting it to the variable `$userADSI`. This differs from the previous examples, where it doesn't actually make the connection to the ADSI adapter, it is just a user object location reference in ADSI format.

You continue by retrieving the ADSI connection string into the group on the computer, by calling `[ADSI] "WinNT://$computer,$groupname, group"` and setting it to the variable `$group`. You then invoke the add method of the `$userADSI` user object in the group defined in `$group` by calling `$group.Add($userADSI)`. After execution, the group defined in `$group` will contain the user referenced in `$userADSI`.

Finally, you call the `add-groupmember` function with the arguments of `$computername`, `svcLocalAccount`, and `MyLocalGroup`. This will add `svcLocalAccount` to the `MyLocalGroup` local group. You also call the `add-groupmember` function with the arguments of `$computername`, `svcLocalAccount`, and `Administrators`. This will add `svcLocalAccount` to the `Administrators` local group.

Removing a user from a group is very similar to adding a user to a group. To remove members from a group, you first have to define where the user object exists on the system using ADSI and store the user object in a variable. This is done through defining a variable and setting it equal to an ADSI path like `[ADSI]"WinNT://SystemName/User"`. You then need to define a variable for the destination group object using an ADSI path. This is done through defining a variable and setting it equal to an ADSI path like `[ADSI]"WinNT://SystemName/MyGroup, Group"`. The final step to removing a user from a group is by leveraging the group object method of `.Remove()`. As an argument to the method, you specify the user object you want to remove from that group. After executing this, the user will be removed from the group.

To create a function to remove a user from a group, do the following:

```
$computername = [system.net.dns]::GetHostName()
Function delete-groupmember { param($computer, $user, $groupname)
    $userADSI= ([ADSI]"WinNT://$computer/$user").path
    $group = [ADSI]"WinNT://$computer/$groupname, group"
    $group.Remove($userADSI)
}
delete-groupmember $computername "svcLocalAccount" "Administrators"
```

The output of this is shown in the following screenshot:

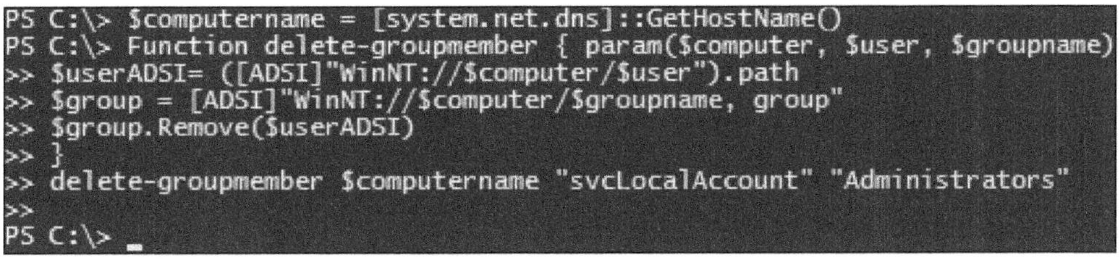
PS C:\> $computername = [system.net.dns]::GetHostName()
PS C:\> Function delete-groupmember { param($computer, $user, $groupname)
>> $userADSI= ([ADSI]"WinNT://$computer/$user").path
>> $group = [ADSI]"WinNT://$computer/$groupname, group"
>> $group.Remove($userADSI)
>> }
>> delete-groupmember $computername "svcLocalAccount" "Administrators"
>>
PS C:\> _

This script displays how to create functions to add local users to local groups. You start by defining the computer name by leveraging the `[system.net.dns]` .NET assembly, using its `GetHostName()` method, and saving the name to the `$computername` variable. You then create a function named `delete-groupmember` with the `param` arguments of `$computer`, `$user`, and `$groupname`. After that, you retrieve the ADSI connection string for the user by calling `([ADSI]"WinNT://$computer/$user").path` and setting it to the variable `$userADSI`. You continue by retrieving the ADSI connection string into the group on the computer by calling `[ADSI]"WinNT://$computer,$groupname, group,"` and setting it to the variable `$group`. You then invoke the `Remove` method of the `$userADSI` user object in the group defined in `$group` by calling `$group.Remove($userADSI)`. After execution, the group defined in `$group` will not contain the user referenced in `$userADSI`. Finally, you call the `delete-groupmember` function with the arguments of `$computername`, `svcLocalAccount`, and `Administrators`. This will delete `svcLocalAccount` from the `Administrators` local group.

Querying for local users and groups

As you are creating users and groups, you may want to verify that a user or group exists prior to creation or deletion. To verify that a user exists, you can leverage the `::Exists` argument to the `[ADSI]` adapter. To do this, you call `[ADSI]::Exists` followed by the ADSI path of the user that you want to modify, such as `WinNt://ComputerName/Username`, and the reference of the `User` object type to complete the ADSI call. This tells the ADSI provider to search `Computername` specified for the object type of `User` for the user named `Username`.

If you want to verify that a group exists, you can leverage the `::Exists` argument to the `[ADSI]` adapter. To do this, you declare `[ADSI]::Exists`, followed by the ADSI location of the user that you want to modify, such as `WinNt://ComputerName/GroupName`, and the reference of `Group` object type to complete the ADSI call. This tells the ADSI provider to search `Computername` specified for the object type of `Group` for the group named `GroupName`.

To search a computer for user and a group object, do the following:

```
$computername = [system.net.dns]::GetHostName()
Function get-ADSISearch { param($computer, $objecttype, $object)
    $test = [ADSI]::Exists("WinNT://$computer/$object, $objecttype")
    If ($test) { Write-host "Local $objecttype Exists. Test Variable
Returned: $test" }
    If (!$test) { Write-host "Local $objecttype Does Not Exist. Test
Variable Returned: $test" }
}
get-ADSISearch $computername "User" "svcLocalAccount"
get-ADSISearch $computername "Group" "MyLocalGroup"
get-ADSISearch $computername "Group" "NotARealGroup"
```

The output of this is shown in the following screenshot:

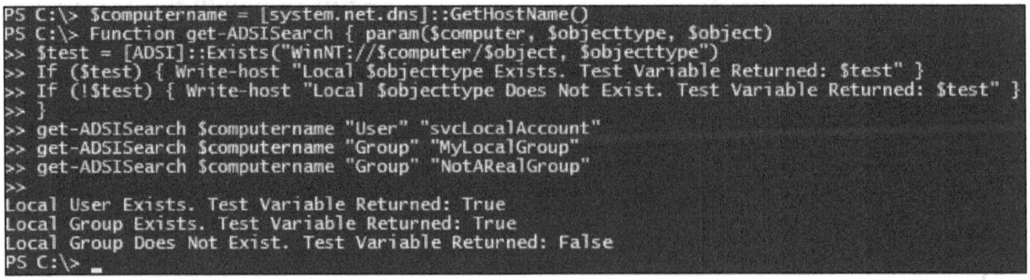

This example displays how to create a function query for a system to see if a user or group has already been created on a system. You start by defining the computer name by leveraging the `[system.net.dns]` .NET assembly, using its `GetHostName()` method, and saving the name to the `$computername` variable. You then create a function named `get-ADSISearch` with the `param` arguments of `$computer`, `$objecttype`, and `$object`. Then, you leverage the ADSI adapter with the `::Exists` method by calling `[ADSI]::Exists("WinNT://$computer/$object, $object type")` and setting it to the variable `$test`. Next, you create an implied True `IF` statement of `($test)` where if `True`, it will use the `write-host` cmdlet to print `Local $objecttype Exists. Test Variable Returned: $test`. You then create an implied False `IF` statement of `(!$test)` where if `False`, it will use the `write-host` cmdlet to print `Local $objecttype Does Not Exist. Test Variable Returned: $test`.

Finally, you test three objects by first calling `get-ADSISearch` function with the arguments of `$computername`, `User`, and `svcLocalAccount`. This will return `True` because the svcLocalAccount user is on the system. The script will print to the screen `Local User Exists. Test Variable Returned: True`. Second, you call the `get-ADSISearch` function with the arguments of `$computername`, `Group`, and `MyLocalGroup`. This will return `True` because the `MyLocalGroup` group exists on the system. The script will print to the screen `Local Group Exists. Test Variable Returned: True`. The third call is to the `get-ADSISearch` function with the arguments of `$computername`, `Group`, and `NotARealGroup`. This will return `False` because the `NotARealGroup` group does not exist on the system. The script will print to the screen `Local Group Does Not Exist. Test Variable Returned: False`.

If you want to view the members of a group, you can leverage an ADSI provider to get the group members. First, you need to define the group you want to query. This is done through defining a group variable and setting it equal to an ADSI path like `[ADSI]"WinNT://SystemName/Groupname"`. You then need to query the members of the group and search through the individual members. This is done through creating an array of the ADSI group object members by invoking the `Members` method. In code, this looks like `@($groupvariable.Invoke("Members"))`.

After you receive the ADSI group object members, you need to retrieve the `Name` property of the individual group members. You pipe the results of the array to a `foreach` loop and get the name property by typing `| foreach {$_.GetType().InvokeMember("Name",'GetProperty',$null, $_, $null)}`. After taking the pipeline and getting the `Name` property from each object, a list of group members' names is printed to the console.

To get the list of the members of a local group, do the following:

```
$computername = [system.net.dns]::GetHostName()
Function get-groupmember { param($computer,$groupname)
    $group = [ADSI]"WinNT://$computer/$groupname"
    @($group.Invoke("Members")) | foreach { $_.GetType().InvokeMember("Na
me",'GetProperty',$null, $_, $null) }

}
$members = get-groupmember $computername "MyLocalGroup"
Write-host "The members for MyLocalGroup are: $members"
$members = get-groupmember $computername "Administrators"
Write-host "The members for Administrators are: $members"
```

The output of this is shown in the following screenshot:

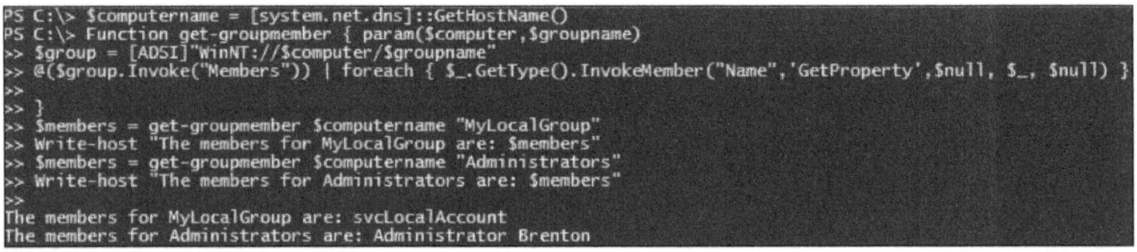
PS C:\> $computername = [system.net.dns]::GetHostName()
PS C:\> Function get-groupmember { param($computer,$groupname)
>> $group = [ADSI]"WinNT://$computer/$groupname"
>> @($group.Invoke("Members")) | foreach { $_.GetType().InvokeMember("Name",'GetProperty',$null, $_, $null) }
>>
>> }
>> $members = get-groupmember $computername "MyLocalGroup"
>> Write-host "The members for MyLocalGroup are: $members"
>> $members = get-groupmember $computername "Administrators"
>> Write-host "The members for Administrators are: $members"
>>
The members for MyLocalGroup are: svcLocalAccount
The members for Administrators are: Administrator Brenton

This example displays how to query the group members of `MyLocalGroup` and `Administrators` group on a computer. You start by defining the computer name by leveraging the `[system.net.dns]` .NET assembly, using its `GetHostName()` method, and saving the name to the `$computername` variable. After that, you create a function named `get-groupmember` with the `param` arguments of `$computer` and `$groupname`. You then retrieve the ADSI connection string for the group by calling `[ADSI]"WinNT://$computer/$groupname"` and setting it to the variable `$group`.

You then create an array of members by typing `@($group.Invoke("Members"))`. Next, you pipe those results to a `foreach` loop and get the `Name` property for each of the results by typing `{$_.GetType().InvokeMember("Name",'GetProperty',$null, $_, $null)}`. This will return the results of the individual member's names within the function. You then close the `get-groupmember` function.

After defining the function, you call the `get-groupmember` function for the `MyLocalGroup` group and set the results to the `$members` variable. You then print to the screen `The members for MyLocalGroup are: $members`. The output to the console is `The members for MyLocalGroup are: svcLocalAccount`.

Finally, you call the `get-groupmember` function for the `Administrators` group and set the results to the `$members` variable. You then print to the screen `The members for Administrators are: $members`. The output to the console is `The members for Administrators are: Administrator Brenton`.

> For detailed information on `GetType()` and `InvokeMember()`, you can refer to `https://msdn.microsoft.com/en-us/library/de3dhzwy(v=vs.110).aspx`.

Managing Windows services

When you are working with Microsoft-based systems, there may be times where you need to interact with Windows services. PowerShell offers a variety of cmdlets that enable you to work with these services. To start, you can review the services on a system by leveraging the `get-service` cmdlet. By calling the `get-service` cmdlet, you can retrieve the full list of services on a system. If you want to obtain a filtered view into a specific service, you can leverage the `-Name` parameter, referencing a specific name of a service. After executing this command, you will see `Status`, `Name`, and `DisplayName` of the service. You may also issue the `-RequiredServices` parameter to display the services that are required to be running, for that particular service to be functional. You may also use `-DependentServices` to view the services that are dependent on that service.

To use the `get-service` cmdlet to query the Windows Audio Service, do the following:

```
Get-service -DisplayName "Windows Audio"
Get-service -DisplayName "Windows Audio" -RequiredServices
(Get-service -DisplayName "Windows Audio").Status
```

The output of this is shown in the following screenshot:

```
PS C:\> Get-service -DisplayName "Windows Audio"

Status   Name               DisplayName
------   ----               -----------
Running  Audiosrv           Windows Audio


PS C:\> Get-service -DisplayName "Windows Audio" -RequiredServices

Status   Name               DisplayName
------   ----               -----------
Stopped  MMCSS              Multimedia Class Scheduler
Running  RpcSs              Remote Procedure Call (RPC)
Running  AudioEndpointBu... Windows Audio Endpoint Builder


PS C:\> (Get-service -DisplayName "Windows Audio").Status
Running
PS C:\> _
```

This example displays how to get information about the Windows Audio Service. You start by calling the `get-service` cmdlet, leveraging the `-DisplayName` parameter, and referencing the `Windows Audio` Windows service. After executing, you see the `Status`, `Name`, and `DisplayName` fields printed to the PowerShell window. You then use the `get-service` cmdlet with the `-DisplayName` parameter referencing `Windows Audio`, and the `-RequiredServices` parameter. After executing the `get-service` command, you will see `Status`, `Name`, and `DisplayName` of all the services that are required for the `Windows Audio` Windows service to function properly. The last call you make leverages the `get-service` cmdlet with the `-DisplayName` parameter referencing the `Windows Audio`. This whole statement is wrapped in parentheses followed by the dot notation of `.Status`. This returns the current status of the Windows Audio Windows service, which is `Running`.

In instances where you want to start, restart, and stop services, you may leverage the `start-service`, `restart-service`, and `stop-service` cmdlets. To start a service, you can call the `start-service` cmdlet, followed by the `-Name` or `-DisplayName` parameters with the corresponding service name. After execution, the service will change status from `Stopped` to `StartPending`, and when it has successfully started, it will change its status to `Running`.

To stop a service, you can call the `stop-service` cmdlet, followed by the `-Name` or `-DisplayName` parameters with the corresponding service name. After execution, the service will change status from `Running` to `StopPending`, and when it has successfully stopped, it will change the status to `Stopped`.

To restart a service, you can call the `restart-service` cmdlet, followed by the `-Name or -DisplayName` parameters with the corresponding service name. After execution, the service will change status from `Running` to `StopPending`, `StopPending` to `Stopped`, `Stopped` to `StartPending`, and when it has successfully restarted, it will change the status to `Running`.

To stop and start the Windows Audio service, do the following:

```
stop-service -DisplayName "Windows Audio"
(Get-service -DisplayName "Windows Audio").Status
start-service -DisplayName "Windows Audio"
(Get-service -DisplayName "Windows Audio").Status
```

The output of this is shown in the following screenshot:

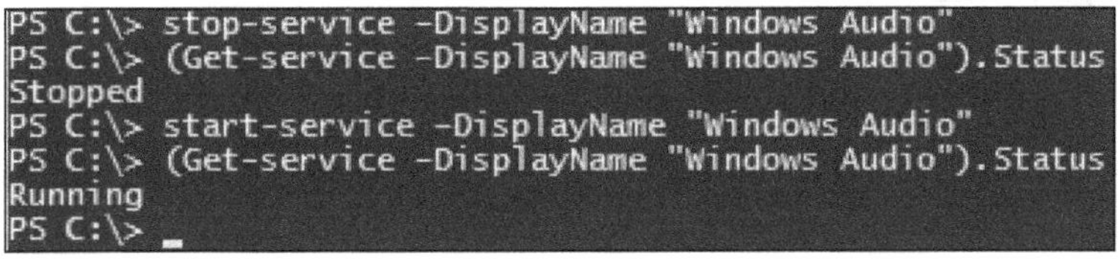
PS C:\> stop-service -DisplayName "Windows Audio"
PS C:\> (Get-service -DisplayName "Windows Audio").Status
Stopped
PS C:\> start-service -DisplayName "Windows Audio"
PS C:\> (Get-service -DisplayName "Windows Audio").Status
Running
PS C:\>

This example shows how to start and stop Windows services. You first stop the Windows Audio service by leveraging the `stop-service` cmdlet, with the `-DisplayName` parameter referencing the `Windows Audio` display name. You then get the current `Status` of the service by executing `get-service`, with the `-DisplayName` parameter referencing the `Windows Audio` display name. You encapsulate that in parentheses and leverage the dot notation of `.Status` to print the current status to the screen. The console will return the status of `Stopped`.

You then start the Windows Audio service by leveraging the `start-service` cmdlet, with the `-DisplayName` parameter referencing the `Windows Audio` display name. You then get the current `Status` of the service by executing `get-service`, with the `-DisplayName` parameter referencing the `Windows Audio` display name. You encapsulate that in parentheses and leverage the dot notation of `.Status` to print the current status to the screen. The console will return the status of `Running`.

You also have the ability to modify different aspects of the Windows services by using the `set-service` cmdlet. The `set-service` cmdlet can modify the service descriptions, start-up types, and even the display names for services. Since Windows does not allow you to modify running services, you first have to leverage the `stop-service` cmdlet to stop the service for editing.

If you want to modify the start-up type for a service, you can leverage the `set-service` cmdlet with `-Name` parameter with the corresponding service name. You then include the `-StartupType` parameter with `Automatic` for automatic start-up, `Manual` for manual start-up, or `Disabled` to disable the service start-up. To view the changes to the service start-up type, you will need to leverage the `get-wmiobject` cmdlet referencing the `win32_service` class, and the `-filter` parameter referencing the `DisplayName='Display Name'`.

> While in most cases, you can leverage the `get-service` cmdlet to display the properties of a service, there are certain properties that are not made available to the cmdlet. As a result, you may have to directly query WMI using `get-wmiobject` to view all of the properties for that service. To view all of the properties available to `get-service` or through WMI, you can pipe | the results to `get-member`, and it will display all available properties that you can view.

To change the Windows Audio `-StartupType` parameter, do the following:

```
(get-wmiobject win32_service -filter "DisplayName='Windows Audio'").
StartMode

stop-service -name "Audiosrv"

set-service -name "Audiosrv" -startup "Manual"

(get-wmiobject win32_service -filter "DisplayName='Windows Audio'").
StartMode

set-service -name "Audiosrv" -startup "Automatic"

(get-wmiobject win32_service -filter "DisplayName='Windows Audio'"
).StartMode

Start-service -name "Audiosrv"
```

The output of this is shown in the following screenshot:

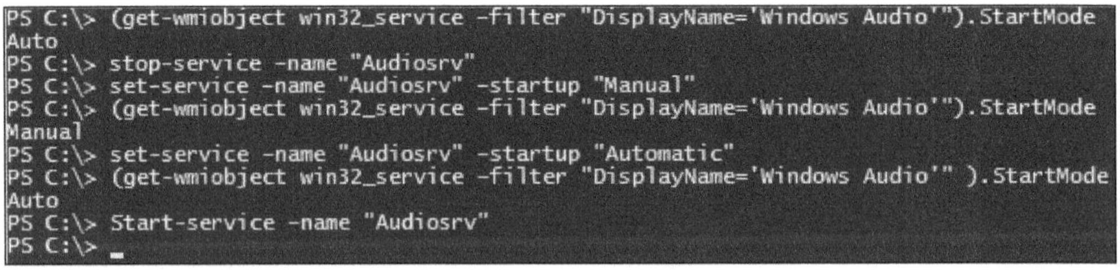
PS C:\> (get-wmiobject win32_service -filter "DisplayName='Windows Audio'").StartMode
Auto
PS C:\> stop-service -name "Audiosrv"
PS C:\> set-service -name "Audiosrv" -startup "Manual"
PS C:\> (get-wmiobject win32_service -filter "DisplayName='Windows Audio'").StartMode
Manual
PS C:\> set-service -name "Audiosrv" -startup "Automatic"
PS C:\> (get-wmiobject win32_service -filter "DisplayName='Windows Audio'").StartMode
Auto
PS C:\> Start-service -name "Audiosrv"
PS C:\>

This example shows how to change the start-up of a Window service on a system. You start by querying the system to see what the existing `StartMode` is. To do this, you have to leverage the `get-wmiobject` cmdlet referencing the `win32_service` class. You leverage the `-filter` parameter with the filter options of `DisplayName='Windows Audio'`. You then encapsulate that statement in parenthesis and leverage the dot notation of `.StartMode` to print to the screen the start mode of a system. The command will print `Auto` to the screen, designating that the service start-up type is set to `Automatic`. Thereafter, you stop the service by calling the `stop-service` cmdlet with the `-name` parameter referencing the `Audiosrv` service name. You then configure the service start-up type to be `Manual` by calling the `set-service` cmdlet with the `-name` parameter referencing `AudioSrv`, and the `-startup` parameter referencing `Manual`. After setting this command, you verify the start-up change by using the `get-wmiobject` cmdlet referencing the `win32_service` class. You leverage the `-filter` parameter with the filter options of `DisplayName='Windows Audio'`. Next, you encapsulate that statement in parenthesis and leverage the dot notation of `.StartMode` to print to the screen the start mode of a system. The command will print `Manual` to the screen designating that the service start-up type is set to `Manual`.

After this, you set the service back to `Automatic` by calling the `set-service` cmdlet with the `-name` parameter referencing `AudioSrv`, and the `-startup` parameter referencing `Automatic`. After setting this command, you verify the start-up change by using the `get-wmiobject` cmdlet referencing the `win32_service` class. You leverage the `-filter` parameter with the filter options of `Displayname='Windows Audio'`. You then encapsulate that statement in parenthesis and leverage the dot notation of `.StartMode` to print to the screen the start mode of a system. The command will print `Auto` to the screen designating that the service start-up type is set to `Automatic`. After final configuration, you start the service by calling the `start-service` cmdlet, with the `-name` parameter referencing the `Audiosrv` service name.

If you want to modify a service's description, you first need to stop the service leveraging the `stop-service` cmdlet. You then call the `set-service` cmdlet with the `-Name` name of the service, and the `-Description` parameter with the description that you want set for the particular service. The description property is unique as it is not made available to the `get-service` cmdlet. To get around this, you need to leverage the `get-wmiobject` cmdlet. To view the description, you can use the `get-wmiobject` cmdlet referencing the `win32_service` class, with the `-filter` parameter referencing `DisplayName='Display Name'`. After executing this script, the description will print to the screen. After setting the description, you can start the service by using the `start-service` cmdlet.

To set the description for the Windows Audio service, do the following:

```
$olddesc = (get-wmiobject win32_service -filter "DisplayName='Windows
Audio'").description
stop-service -DisplayName "Windows Audio"
Set-service -name "Audiosrv" -Description "My New Windows Audio
Description."
(get-wmiobject win32_service -filter "DisplayName='Windows Audio'").
description
Set-service -name "Audiosrv" -Description $olddesc
(get-wmiobject win32_service -filter "DisplayName='Windows Audio'").
description
start-service -DisplayName "Windows Audio"
```

The output of this is shown in the following screenshot:

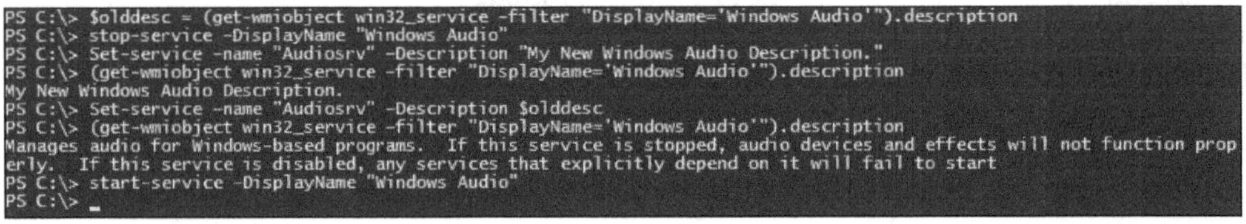
PS C:\> $olddesc = (get-wmiobject win32_service -filter "DisplayName='Windows Audio'").description
PS C:\> stop-service -DisplayName "Windows Audio"
PS C:\> Set-service -name "Audiosrv" -Description "My New Windows Audio Description."
PS C:\> (get-wmiobject win32_service -filter "DisplayName='Windows Audio'").description
My New Windows Audio Description.
PS C:\> Set-service -name "Audiosrv" -Description $olddesc
PS C:\> (get-wmiobject win32_service -filter "DisplayName='Windows Audio'").description
Manages audio for Windows-based programs. If this service is stopped, audio devices and effects will not function prop
erly. If this service is disabled, any services that explicitly depend on it will fail to start
PS C:\> start-service -DisplayName "Windows Audio"
PS C:\>

This example displays how to change the description for a Windows service, and set it back to the original description. You start by querying the system to see what the existing description is. To do this, you have to leverage the `get-wmiobject` cmdlet referencing the `win32_service` class. You leverage the `-filter` parameter with the filter options of `DisplayName='Windows Audio'`. You then encapsulate that statement in parenthesis and leverage the dot notation of `.description`. The output, which is the Windows service description, is then set to the variable `$olddesc`. You then stop the service with the `stop-service` cmdlet, and the `-DisplayName` parameter referencing `Windows Audio`. To set the description, you use the `set-service` cmdlet with the `-name` parameter set to `Audiosrv`, and the `-description` parameter set to `My New Windows Audio Description`.

After setting the description, you query the system with the `get-wmiobject` cmdlet referencing the `win32_service` class, and the `-filter` parameter with the filter options of `DisplayName='Windows Audio'`. You then encapsulate that statement in parenthesis and leverage the dot notation of `.description`. The output from this will be the current description, which is `My New Windows Audio Description`. To set the description back to the original, you use the `set-service` cmdlet with the `-name` parameter set to `Audiosrv`, and the `-description` parameter referencing the `$olddesc` variable. After setting the description back to the original description, you query the system with the `get-wmiobject` cmdlet referencing the `win32_service` class, and the `-filter` parameter with the filter options of `DisplayName='Windows Audio'`. You then encapsulate that statement in parenthesis and leverage the dot notation of `.description`. The output from this will be the current description, which is `Manages audio for Windows-based programs`. If this service is stopped, audio devices and effects will not function properly. If this service is disabled, any services that explicitly depend on it will fail to start. You complete this process by starting the Windows Audio service. You use the `start-service` cmdlet with the `-DisplayName` parameter referencing `Windows Audio`.

Managing Windows processes

There may be times when, during scripting, you need to check if there is a running process on a system. PowerShell offers the `get-process` cmdlet to search for available processes on a system. By running the `get-process` cmdlet alone, you will get a report of all the running services on the system. The default record set that is returned about the running services include:

- **Handles**: The number of thread handles that are being used by a particular process
- **NPM (K)**: Non Paged Memory is the memory that is solely in physical memory, and not allocated to the page file that is being used by a process
- **PM (K)**: Pageable Memory is the memory that is being allocated to the page file that is used by a process
- **WS(K)**: Working Set is the memory recently referenced by a process
- **VM(M)**: Virtual Memory is the amount of virtual memory that is being used by a process
- **CPU(s)**: Processor time, or the time the CPU is utilizing a process
- **ID**: An assigned Unique ID to a Process
- **Process name**: The name of the process in memory

Typically, when you query the active running processes on a system, you will be looking for a particular process. To do this, you can leverage the `get-process` cmdlet with the `-name` parameter referencing `process name` to view information about that particular process. You can also leverage the asterisk (`*`) to be a wild card to query processes that are like the partial word you specify. You may also directly reference the Process ID of a process if you invoke the `-ID` parameter with an ID of a process. If you want more information about the process that is running, you can also leverage the `-fileversioninfo` parameter to pull `ProductVersion`, `FileVersion`, and `Filename information` from the process. In instances where you need to find all of the modules, or DLL references that are loaded by a process, you may also leverage the `-module` parameter.

To search for a process by using a wild card and get a process by a process ID, do the following:

```
$process = get-process powersh*
$process
get-process -id $process.id
```

The output of this is shown in the following screenshot:

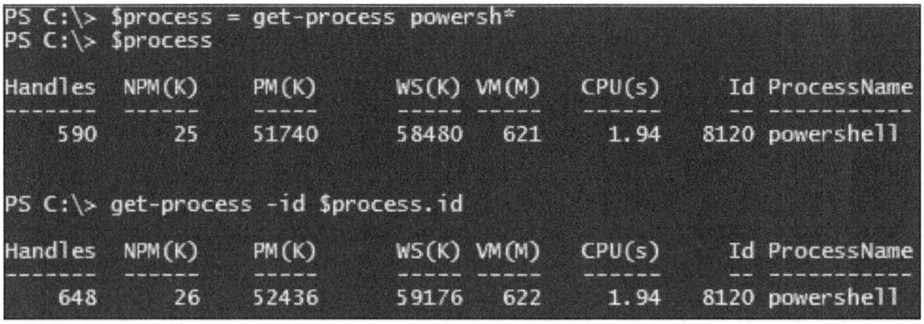
PS C:\> $process = get-process powersh*
PS C:\> $process
Handles NPM(K) PM(K) WS(K) VM(M) CPU(s) Id ProcessName
590 25 51740 58480 621 1.94 8120 powershell
PS C:\> get-process -id $process.id
Handles NPM(K) PM(K) WS(K) VM(M) CPU(s) Id ProcessName
648 26 52436 59176 622 1.94 8120 powershell

This script displays how to search for a process by a wildcard and obtain the process ID. You also view that same service by calling the process ID of that service. You start by using the `get-process` cmdlet with the `powersh*` searching wild card. The system returns the PowerShell process into the `$process` variable. You then call the `$process` variable to view the information about the PowerShell process. Next, you leverage the `get-process` cmdlet with the `-id` parameter pointing to the `$process` variable referencing the dot notation of `.id`. This returns the same PowerShell process information, as `$process.id` that is being referenced is the process ID of the first search result. After executing this script, you will see the `Handles`, `NPM`, `PM`, `WS`, `VM`, `CPU`, `ID`, and `ProcessName` information for the PowerShell process.

To get a process using a wildcard and get its `FileVersionInfo` information, do the following:

```
$process = get-process powersh*
get-process -id $process.id -FileVersionInfo
```

The output of this is shown in the following screenshot:

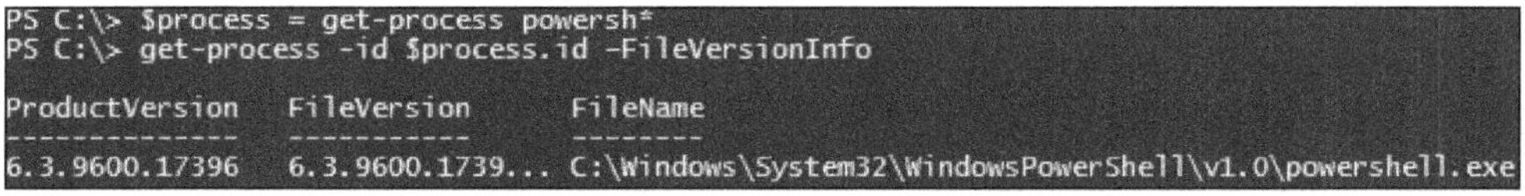

PS C:\> $process = get-process powersh*
PS C:\> get-process -id $process.id -FileVersionInfo
ProductVersion FileVersion FileName
6.3.9600.17396 6.3.9600.1739... C:\Windows\System32\WindowsPowerShell\v1.0\powershell.exe

This script displays how to search for a process by using a wild card and then use that information to view the file version information. You first start by using the `get-process` cmdlet with the `powersh*` searching wild card. The system returns the PowerShell process into the `$process` variable. You then call the `get-process` cmdlet, and leverage the `-id` parameter pointing to the `$process` variable referencing the dot notation of `.id`. You also call the `-FileVersionInfo` parameter to display the advanced information about the PowerShell process. After executing this script, you will see the `ProductVersion`, `FileVersion`, and `FileName` information about the PowerShell process.

To get a process by a wild card, and get the number of modules for that process, do the following:

```
$process = get-process powersh*
$modules = get-process -id $process.id -module
$modules.count
```

The output of this is shown in the following screenshot:

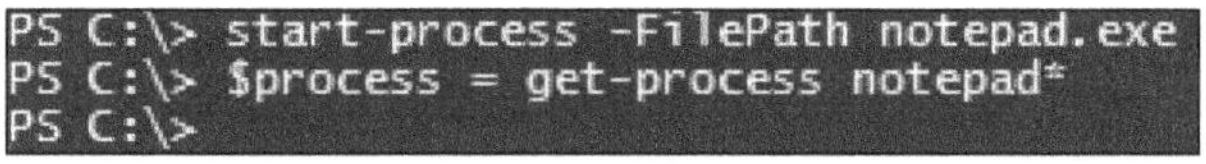

This script shows how to search for a process by using a wild card and then use that information to view the module information. You start by using the `get-process` cmdlet with the `powersh*` searching wild card. The system returns the PowerShell process into the `$process` variable. You then call the get-process cmdlet, leverage `the -id` parameter pointing to the `$process` variable referencing the dot notation of `.id`, and call the `-module` parameter. You then save the result in a variable named `$modules`. The final step is to count the number of modules that are linked to the PowerShell process by using `$modules.count`. After executing this script, you will see that there are `77` module items that make up the PowerShell process.

To start a new process, or invoke a program, you can leverage the `start-process` cmdlet. The proper syntax for using this cmdlet is calling the `start-process` cmdlet and providing the `-filepath` parameter pointing to the location of the item you want to execute. You can then call the optional `-argumentlist` parameter, referencing the parameters that are needed to execute the item, the optional `-verb` parameter to invoke any verbs associated with the file type (such as `Edit`, `Open`, `Play`, `Print`, and `RunAs`), the optional `-NoNewWindow` parameter to not spawn the command in a new PowerShell console, and the optional `-wait` parameter to wait for the process to complete before continuing with the script. If you do not execute the `-wait` parameter, the script will continue to the next step without waiting for the current step to be successful. After starting a process, the process will receive a process ID for which you can reference with the other process cmdlets.

To start a new notepad process, do the following:

```
start-process -FilePath notepad.exe
$process = get-process notepad*
```

The output of this is shown in the following screenshot:

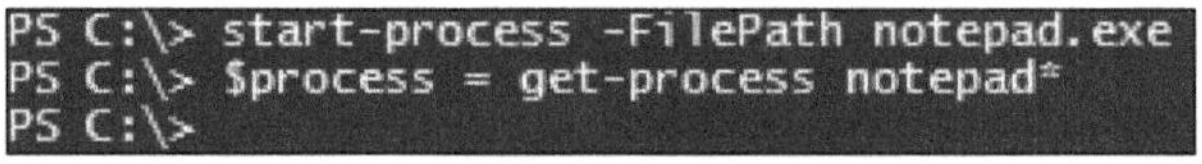
PS C:\> start-process -FilePath notepad.exe
PS C:\> $process = get-process notepad*
PS C:\>

This script displays how to start a notepad process, and search for the notepad process by using a wild card. You start by using the `start-process` cmdlet with the `-filepath` parameter referencing the `notepad.exe` process. After execution, it will launch `notepad.exe`. You then use the `get-process` cmdlet with the `notepad*` searching wild card. The system returns the PowerShell process object into the `$process` variable.

To stop a process, or stop a program, you can leverage the `stop-process` cmdlet. The proper syntax for using this cmdlet is calling the `stop-process` cmdlet and providing the `-filepath` parameter pointing to the location of the item you want to terminate. You may also leverage the `-processname` parameter to stop a service by its process name or use wildcards with the `-processname` parameter to end processes that are like the partial word you specify. You can specify the `-id` parameter to terminate a process by its Process ID as well. By default, if you kill a process, it will prompt you for confirmation. The `-force` parameter will force the termination of the process without prompting the user.

To stop the running notepad process, do the following:

```
start-process -FilePath notepad.exe
$process = get-process notepad*
stop-process -ID $process.id
```

The output of this is shown in the following screenshot:

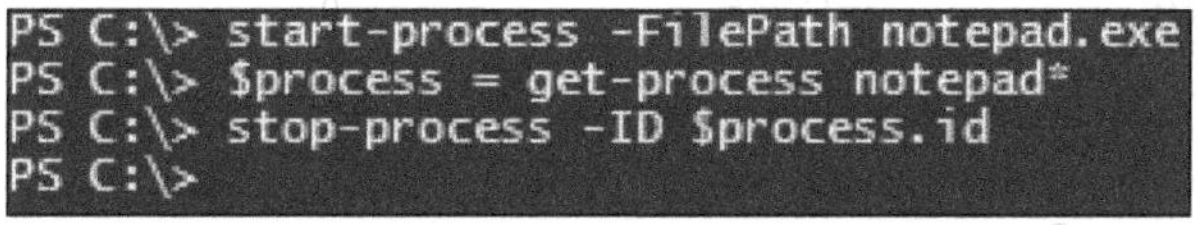
PS C:\> start-process -FilePath notepad.exe
PS C:\> $process = get-process notepad*
PS C:\> stop-process -ID $process.id
PS C:\>

This script displays how to start a notepad process, search for the notepad process by a wild card, and then use that information to stop the notepad process. You start by using the `start-process` cmdlet with the `-filepath` parameter referencing the `notepad.exe` process. After execution, it will launch `notepad.exe`. You then use the `get-process` cmdlet with the `notepad*` searching wild card. The system returns the PowerShell process into the `$process` variable. Next, you call the `stop-process` cmdlet, and leverage the `-id` parameter pointing to the `$process` variable referencing the dot notation of `.id`. After executing this script, you will see the notepad open and close.

Installing Windows features and roles

Windows Server 2012 SP2, and PowerShell 4.0 introduced new cmdlets to install Windows features through the use of scripts. This provides a further layer of automation to the PowerShell toolset as you can dynamically and completely build servers with a single script.

> If you want to manage the Windows features cmdlets from a Windows 8.1 system, you will first need to install Remote Server Administration Tools. Then you will have to enable Server Manager the feature. This will enable you to manage server-based operating systems such as Windows Server 2012 R2. These can be found at `http://www.microsoft.com/en-us/download/details.aspx?id=39296`.

To view the features that are available for installation and uninstallation through the cmdlets, you can leverage the `get-windowsfeature` cmdlet. When you call the `get-windowsfeature` cmdlet without parameters, you will find that there are over `260` items that can be individually installed. Each feature on the system is broken up into `Display Names`, `Names`, and `Install State`. These features also have sub-features that can also be installed, uninstalled, or viewed. If you want to dig deeper into a specific feature, you can leverage the `-name` parameter which will pull up the specific information for that particular service.

To view all the Windows feature information that match the word Telnet, do the following:

```
$featureinfo = get-WindowsFeature | Where {$_.DisplayName -match
"Telnet"}
foreach ($feature in $featureinfo) {
    Write-host "Feature Display Name:" $feature.DisplayName
    Write-host "Feature Name:" $feature.Name
    Write-host "Feature Install State:" $feature.InstallState
    Write-host ""
}
```

The output of this is shown in the following screenshot:

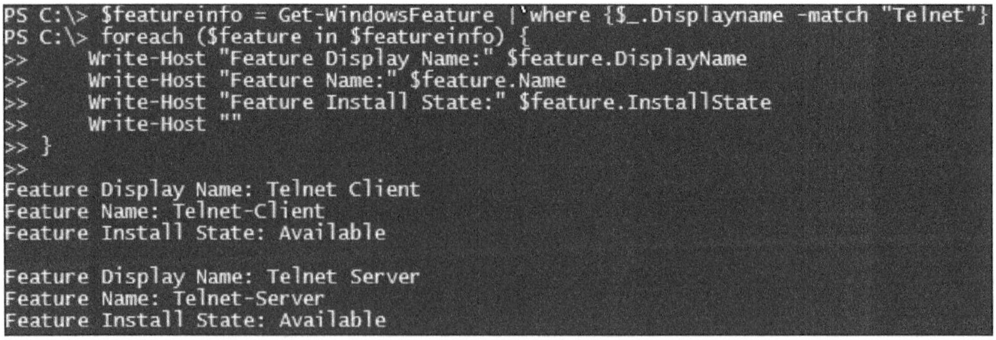

This example displays how to query properties about services on a system. You start by getting the Windows features that match the word `Telnet`. You leverage the `get-WindowsFeature` cmdlet, pipe | the results to the statement where `{$_.Displayname -match "Telnet"}`. You place the output of that command into the `$featureinfo` variable and then create a `foreach` loop to query each `$feature` in `$featureinfo`. You then call the `write-host` cmdlet and print to screen `Feature Display Name:` with the `$feature` variable referencing the dot notation of `.Displayname`. Thereafter, you use the `write-host` cmdlet, print to screen `Feature Name:` with the `$feature` variable referencing the dot notation of `.name`.

Finally, you use the `write-host` cmdlet, print to screen `Feature Install State:` with the `$feature` variable referencing the dot notation of `.InstallState`. After executing this command, the console will print to screen `Feature Display Name`, `Feature Name`, and `Feature Install State` for both `Telnet-Client` and `Telnet-Server`.

If you want to install a feature, you can use the `install-windowsfeature` cmdlet, with the `-name` parameter referencing the feature you want to install. You can also designate the `-InstallAllSubFeature` parameter, which installs all of the sub-features for the feature you are installing on the system. You can designate the `-IncludeManagementTools` parameter to include the management tools for the specific feature you are installing. It also allows for a configuration file with `-ConfigurationFilePath` for advanced configuration options for individual feature installations. The `install-windowsfeature` cmdlet also supports offline editing of VHD's features. If you specify the `-vhd` parameter pointing to a VHD location, you can add a feature in an offline servicing mode.

To install windows features, do the following:

```
Install-windowsFeature -name Telnet-Client -IncludeAllSubFeature
-IncludeManagementTools
install-windowsFeature -name Telnet-Server -IncludeAllSubFeature -
IncludeManagementTools
```

The output of this is shown in the following screenshot:

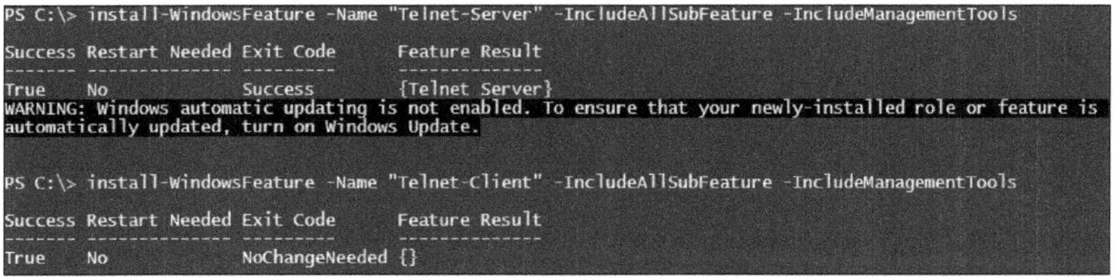

PS C:\> install-WindowsFeature -Name "Telnet-Server" -IncludeAllSubFeature -IncludeManagementTools
Success Restart Needed Exit Code Feature Result
True No Success {Telnet Server}
WARNING: Windows automatic updating is not enabled. To ensure that your newly-installed role or feature is automatically updated, turn on Windows Update.
PS C:\> install-WindowsFeature -Name "Telnet-Client" -IncludeAllSubFeature -IncludeManagementTools
Success Restart Needed Exit Code Feature Result
True No NoChangeNeeded {}

This example displays how to install the `Telnet-Server` and `Telnet-Client` Windows features, and their management tools, on a system. You start by leveraging the `install-windowsfeature` cmdlet with the `-name` parameter pointing to `Telnet-Server`. You then use the `-IncludeAllSubfeature` parameter to install all the sub-features, and the `-IncludeManagementTools` parameter to install all the management tools. You proceed to install `Telnet-Client` by using the `install-windowsfeature` cmdlet with the `-name` parameter pointing to `Telnet-Client`. You then use the `-IncludeAllSubFeature` parameter to install all the sub-features, and the `-IncludeManagementTools` parameter to install all the management tools.

After running this script, both `Telnet-Server` and `Telnet-Client`, and their sub-features and management tools, will be installed on the system.

To uninstall a Windows feature, you can leverage the `uninstall-windowsfeature` cmdlet with the `-name` parameter to specify a Windows feature you want to remove. You can specify the `-restart` parameter to restart the system after the feature is uninstalled. You may also want to use the `-IncludeManagementTools` parameter to also uninstall the management tools for the feature.

To uninstall windows features, do the following:

```
Uninstall-WindowsFeature -Name "Telnet-Server"
uninstall-WindowsFeature -Name "Telnet-Client"
```

The output of this is shown in the following screenshot:

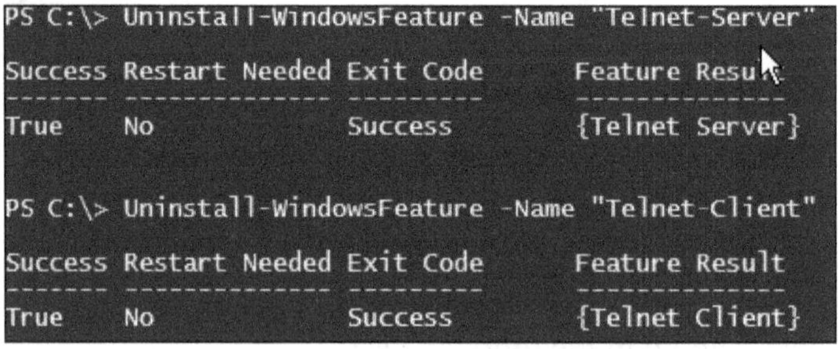
PS C:\> Uninstall-WindowsFeature -Name "Telnet-Server"
Success Restart Needed Exit Code Feature Result
True No Success {Telnet Server}
PS C:\> Uninstall-WindowsFeature -Name "Telnet-Client"
Success Restart Needed Exit Code Feature Result
True No Success {Telnet Client}

This example displays how to uninstall the `Telnet-Server` and `Telnet-Client` Windows features from a system. You start by using the `uninstall-windowsfeature` cmdlet and using the `-name` parameter pointing to `Telnet-Server`. After execution, the console prints to the window the `Success`, `Restart Needed`, `Exit Code`, and `Feature Result` properties. You then use the `uninstall-windowsfeature` cmdlet using the `-name` parameter pointing to `Telnet-Client`. After execution, the console prints to the window the `Success`, `Restart Needed`, `Exit Code`, and `Feature Result` properties. After running this code, both the `Telnet-Server` and `Telnet-Client` Windows Features are successfully uninstalled from the system.

Summary

This chapter provided a good view of how to manage the basic functions of Microsoft systems. You first learned how to leverage the active directory services interface (ADSI) adapter to make a connection to the local system. You learned how to use the ADSI adapter to create an ADSI adapter variable. You now understand how to leverage the `.Create()` method to create new users and groups and how to use the `.Delete()` method to delete users and groups. You also got to know how to set a password by leveraging the `.Description ()` method and how to set the data into the SAM using the `.setinfo()` method. You then learned how to search a system using the ADSI adapter, by leveraging the `::Exists` argument, to search for users and groups on a system.

The next section of the chapter explored windows services and processes. You started by learning about Windows Services and how to use the `get-service`, `set-service`, `stop-service`, and `start-service` cmdlets. You learnt how to change the description and the start-up parameters for Windows services. You then dived into Windows processes and got familiar with how to use the `get-process`, `start-process`, and `stop-process` cmdlets. You also understood about the different process properties of `Handles`, `Non-paged Memory`, `Pageable Memory`, `Working Set`, `Virtual memory`, `CPUs`, `Processor ID`, and `Process name`. Additionally, you learned how to search for processes on a system by leveraging wildcards and calling the `-id` parameter.

You finished this chapter learning about Windows features, and PowerShell's interaction with them. You found out about the `get-windowsfeature`, `install-windowsfeature`, and `uninstall-windowsfeature` cmdlets. You also understood how to query, install, and uninstall the `Telnet-Client` and `Telnet-Server` features. At the end of this chapter, you should have a basic understanding of managing Microsoft systems with PowerShell. In the next chapter, you will learn about automation leveraging PowerShell. This includes internally invoking scripts as well as desired state configuration.

13
Automation of the Environment

One of the fastest growing uses for PowerShell is the automation of network environments. Whether it is automating mundane tasks or dynamically provisioning entire systems, PowerShell provides limitless options for developers to put their creative touch on system automation.

In this chapter, you will learn the following:

- Invoking programs for automation
- Using desired state configuration
- Detecting and restoring drifting configurations

Invoking programs for automation

When you want to automate the provisioning of systems, Microsoft provides many tools that enable you to execute items in a sequence. With **Microsoft Deployment Toolkit** (**MDT**), **Deployment Workbench**, **System Center Configuration Manager**, **Desired Configuration Management**, and **System Center Orchestrator**, you have the ability to stage different tasks in sequential order. This allows administrators to pre-stage prerequisites on a system, before installing additional software. While these tools are extremely effective, there are instances where you may not have access to, or licensing for, the use of these products. This section explores alternative options for dynamically provisioning systems, and how to sequence a series of scripts.

The following graphic represents how you can have a parent child relationship between scripts:

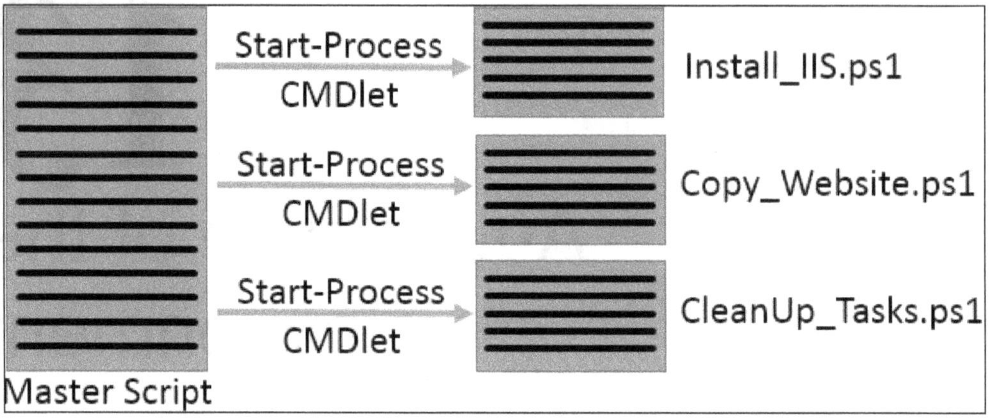

The first and most important step in architecting an automation solution is to create a master script, to invoke the subsequent steps in the build process. While you could create all the steps for the automation into a giant script, it can be extremely cumbersome to troubleshoot. It is recommended that you break apart all the individual components you are automating into individual scripts, and invoke these scripts from a master file. This allows you to only troubleshoot or update the individual components, and makes management of the automation solution much easier.

The three most popular cmdlets that are used for invoking automation through PowerShell are the `start-process`, `invoke-item`, and `invoke-expression` cmdlets. The `start-process` cmdlet is used to invoke one or multiple processes on a system. This is one of the most flexible cmdlets, which allows the most number of arguments, triggers, and verbs to execute the task at hand. The proper syntax for using this cmdlet is calling the `start-process` cmdlet, providing the `-filepath` trigger pointing to the location of the item you want to execute. You can then call the optional `-argumentlist` trigger, referencing the triggers that are needed to execute the item, the optional `-verb` trigger to invoke any verbs associated with the file type (such as `Edit`, `Open`, `Play`, `Print`, and `RunAs`), the optional `-NoNewWindow` trigger to not spawn the command in a new PowerShell window, and the optional `-wait` trigger to wait for the process to complete before continuing with the script. If you do not execute the `-wait` trigger, the script will continue to the next step without waiting for the current step to be successful.

To launch an administrator PowerShell window, do the following:

```
$filepath = "powershell.exe"
$arguments = "-ExecutionPolicy RemoteSigned"
start-process -filepath $filepath -Verb RunAs -ArgumentList $arguments
```

The output of this is shown in the following screenshot:

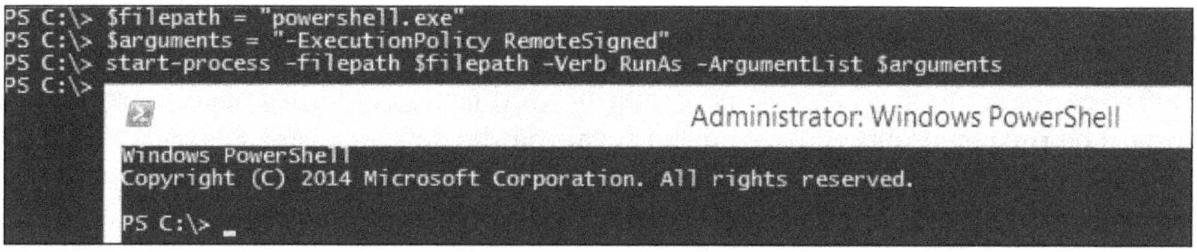
PS C:\> $filepath = "powershell.exe"
PS C:\> $arguments = "-ExecutionPolicy RemoteSigned"
PS C:\> start-process -filepath $filepath -Verb RunAs -ArgumentList $arguments
PS C:\>
Administrator: Windows PowerShell
Windows PowerShell
Copyright (C) 2014 Microsoft Corporation. All rights reserved.
PS C:\> _

The preceding example displays how to properly launch an administrator PowerShell window, with the execution policy of `RemoteSigned`, using the `start-process` cmdlet. You start by declaring the `$filepath` variable and setting it equal to `powershell.exe`. You then declare the `$arguments` variable and set it to `-ExecutionPolicy RemoteSigned`. Finally, you call the `start-process` cmdlet with the `-filepath` trigger referencing `$filepath`, the `-Verb` trigger set to `RunAs`, and `-argument` set to `$arguments`. After running the command, a new administrator PowerShell window will launch on your system. This is useful in instances where you need a PowerShell window to invoke with a specific execution policy level and under the administrator account.

The `invoke-item` cmdlet differs from the `start-process` cmdlet in the way that it is solely designed to natively open files using the default open action. The proper syntax for this cmdlet is to call the `invoke-item` cmdlet and reference a file path to an executable. If the executable that you are invoking is in the `System32` directory of the system you are executing it on, you can just reference the executable name, and it will launch accordingly.

> The `invoke-item` cmdlet is deprecated and may be removed in subsequent releases of PowerShell. PowerShell natively invokes executables by calling the executable path as a line in a script, which makes the `invoke-item` cmdlet likely to go away.

To leverage `invoke-item` to launch calculator, do the following:

```
invoke-item "c:\windows\system32\calc.exe"
```

The output of this is shown in the following screenshot:

The above example displays how to properly use the `invoke-item` cmdlet to launch the Windows calculator. You start by typing `invoke-item`, followed by the location of the Windows calculator of `c:\windows\system32\calc.exe`. After running this script, the Windows calculator will launch.

The `invoke-expression` cmdlet is primarily used to execute lines of code from a string. The proper syntax of this cmdlet is calling the `invoke-expression` cmdlet, and referencing a string `$variable` that contains code. This string can contain a PowerShell command or even a command-line expression. This cmdlet differs from `invoke-item` and `start-process` in the way that it natively executes command-line code, without having to call the `CMD.exe` or `PowerShell.exe` executable with the appropriate triggers:

```
$string = "ping 127.0.0.1"
invoke-expression $string
```

The output of this is shown in the following screenshot:

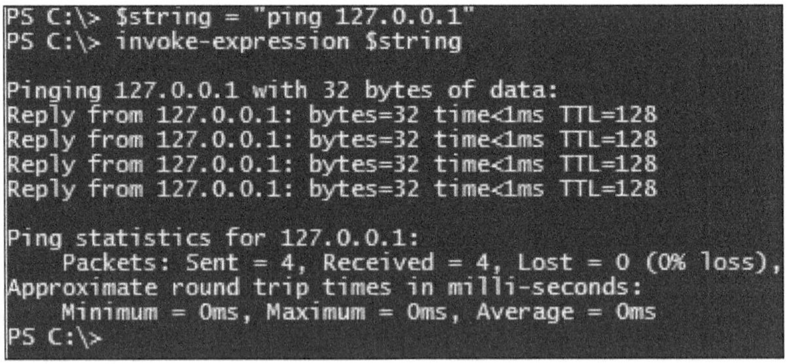

PS C:\> $string = "ping 127.0.0.1"
PS C:\> invoke-expression $string
Pinging 127.0.0.1 with 32 bytes of data:
Reply from 127.0.0.1: bytes=32 time<1ms TTL=128
Reply from 127.0.0.1: bytes=32 time<1ms TTL=128
Reply from 127.0.0.1: bytes=32 time<1ms TTL=128
Reply from 127.0.0.1: bytes=32 time<1ms TTL=128
Ping statistics for 127.0.0.1:
Packets: Sent = 4, Received = 4, Lost = 0 (0% loss),
Approximate round trip times in milli-seconds:
Minimum = 0ms, Maximum = 0ms, Average = 0ms
PS C:\>

This example displays how to use the `invoke-expression` cmdlet to run a command from a string. You start by declaring a variable of `$string` and setting it equal to `ping 127.0.0.1`. You then call the `invoke-expression` cmdlet with the `$string` variable. After executing this script on your system, you will see a loopback ping response in your PowerShell console.

> It is important to note that the `invoke-expression` cmdlet presents a security vulnerability when used in scripts. If the expression is dynamically generated, or generated as a result of user input, one could theoretically invoke a variety of actions on a server, simply by inserting code into the user-defined fields.

The following graphic represents how the variables and functions defined in a parent can be shared with the child script:

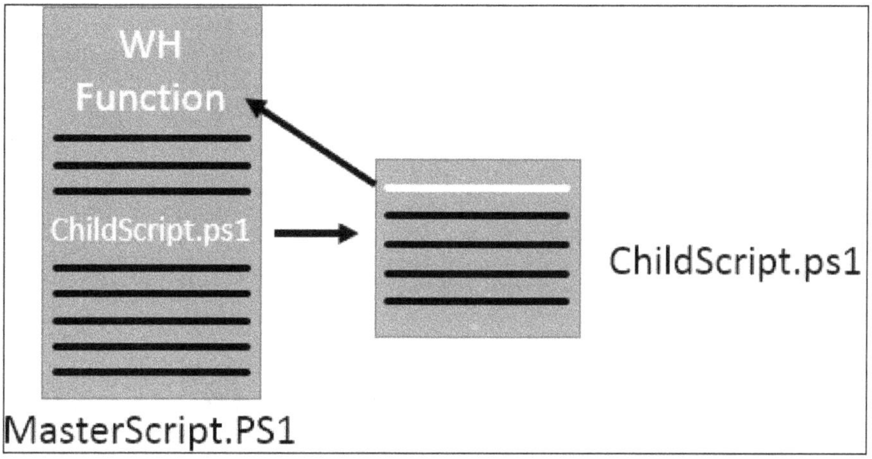

When you are chaining multiple scripts together, you have the ability to share all the variables and functions that you define in the parent script with the child script. This is a result of PowerShell sharing the same memory session between all invoked PowerShell windows from a parent window. While this makes all the items available to the child script, if you define the same named variables and functions in the child script, then the child script's version of those items will prevail. However, when the child script closes, PowerShell will dispose of the child script's version and the parent's version of the variable, method, and functions will be made available for further use.

To show how scripts can share functions, you will need to stage your computer with two files. To do this, you will need to follow these steps:

1. Create the directory of `c:\temp\scripts\` (if it doesn't already exist).
2. Create a PowerShell file in `c:\temp\scripts\` named `masterscript.ps1`. Place the following code in `masterscript.ps1`:

```
function wh { param([string]$message)
    write-host "Wh Function Output is: $message"
}
write-host "MasterScript.ps1: Launching Child Script..."
invoke-expression -command c:\temp\scripts\childscript.ps1
```

3. Create a PowerShell file in `c:\temp\scripts\` named `childscript.ps1`. Place the following code in `childscript.ps1`:

```
wh "From ChildScript.ps1: The wh Function resides in MasterScript.
ps1 file."
wh "From ChildScript.ps1: Childscript.ps1 is accessing the wh
Function successfully from memory."
pause
```

After both the files have been created, you leverage the `invoke-expression` cmdlet with the `-command` trigger set to `c:\temp\scripts\masterscript.ps1` to launch the `masterscript.ps1` file.

To run the `masterscript.ps1` file, which will execute the `childscript.ps1` file, do the following:

```
invoke-expression -command c:\temp\scripts\masterscript.ps1
```

The output of this is shown in the following screenshot:

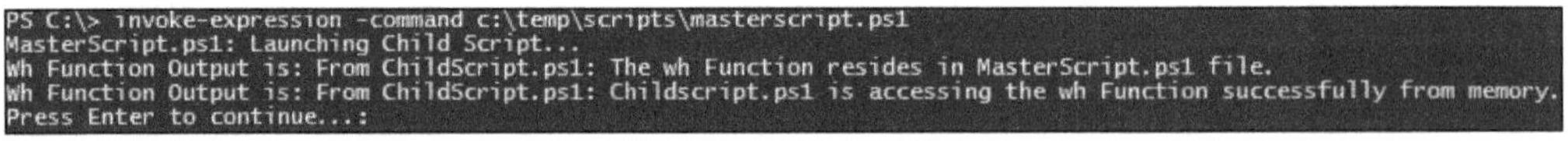
PS C:\> invoke-expression -command c:\temp\scripts\masterscript.ps1
MasterScript.ps1: Launching Child Script...
Wh Function Output is: From ChildScript.ps1: The wh Function resides in MasterScript.ps1 file.
Wh Function Output is: From ChildScript.ps1: Childscript.ps1 is accessing the wh Function successfully from memory.
Press Enter to continue...:

This script displays how to share a function between a parent and child script. You start by manually invoking the script by using the `invoke-expression` cmdlet, using the `-command` parameter with the argument of `c:\temp\scripts\masterscript.ps1`. After executing this script, the `masterscript.ps1` file will print to the screen `MasterScript.ps1: Launching Child Script...` and launch the `childscript.ps1` file. The `childscript.ps1` file will then invoke the `wh` function with text overloads in the `masterscript.ps1` file.

The console will then print to the screen `Wh Function Output is: From ChildScript.ps1: The wh Function resides in MasterScript.ps1 file.` and `Wh Function Output is: From ChildScript.ps1: Childscript.ps1 is accessing the wh Function successfully from memory.` This properly displays the `childscript.ps1` file, successfully utilizing the `Wh` function defined in `masterscript.ps1` file.

As you are building a series of scripts to automate your environment, you can share the large repeating functions across your scripts to reduce their overall size. This not only reduces the complexity of the individual scripts, but requires you to only update the large repeating functions in one location as you improve them. This creates greater efficiencies with scripting and will produce more reliable scripts.

Using desired state configuration

Desired state configuration (**DSC**) is a management layer which enables you to dynamically build computer environments using a common language. This management layer was designed to create *configuration baselines*, which enforce a set of configuration standards for a system. Simply put, it makes sure that the files, folders, services, registry, and applications that you expect to be installed or removed from a system, are in their expected state. If DSC determines that these items are not in their *desired state*, it will automatically correct the system to ensure it follows the *desired configuration*.

There are three core phases for a proper implementation of DSC. These phases include:

- **Authoring phase**: The authoring phase is the process where you create the configuration. The configuration will have a subset of configuration items such as files, folders, services, registry, and applications. This is where you create *what is desired* to be configured for a particular configuration.
- **Staging phase**: The staging phase is the process by which the system compares the desired state against the current running configuration. DSC then determines what items in the configuration need to be enforced. The files are then staged to be pushed to a server or pulled from a server.
- **Remediation phase**: The remediation phase is the enforcement state. It updates the configuration of a system, so that it matches the desired configuration.

The authoring phase enables you to create a configuration, where you can specify any number of resources for configuration of a system. PowerShell's 4.0 implementation of DSC has 12 resources that you can configure, to automate and enforce the installation of items on a system.

These resources available to DSC include:

- **Archive resource**: This resource is responsible for unzipping files in a specified path during the configuration. The mandatory properties for this resource are `Ensure`, `Destination`, and `Path`. The optional properties are `Checksum`, `DependsOn`, `Validate`, and `Force`.
- **Environment resource**: This resource is responsible for modifying the environment variables during the configuration. The mandatory properties for this resource are `Ensure`, `Path`, and `Value`. The optional property is `DependsOn`.
- **File resource**: This resource is responsible for managing files and folders during the configuration. The mandatory properties for this resource are `Type`, `Ensure`, `SourcePath`, and `DestinationPath`. The optional properties are `Recurse`, `Attributes`, `Checksum`, and `DependsOn`.
- **Group resource**: This resource is responsible for configuration of local groups during the configuration. The mandatory properties for this resource are `Ensure` and `GroupName`. The optional properties are `Credential`, `Description`, `Members`, `MembersToExclude`, `MembersToInclude`, and `DependsOn`.
- **Log resource**: This resource is responsible for logging the information pertaining to the configuration, on the system during the configuration. The mandatory property for this resource is `Message`. The optional property, almost always used with the log resource, is `DependsOn`.
- **Package resource**: This resource is responsible for working with software installation packages such as MSI's and `setup.exe` during the configuration. The mandatory properties for this resource are `Ensure`, `Path`, `Name`, and `ProductID` (for MSI's). The optional properties are `Arguments`, `Credential`, `LogPath`, `DependsOn`, and `ReturnCode`.
- **WindowsProcess resource**: This resource is responsible for working with Windows processes during the configuration. The mandatory properties for this resource are `Ensure`, `Arguments`, and `Path`. The optional properties are `Credential`, `StandardErrorPath`, `StandardInputPath`, `StandardOutputPath`, `WorkingDirectory`, and `DependsOn`.
- **Registry resource**: This resource is responsible for working with the registry during the configuration. The mandatory properties for this resource are `Ensure`, `Key`, and `ValueName`. The optional properties are `Force`, `Hex`, `ValueData`, `ValueType`, and `DependsOn`.

- **WindowsFeature resource**: This resource is responsible for working with the Windows features during the configuration. The mandatory properties for this resource are `Name` and `Ensure`. The optional properties are `Credential`, `IncludeAllSubFeature`, `LogPath`, `Source`, and `DependsOn`.
- **Script resource**: This resource is responsible for executing PowerShell script blocks during the configuration. Depending on usage, the mandatory properties of this resource may be `SetScript`, `GetScript`, or `TestScript`. The optional properties are `Credential` and `DependsOn`.
- **Service resource**: This resource is responsible for managing the Windows Services during the configuration. Depending on usage, the mandatory properties for this resource are `Name` or `State`. The optional properties are `BuiltInAccount`, `Credential`, `StartupType`, and `DependsOn`.
- **User resource**: This resource is responsible for configuration of local users during the configuration. The mandatory properties for this resource are `UserName`, `Ensure`, and `Password`. The optional properties are `Description`, `Disabled`, `Fullname`, `PasswordChangeNotAllowed`, `PasswordChangeRequired`, `PasswordneverExpires`, and `DependsOn`.

Each of these resources has optional and mandatory properties. The mandatory properties must be set in your configuration, or the resource will not properly configure. Properties define the action that needs to be performed for that resource.

> For more information on the properties for each of these resources, you can view the Microsoft TechNet article at `http://technet.microsoft.com/en-us/library/dn249921.aspx`.

Authoring phase

The four required components to author a new DSC configuration item are declaring a name for the configuration, defining the nodes, referencing configuration resources, and setting the properties for those resources.

The following code represents the proper syntax of a DSC configuration item:

```
configuration InstallTelnet {
    param($computers)
    Node $computers {
        WindowsFeature Telnet-Client {
            Name = "TelnetClient"
            Ensure = "Present"
```

```
                IncludeAllSubFeature = "True"
            }
        }
    }
    InstallTelnet -computers MyComputer
```

The name for the configuration is called much like a function in PowerShell. You start by declaring `configuration NameOfConfiguration {`. The name of configuration should represent the overall configuration you are trying to achieve. In the preceding example, you are going to install telnet, so you name the configuration `InstallTelnet`.

You may also wish to define the optional `param()` code block to define parameters for the configuration item. In the previous example, you created a `param()` code block with the `$computers` parameter to specify the computers for the node component.

The node component specifies which systems the configuration will generate the MOF files for. To specify the nodes, you use the syntax of `node Value {`. The `Value` parameter, specified in the syntax for the `node` component, can contain a string, a variable, or an array. In the preceding example, you leverage an array named `$computers`, for which individual MOF files will be created.

The next step is to call the individual configuration resources. This is done by calling configuration resource such as `WindowsFeature Telnet-Client {`. The `WindowsFeature` portion tells PowerShell you are leveraging the `WindowsFeature` resource. When you specify `Telnet-Client`, it is the reference name of that particular configuration resource. The name of the configuration resource can be referenced by other parts of your script for properties like `DependsOn`. This means that you can setup dependencies on other configuration resources, so that items install in order.

After you define the configuration resource, the last component requires you to define its mandatory properties. The proper syntax for adding properties is `propertyname = Value`. The property name must reflect an actual mandatory or optional property for that resource. Subsequent properties for the resource can be declared on an additional line below the other properties. In the preceding example, there are three mandatory properties defined. The `Name` property is set to `TelnetClient`, the `Ensure` property is set to `Present`, and the `IncludeAllSubFeature` is set to `True`. You then close the bracket for configuration resource, node, and the configuration item itself. At this point, you have successfully created a configuration item.

After creating the configuration items, proceed to execute the configuration to create MOF files for the individual nodes. During this phase, the configuration is validated against all nodes that will receive the packages. To start the validation, you call the name of configuration item of `NameOfConfiguration`, and then any of the variables you want to include in the `param()` block for the configuration item. In the previous example, you call the configuration item of `InstallTelnet` and specify the `-computers` parameter with the `MyComputer` argument.

After calling the configuration item, the system will automatically generate a folder with the configuration item name as the folder name. Inside that folder, you will find a **MOF** file named after every node. This file is used during the staging and remediation phase to change the systems.

If you want to create a configuration item for `Telnet-Client` and `Telnet-Server`, do the following:

```
configuration InstallTelnet {
    param($computers)
    Node $computers {
        WindowsFeature Telnet-Client
        {
            Name = "Telnet-Client"
            Ensure = "Present"
            IncludeAllSubFeature = "True"
        }
        WindowsFeature Telnet-Server
        {
            Name = "Telnet-Server"
            Ensure = "Present"
            IncludeAllSubFeature = "True"
            DependsOn = "[WindowsFeature]Telnet-Client"
        }
    }

}
$computer = $env:computername
InstallTelnet -computers $computer
```

The output of this is shown in the following screenshot:

```
PS C:\scripts> configuration InstallTelnet {
>>     param($computers)
>>     Node $computers {
>>         WindowsFeature Telnet-Client
>>         {
>>             Name = "Telnet-Client"
>>             Ensure = "Present"
>>             IncludeAllSubFeature = "True"
>>         }
>>         WindowsFeature Telnet-Server
>>         {
>>             Name = "Telnet-Server"
>>             Ensure = "Present"
>>             IncludeAllSubFeature = "True"
>>             DependsOn = "[WindowsFeature]Telnet-Client"
>>         }
>>     }
>> }
>>
PS C:\scripts> $computer = $env:computername
PS C:\scripts> InstallTelnet -computers $computer


    Directory: C:\scripts\InstallTelnet


Mode                LastWriteTime     Length Name
----                -------------     ------ ----
-a---        12/31/2014   2:43 PM       1910 DEMODC1.mof
```

This example displays how to properly leverage **Desired State Configuration** and the `WindowsFeature` resource, to create a MOF file for installing the Telnet client and server on a system. You start by declaring the configuration item of configuration `InstallTelnet {`. You then accept in a parameter of `$computers` leveraging the `param($computers)` line of code. The next step is declaring the `node`, which will be the content of the parameter, which would be `Node $computers {`. You then declare the `WindowsFeature` resource and reference `Telnet-Client WindowsFeature`. To complete the configuration of `WindowsFeature`, you set the `name` property to `Telnet-Client`, the `Ensure` property to `Present`, and the `IncludeAllSubFeature` property to `True`.

You continue by declaring another `WindowsFeature` resource and reference `Telnet-Server WindowsFeature`. To complete the configuration of `WindowsFeature`, you set the `name` property to `Telnet-Server`, the `Ensure` property to `Present`, the `IncludeAllSubFeature` property to `True`, and the `DependsOn` property to `[WindowsFeature]Telnet-Client`.

You then leverage the `$env:computername` function and set it to the `$computer` variable. You complete this script by calling the configuration item of `InstallTelnet`, the `-computers` trigger, followed by the `$computer` variable. After execution, you will find that there will be a folder named `InstallTelnet`, with a MOF file named as `computername.MOF`.

Staging and remediation phase

The two different types of deployment mechanisms that DSC supports for configuring systems are pull and push types. The main difference between pull and push methodology is where the command is being processed. In the pull methodology, you set up a pull server like **System Center Configuration Manager** (**SCCM**) or a PowerShell DSC Pull Server, and it will synchronize with the appropriate clients for the configuration. A pull server often offers built-in reporting of compliance, and can schedule a time where the configuration item can be pulled from the server.

With the push method, you are leveraging the `start-dscconfiguration` cmdlet to push the configuration, in real-time, to the specified nodes. The proper syntax for the cmdlet is referencing the `start-dscconfiguration` cmdlet, specifying the `-path` trigger, referencing the location where the MOF files were created, and referencing the configuration item name. You may also specify the `-wait` trigger to wait for that configuration to complete before proceeding to the next line of code, the `-force` trigger to override any confirmation of changes, and the `-verbose` trigger to print to the screen the verbose output from PowerShell, configuring the individual systems.

The remediation phase is where the configuration item hits the local system, is evaluated, and is applied to a system. The remediation phase is complete after the configuration item successfully configures a system. This is the phase when you detect if a configuration has drifted from the desired state. It will reapply the configuration to ensure compliance to that desired state.

To push a configuration item to a local system, do the following:

```
start-DscConfiguration -path .\InstallTelnet -wait -force
```

The output of this is shown in the following screenshot:

PS C:\scripts> start-DscConfiguration -path .\InstallTelnet -wait -force

This example displays how to properly leverage the push methodology to configure systems in an environment. After generating the MOF file, you are ready to make the configuration item changes. You start by calling the `start-dscConfiguration` cmdlet, with the `-path` trigger pointing to the root location of where the MOF files were generated. In this case, it is `.\InstallTelnet`. You then declare the `-wait` trigger, so the script doesn't continue to the subsequent lines in the script until Telnet is fully installed. Last, you issue the `-force` trigger to suppress any confirmation messages. After execution, the server will have both the Telnet-Server and Telnet-Client Windows features installed on it.

> It is important to note that after you run the `start-dscConfiguration` cmdlet, the MOF files are still present on a system after execution. You may want to consider deleting these files after execution. The MOF files are created in clear text and may contain sensitive information about the system you are configuring.

Detecting and restoring drifting configurations

PowerShell's integration with DSC provides the ability to evaluate the current state of the desired configuration on a system. After the configuration has been set on the system, you have the ability to check the current configuration using the `get-dscconfiguration` cmdlet. By simply calling `get-dscconfiguration`, the PowerShell cmdlet will evaluate what DSC items have been designated for the system, and how they were configured.

You may also want to determine if the system has drifted from the existing configuration set. Drifting happens when engineers modify a system, or additional software changes the configuration of that server. To test the existing configuration set, you can leverage the `test-dscconfiguration` cmdlet. The `test-dscconfiguration` cmdlet will either return `True`, which means that the system is configured as desired, or `False`, which means the system no longer adheres to the desired configuration for the system.

When you determine that a configuration has drifted from the desired state of configuration, you have the ability to restore the original configuration itself. This is done through leveraging the `restore-dscconfiguration` cmdlet. Often, `test-dscconfiguration` is used in conjunction with the `restore-dscconfiguration` cmdlets, as you can immediately remediate issues if the test returns `False`.

The `get-dscconfiguration`, `test-dscconfiguration`, and `restore-dscconfiguration` cmdlets support `cimsessions`. You can declare a `cimsession` using the `new-cimsession` cmdlet to query multiple systems configuration. By using the optional `-cimsession` trigger with the `get-dscconfiguration`, `test-dscconfiguration`, and `restore-dscconfiguration` cmdlets, you can retrieve information and reconfigure items over a session for remote systems.

`get-dscconfiguration`

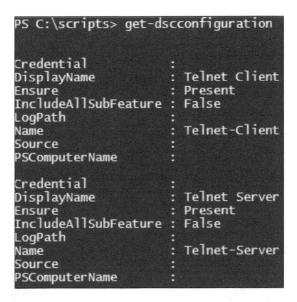

```
PS C:\scripts> get-dscconfiguration


Credential           :
DisplayName          : Telnet Client
Ensure               : Present
IncludeAllSubFeature : False
LogPath              :
Name                 : Telnet-Client
Source               :
PSComputerName       :

Credential           :
DisplayName          : Telnet Server
Ensure               : Present
IncludeAllSubFeature : False
LogPath              :
Name                 : Telnet-Server
Source               :
PSComputerName       :
```

In this example, you are querying a system that you set a desired state configuration item on, using the `get-dscconfiguration` cmdlet. After executing the command, you will see the expected desired state configuration printed to screen. You will also see the expected configuration of those individual resources on the system. In this case, you see that the DSC resources of `Telnet-Client` and `Telnet-Server` are expected to be `Present` in the system:

`test-dscconfiguration`

```
PS C:\scripts> test-dscconfiguration
True
PS C:\scripts>
```

In this example, you are querying a system that you set a desired state configuration item on, using the `test-dscconfiguration` cmdlet. After executing the command, you will see that the existing configuration matches the expected configuration with the cmdlet returning `True`:

```
Remove-WindowsFeature -name Telnet-Server
write-host "Telnet-Server Feature Has Been Manually Removed From The
System"
$testresult = test-dscconfiguration
if ($testresult -like "False") {
    Restore-dscconfiguration
}
$testresult = test-dscconfiguration
if ($testresult -like "True") {
    write-host "Telnet-Server Successfully Restored on The System"
}
```

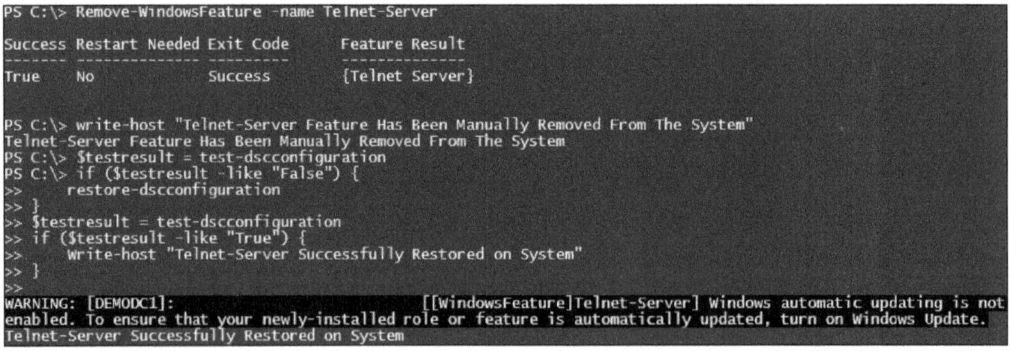

```
PS C:\> Remove-WindowsFeature -name Telnet-Server

Success Restart Needed Exit Code      Feature Result
------- -------------- ---------      --------------
True    No             Success        {Telnet Server}


PS C:\> write-host "Telnet-Server Feature Has Been Manually Removed From The System"
Telnet-Server Feature Has Been Manually Removed From The System
PS C:\> $testresult = test-dscconfiguration
PS C:\> if ($testresult -like "False") {
>>     restore-dscconfiguration
>> }
>> $testresult = test-dscconfiguration
>> if ($testresult -like "True") {
>>     Write-host "Telnet-Server Successfully Restored on System"
>> }
>>
WARNING: [DEMODC1]:                            [[WindowsFeature]Telnet-Server] Windows automatic updating is not
enabled. To ensure that your newly-installed role or feature is automatically updated, turn on Windows Update.
Telnet-Server Successfully Restored on System
```

This example displays how to restore a configuration when a system drifts from the desired state. You start by executing a manual command to remove `Telnet-Server` from the system. This is done by using the `Remove-WindowsFeature` cmdlet with the `-name` trigger set to `Telnet-Server`. You then print to the screen `Telnet-Server Feature Has been Manually Removed From The System`.

Thereafter, you would query the existing configuration to determine if it has drifted from the initial configuration, using the `test-dscconfiguration` cmdlet and storing the result in the `$testresult` variable. Next, you create an `IF` statement to determine if the `$testresult` variable is set to `False`. If it is set to `False`, it means the configuration has drifted, and you execute the `restore-dscconfiguration` cmdlet to restore it to the desired state. After the `restore-dscconfiguration` cmdlet is done executing, you re-execute `test-dscconfiguration` and store it in `$testresult` to determine if the configuration has been restored. If the `$testresult` variable is set to `True`, you then print to the screen `Telnet-Server Successfully Restored on System`. After executing the script, you manually remove `Telnet-Server`, validate the drift in configuration, and restore `Telnet-Server` back on the server using Desired State Configuration.

Summary

This chapter explained many different facets of automation in environments. You started by learning how to invoke programs for automation. You learned about the cmdlets `start-process`, `invoke-item`, and `invoke-expression`, and how they can be used to initiate actions on a system. Next, you understood how to chain multiple PowerShell scripts together in a child and parent relationship. You also learnt how to share functions, methods, and variables between multiple scripts, and how to invoke them between each other.

The chapter proceeded to dive into DSC and explained about its three phases, and the variety of resources you can apply to your configurations. You also learned how to detect a drifting configuration and how to restore it if it drifts from the desired state. In the next chapter, you will learn some of the recommended best practices for PowerShell. These best practices will help create efficiencies in your scripts and make your scripts portable between engineers.

14
Script Creation Best Practices and Conclusion

This chapter explores the best practices for script creation. It begins by discussing the ways to create comment headers in your scripts. It then dives into how to comment on code in your scripts and different situations where you may need detailed comments. You will then explore the best practices for script creation and provide other considerations that developers need to have in order to develop their scripts. This chapter then explains source control and maintaining revisions, and concludes with the best practices for automation with PowerShell.

Best practices for script management

When you are creating and maintaining scripts, you may create multiple iterations of your scripts. Whether it is bug fixes or adding new functionality, it's sometimes difficult to keep track of all of the different versions of your code. This section explores tips for better managing your scripts and provides insight into tricks that you can do to make your iterations more reliable.

commenting headers

The first recommendation is to create headers for the detailed tracking information about the PowerShell script itself. Headers can track information about the script's creation, authors, changes, and other useful information that will enable you to quickly determine what the script is doing. PowerShell has built-in block comment support, which integrates with the `get-help` cmdlet.

The required components for this include:

- **Comment block location**: The comment block must be the first item defined at the top of your script. If you use parameter blocks, you will need to specify the parameter blocks after the comment block.
- **Start comment block**: In order to integrate with the help system, you need to specify the starting of the comment block. To start a comment block, you type `<#`.
- **.SYNOPSIS**: To create a synopsis for the script, type `.SYNOPSIS` on a line and then on a subsequent line, type a one line description of what the script is for.
- **.DESCRIPTION**: To create a full description for the script, type `.DESCRIPTION` on a line and then on a subsequent line, type a description of the script's functions so that any editor who looks at the script will know the script's basic functions. If it is a complicated script or a script that invokes other scripts, describe the overall process for the script. You may also want to include author information such as the author's name, author's position, author's company and contact information, initial release number, and date of the initial release.
- **.PARAMETER**: To describe a parameter for the script, you can type `.PARAMETER`, the parameter name on a line and then on a subsequent line, type a description of that parameter. If you have multiple parameters, you can define multiple `.PARAMETER` statements referencing parameter names.
- **.EXAMPLE**: To provide an example of usage for your script, you can type `.EXAMPLE` and on a subsequent line, type a usage example of the script. If you have multiple examples, you can define multiple `.EXAMPLE` statements.
- **.NOTES**: To provide notes for execution caveats, you can type `.NOTES` and on a subsequent line, type a usage note to execute the script.
- **.LINK**: If you have other help topics you want to link to, you can type `.LINK` and on a subsequent line, provide a URL to another help topic.
- **Ending comment block**: In order to integrate with the help system, you need to specify the ending of the comment block. To end a comment block, you need to type `#>`.

The following graphic displays a properly commented header that will integrate with the help system:

```
<#
.SYNOPSIS
This script scans the network file shares for clear text files, and determined if there
are clear text username and passwords in the files.

.DESCRIPTION
This script scans the network file shares for clear text files, and determined if there
are clear text username and passwords in the files.

Author: Brenton J.W. Blawat / Packt Publishing / Author / email@email.com
Revision: 1.3a - Initial Release of Script / 5-27-2016
Revision: 1.4 - Paul Brandes / Company XYZ / Consultant / email@company.com / 10-27-2016
R1.4 Details: Corrected the scanning function to accommodate large UNC paths and process
paths over 248 character

.PARAMETER PATH
The optional path parameter enables you to specify a path to the file structure to scan.

.EXAMPLE
powershellscript.ps1 /path \\uncpath\folder\

.NOTES
You must have administrative rights to the paths you are scanning. You must run the script
in an Administrator powershell window.
#>
```

This properly shows the syntax of a comment block that is usable via the PowerShell help system. You start by defining the comment block of `<#`. You then create a `.SYNOPSIS` section with a synopsis of the script. You then create a `.DESCRIPTION` section and provide a detailed description of the script. You also provide the author, revision, and editing revisions to the script. Following that section, you define a `.PARAMETER PATH` section, which provides detailed information about the `PATH` parameter in the script. You create an `.EXAMPLE` section to provide an example for usage, and you create a `.NOTES` section to provide information about the required execution environment. You then close the comment block by issuing `#>`.

Commenting code

The second recommendation is to keep track of changes in the PowerShell scripts in-line with the code. While most developers are great at providing comments pertaining to the overall functions, there are some guidelines that should be followed for commenting code in-line with the code, which are given here:

- **Comment the usage of all functions**: As you are developing functions to use within your scripts, it is recommended that you comment on how to use these items. This should include all mandatory parameters and all optional parameters being fed into the function. You should also specify the input and the output of the function.

- **Comment bug fixes**: When you are creating code to fix known bugs with the script or bugs within the system you are trying to configure, it is helpful to document the bug properly. Create a comment that references a bug number, TechNet article, or URL to provide insight into why you are performing code that might seem out of place in the script.
- **Comment backwards compatibility**: It is very common for environments to have a mixed variety of PowerShell versions in the environment. When you are creating code to provide backwards compatibility, it is recommended that you fully comment on what you're engineering for previous versions of PowerShell. This will provide insight into why you are not using a more efficient way of coding the script through new cmdlets.
- **Comment complex math calculations or formulas**: There may be instances where you need to leverage complex equations for data within PowerShell. It is recommended that you fully comment on the equations so that others can understand how you are deriving the data.
- **Comment the third-party modules**: When you are importing third-party modules for use in your PowerShell scripts, it is recommended that you provide the URL of the location where you downloaded the modules and other details about the module. This can include how you are using it, why you are using it, and where licensing information is for the third party module.
- **Comment .NET references**: In instances where you need to call .NET reflection assemblies to perform code, it is recommended that you comment on the individual lines of the code. Since most PowerShell users don't have a traditional .NET development background, it's important to comment on the individual lines of PowerShell code using .NET objects and what they are used for.
- **Comment in third person present tense**: When you are creating comments for your scripts, always try to create all comments in third person and present tense. This will keep the code more factual to *what is* being implemented instead of *what was* implemented. It also provides the developers the opportunity to identify themselves inside the comments, which is easier when non-identifying *I or me* words are not used. Only in cases of backwards compatibility, it is acceptable to use the past tense for historical information.

Best practices for script creation

As you are developing your scripts, there are standardized best practices that should be followed during the coding stage. These best practices provide robust and structured scripts, which will have predictable results. This section explores some of the recommendations for efficient PowerShell coding and provides guidance on how to avoid programming headaches.

Script structure

When you are creating scripts, you should adhere to a strict script structure. The structure of the script dictates the order of execution and how things are processed. It is recommended that you structure your scripts as shown here:

1. **Declare the script header**: To start the scripting process, declare a header and include everything that is pertinent to the script. This may include a description, revision information, author, editor, and additional notes.
2. **Declare the input parameters**: After the header, declare your input parameters if required by the script. Not only is this necessary, but it helps developers identify what is being input into the script and what fields are required for proper exaction of the script.
3. **Declare the global variables**: You should declare your global variables after the input parameters. As the variables are declared in a function, only stay within the boundary of function; the variables you need to use globally should be defined here.
4. **Declare the functions in order**: The next portion of the structure is declaring your functions. If you have functions that call each other, you will want to declare the functions that are called first in the script. This ensures that your scripts will not error out due to the function not being declared prior to execution.
5. **Start the execution of script**: After declaring the functions, you can start the execution of the script. This section will call the other functions that use the global variables and parameters to complete the tasks for the script.
6. **Declare the end of the script**: After execution, it is recommended that you create an indicator that specifies that the script runs successfully. Whether it is logging an exit code to a file or pausing the script at the end, it is important for you to create logic declaring proper or improper execution of your script.

Other important best practices for script creation

In addition to creating a proper script structure, there are a few other recommendations that should be considered when you are developing your scripts. These items include:

- **Limiting the use of cmdlet aliases**: While aliases provide the ability to shorten the overall size of a script, they also add complexity for those who are not familiar with a particular alias. This can also cause problems while editing scripts you haven't visited in a while if you have forgotten what the alias relates to. Another reason why you should avoid aliases is because they are not always portable from one machine to the next. This can be due to conflicting PowerShell versions or because the aliases are not defined on other machines. It's recommended to use aliases only during testing and manual PowerShell interactions.
- **Know when and when not to use a script**: While PowerShell is an excellent tool for automation and management, there are times where it may not be in your best interest to create a script. In the instance of software deployment tools, instead of executing a PowerShell script that invokes a MSIEXEC installation, it's sometimes easier to just place the MSIEXEC installation command in the deployment tool itself. This reduces the number of steps that are required to determine what task is being completed. Always take time to determine if a PowerShell script is required for the task at hand.
- **Never assume that a path is available**: When you are working with PowerShell, one of the most useful tools is the `test-path` cmdlet. This cmdlet allows you to validate files, folders, and registry items on systems before using them. Always plan for the worst case scenario and build the logic into your script to `test-path` before using files, folders, and registry items.
- **Never statically set up information in a script**: As you are developing your scripts, it is easy to statically set up information in your scripts. This information may include locations to a file, folder, registry, or usernames and passwords. Unless it's absolutely required for script execution, it is recommended that you leverage relative paths, systems variables, answer files, and prompts for usernames and password.
- **Use answer files for script static information**: When you are scripting, it's important to keep the PowerShell scripts as generic as possible. For reusability. When you need to feed information into a script, it is recommended that you use answer files that contain all of the information needed to process the script. These answer files may contain items such as path locations, domain credentials, a list of computers, and other items that would otherwise be static in a script.

- **Encrypting usernames and passwords**: In cases where you need to provide credentials to resources in your scripts, it is recommended that you always encrypt the strings when they are declared in the scripts or answer files. When you need to use them, you can decrypt these strings on the fly and store the usernames and passwords in a variable (memory). When the PowerShell script closes after execution, the PowerShell garbage collector will clear the variables from memory, and the usernames and passwords will no longer be decrypted on the system.

> For more information on encrypting and decrypting strings, you can view the following Microsoft TechNet article:
> `https://gallery.technet.microsoft.com/scriptcenter/PowerShell-Script-410ef9df`

- **Segments of code being reused belong to a function**: As you are developing your code, you may find sections where you repeat multiple lines of code. As a best practice rule of thumb, if you need to repeat a task multiple times, create a new function to process the work. This not only keeps the length of your script down, but it also ensures that any code changes to that code can be found in one location instead of in multiple locations in your script.
- **Display progress indicator on the screen**: For most PowerShell operations, you should be able to calculate a progress percentage to leverage the `write-progress` cmdlet. This provides the end users with the ability to approximately gauge the progress of the script. In instances where you are running the script and it's difficult to update the progress percentage, it is recommended that you leverage the `write-debug` cmdlet to print a status to the screen. This way, you can give the script user an approximate duration of the operation that is occurring on the screen.

> More information on the `write-progress` cmdlet can be found at `https://technet.microsoft.com/en-us/library/hh849902.aspx`.

- **Always use exception handling**: Exception handling is one of the most important components to be learned when becoming a PowerShell expert. Typically while scripting, 40 percent of your time goes to making the script work as intended and the remaining 60 percent is catching scenarios of the script failing. Whether it is validating the data extracted in the script, the files, folders, and registry items that exist before use, or to see if your changes were successful, it is essential for you to leverage exception handling.

- **Limit the use of regular expressions**: While regular expressions are very helpful in validating data, there is a large learning curve. Limit the use of regular expressions in your scripts. When you need to use them, fully comment them so others can quickly understand their function in your scripts.
- **Use the invoke-expression cmdlet cautiously**: There are well known security implications of leveraging the `invoke-expression` cmdlet in your scripts. If you need to leverage `invoke-expression`, reduce the privileges account running the block of code and ensure that all part of the expression cannot be modified by user input.

Controlling source files

It is well known in the industry that you should be using source control on all code that you are developing. In the industry, however, many developers ignore the need for source control for network, batch, VB, and PowerShell scripts, as they can be easily recreated. PowerShell is developing as a language, and the need for source control will be growing as the technology evolves. There are some general recommendations for controlling the source files while you are developing. Some of these items include:

- **Use source control software (if available)**: If there are source control systems that are available in your organization, you should strongly consider using them. This allows you and multiple other individuals to check out and add to the PowerShell scripts. It also allows you to track changes between different iterations of the code. These source control tools have many built-in features that can expedite the development of large and complex scripts.
- **Use Secured cloud storage systems:** An easy method to continually have a backup copy of your files is to leverage secured cloud storage systems. Some of these cloud systems also include a roll-back feature that provides source revision backups on the fly.
- **Revision major releases**: When you complete scripts for use in the environment, you should generate a new release number for those scripts. Archive the existing release and build a new folder structure for the next iteration of the scripts. This ensures that you are able to roll back to the previous versions of the script with minimal effort.

Best practices for software automation

Automation through PowerShell can be a very powerful tool when it's done right. There are few things that you can do, however, they will reduce the complexity of large automation scripts and increase reliability of execution. This section explores two things you can do that will greatly improve your success with automation when using PowerShell.

The first consideration is breaking apart scripts that contain 2000+ lines into smaller scripts. This allows you to better troubleshoot what items are failing and also makes the scripts more reusable for different tasks in your environment. For most purposes, you can break your large scripts into multiple scripts by what you're trying to accomplish. If you are installing a large software system, you could break the script into the prerequisite software scripts and main software scripts. If you are configuring different Windows features, you could break each individual feature installation and configuration into a separate script. The segmentation of code will help your productivity and will help you quickly ease the learning curve of complex automation operations.

While breaking your scripts into smaller scripts is recommended, it is also recommended that you don't create so many scripts that the automation becomes unmanageable. If you find yourself creating 20 or more scripts for an automation task, you should try to consolidate the scripts into more manageable sections.

> In instances where you reuse large segments of code in all of your scripts, you may consider writing your own PowerShell module. For more information on PowerShell modules, you can go to `https://msdn.microsoft.com/en-us/library/dd878297(v=vs.85).aspx`.

In addition to breaking apart large scripts, the second consideration is including four sections in your automation scripts. These sections are:

- **Prerequisite check**: This section of the script will check the system for prerequisite hardware and software items. It should include a check for items such as running or available services, installed software, or available resources such as the hard drive or memory. This ensures that the system is ready to proceed with the automation tasks.
- **Pre-installation tasks**: This will remediate anything in the prerequisite check that is not satisfactory. This could include starting and stopping services, backing up the system files or registry prior to installation, installing prerequisite software, and checking for pending restarts.

- **Installation**: This section of the script should install or configure the items that you desire on the system. This may include registry entries, executing MSI files, copying files and folders to the system, or even executing batch operations.
- **Post-installation tasks**: This section of the script will execute all cleanup tasks for the installation. This may include cleaning up after the prerequisites and the installation or starting services that were stopped in the previous steps.

While following these considerations for creation of scripts, you will have a much more consistent approach to script creation. This approach ensures that you check to make sure the script won't take down a system, you are able to update the system as intended, and you are leaving the system in a stable state after execution.

It is also important to note that some scripts may not require all of the sections. If the script you are creating doesn't require all of the sections, just leave the sections commented out or remove them entirely from the script. Use your best judgment in creating the scripts with the complexity that you need for the task at hand.

Summary

This chapter explored multiple best practices for developing scripts in PowerShell. It started by explaining how you should have commented headers in all of your scripts. It also explained that the headers should have highlighted script headers, a brief description, script author information, revision information, and usage information. It then displayed a suggested header, formatted using those best practices.

You then learned about commenting on code and different guidelines to follow for that. You proceeded to learn about the best practices for script creation. You then explored several recommendations for controlling source files. This chapter ends by explaining the best practices for automation. You learned that when you are automating large systems, you should split the scripts apart into smaller, more manageable scripts.

Mastering Windows PowerShell Scripting – conclusion

PowerShell is quickly becoming the language of choice to support Microsoft systems in organizations. With Microsoft's deep integration of PowerShell in their products, PowerShell knowledge will be a required skill set in the years to come. This book has taught you the fundamentals of PowerShell scripting and is geared towards real world scenarios of how Fortune 500 companies leverage PowerShell.

In the beginning chapters, you learned the basics of PowerShell. You started by learning variables, hashes, and arrays. You also learned the data parsing, manipulation, and comparison operators. You then attained the knowledge of how to use functions, switches, and loop structures. You proceeded with working with more complex items such as regular expressions, error and exception handling, and session-based remote management.

The second half of the book was focused on managing different components of the Microsoft operating system. You started by mastering how to manage files, folders, and registry items. You then learned how to control permissions with access control lists and applying basic and advanced attributes to files and folders using PowerShell. You then dived into Windows Management Instrumentation, XML manipulation, Windows processes, Windows services, and local users and group management.

The last section of this book explained different PowerShell automation techniques and taught you how to use the desired configuration management to create and enforce configuration baselines. It concluded with providing a list of best practices and final recommendations for scripting with PowerShell.

Staying connected with the author

As the author of this book, Brenton Blawat always extends a helping hand to the community. You can follow Brenton on twitter `@brentblawat` or his blog at `http://www.bittangents.com`. The author is always open for discussions on the book and will provide feedback to readers, as time allows. To ask book related PowerShell questions, you can visit `http://www.masteringposh.com`.

If you found this book helpful, the author also encourages you to leave your feedback on the site where you purchased the book. Every comment helps spread the word about the book and helps point the community towards helpful methods to learn PowerShell.

The author sincerely thanks you for purchasing and reading *Mastering Windows PowerShell Scripting*.

Happy coding!

Index

Symbols

-and comparison operator 42, 43
 # commenting headers 241-243
-contains operator 39-42
-like operator 41, 42
-match operator 39-42, 66
-or comparison operator 42, 43

A

access control lists (ACL)
about 137
copying 148-150
ACL rules
adding 150-156
removing 150-156
Active Directory cmdlets
URL 195
active directory services interface (ADSI) 195
anchors, regular expression 78-81
arrays
about 6
jagged arrays 7
single dimension arrays 6, 7
values, updating 8, 9
attributes
retrieving 138-141
authoring phase 231-234
automation
programs, invoking 223-229

B

best practices
for functions 62
for looping structures 62, 63
for script creation 245
for script management 241
for software automation 249
for switches 62, 63
best practices, for script creation
about 245-247
script structure 245
source files, controlling 248
bytes
formatting 26, 27

C

characters
of regular expressions 66, 67
of regular expressions quantifiers 73
CIM Object Manager (CIMOM) 160
CIM sessions
creating 107-109
creating, with session options 109-111
NoEncryption parameter 110
Protocol parameter 109
ProxyAuthentication parameter 109
ProxyCredential parameter 110
removing 113, 114
UseSSL parameter 110
using, for remote management 111-113
utilizing 104-107
class methods, WMI
invoking 174, 175

code testing, methodologies
about 96
containers, hit testing 98, 99
frequency, testing 97, 98
production testing, avoiding 99, 100
WhatIf argument, testing 96, 97
comma separated values (CSV) 17
Common Information Model (CIM) 103
Common Language Runtime (CLR) 88
comparison operators
-and comparison operator 42, 43
-contains operator 39- 42
-like operator 39-42
-match operator 39-42
-or comparison operator 42, 43
basics 35, 36
best practices 43, 44
equal comparison operator 36-38
greater than comparison operator 38, 39
less than comparison operator 38, 39
not equal comparison operator 36-38
containers
about 1
selecting, for scripts 13, 14

D

data types
forcing 30, 31
date manipulation 27-30
Deployment Workbench 223
Desired Configuration Management 223
desired state configuration. *See* **DSC**
Distributed Component Object Model (DCOM) 104
Distributed Management Task Force (DMTF) 162
Document Object Model (DOM) 180
Do/Until looping structure
creating 53
format 54, 55
Do/While looping structure
creating 52
format 52, 53
drifting configurations
detecting 236-239
restoring 236-239
drivers (DLL) 161
DSC
archive resource 230
authoring phase 229
environment resource 230
file resource 230
group resource 230
log resource 230
package resource 230
registry resource 230
remediation phase 229
resources, URL 231
script resource 231
service resource 231
staging phase 229
user resource 231
using 229-231
WindowsFeature resource 231
WindowsProcess resource 230

E

equal comparison operator 36-38
error and exception handling
legacy exception handling 93
parameters 88-90
Try/Catch block 90
eXtensible Markup Language (XML) 177

F

files
copying 125-128
creating, with PowerShell 119-121
deleting 132-135
extended attributes, setting 143-147
extended attributes, viewing 141-143
mode, setting 143
moving 125-128
permissions, managing 147, 148
renaming 128-131
verifying 123, 124
file structure, XML
about 177-180
XML parser 177, 178

folders
copying 125-128
creating, with PowerShell 119-121
deleting 132-135
extended attributes, setting 143-147
extended attributes, viewing 141-143
mode, setting 143-147
moving 125-128
renaming 128-131
verifying 123, 124
ForEach loop structure
about 55
format 55
functions
about 45
best practices 62
declaring 46-51
reference link, for advanced parameters 50

G

greater than comparison operator 38, 39
grouping constructs, regular expression
about 70-72
using, examples 71
groups
managing 195
querying for 204-207

H

hashes 10-13
Hypertext Markup Language (HTML) 177

I

Internet Corporation for Assigned Names and Numbers (ICANN) format 84, 85

J

jagged arrays 7

L

legacy exception handling 93-96
less than comparison operator 38, 39
local groups
managing 198-203
local users
managing 195-198
querying for 204-206
looping structures
about 52
best practices 62, 63
Do/Until 52-55
Do/While 52, 53
For 52, 56
ForEach 52-56

M

Managed Object Format (MOF) 160, 233
Microsoft Deployment Toolkit (MDT) 223
mode attributes 139

N

named values
adding, to registry keys 121-123
deleting 131-135
renaming 128-131
namespace 160
New Technology File System (NTFS) 141
not equal comparison operator 36-38
numbers
formatting 25, 26
manipulation 24, 25

O

objects
storing, in variables 4, 5

P

parameters
ErrorAction 88
ErrorVariable 89
Try/Catch block, using with 92, 93
WarningAction 88
WarningVariable 89
parsing 24, 25
piping
about 32
variables 32-34

PowerShell
comparison operators 35, 36
modules, URL 249
properties
retrieving 138-141

R

ranges, regular expression 70-72
registry items
creating, with PowerShell 119-121
verifying 123, 124
registry keys
named values, adding 121-123
renaming 128-131
registry permissions
managing 147, 148
registry provider 118
regular expression quantifiers
about 72-77
characters 73
regular expressions
about 65-70
anchors 78
examples 82-85
grouping construct 70-72
quantifiers 72-77
ranges 70-72
remediation phase 235
Remote Procedure Call (RPC) 103
Replace() method
used, for replacing strings 16

S

script management
best practices 241
scripts
container, selecting 13, 14
creation, best practices 245
Security Account Manager (SAM) 170, 196
serviceExample function 90
single dimension arrays 6, 7
split() method
used, for splitting strings 17
staging phase 235
static fields 24
strings
counting 18, 19
false method 22, 23
manipulation 15, 16
replacing, Replace() method used 16
splitting, split() method used 17
trimming 18, 19, 20
true method 22, 23
structures
usage, combining of 58-61
Substring() method 21, 22
switches
about 57
best practices 62, 63
System Center Configuration Manager (SCCM) 160, 223, 235
System Center Orchestrator 223

T

time manipulation 27-30
toLower() method 16
toUpper() method 16
TrimEnd() method 20
Trim() method 19, 20
TrimStart() method 20
Try/Catch block
using 90, 91
using, with parameters 92, 93

U

User Account Control (UAC) 119

V

variables
about 2, 3
stored objects 4, 5
piping 32-34

W

WhatIf argument
testing 96, 97

Windows
features, installing 217-220
processes, managing 213- 216
services, managing 207-213
Windows Management Instrumentation (WMI)
about 159
class methods, invoking 174
classes, searching 163-166
objects 161, 162
searching 163-166
structure 159
Windows Remote Management (WinRM) 103
WMI components
WMI consumers 159
WMI infrastructure 159
WMI providers 159
WMI property instances
creating 167-171
modifying 167-172
removing 167-173
WMI Query Language (WQL) 175
World Wide Web Consortium (W3C) 177
write-progress cmdlet
URL 247

X

XML
content, adding 185-188
content, modifying 189-191
content, removing 192, 193
files, reading 181-85
XML parser 177

Thank you for buying

Mastering Windows PowerShell Scripting

About Packt Publishing

Packt, pronounced 'packed', published its first book, *Mastering phpMyAdmin for Effective MySQL Management*, in April 2004, and subsequently continued to specialize in publishing highly focused books on specific technologies and solutions.

Our books and publications share the experiences of your fellow IT professionals in adapting and customizing today's systems, applications, and frameworks. Our solution-based books give you the knowledge and power to customize the software and technologies you're using to get the job done. Packt books are more specific and less general than the IT books you have seen in the past. Our unique business model allows us to bring you more focused information, giving you more of what you need to know, and less of what you don't.

Packt is a modern yet unique publishing company that focuses on producing quality, cutting-edge books for communities of developers, administrators, and newbies alike. For more information, please visit our website at `www.packtpub.com`.

About Packt Enterprise

In 2010, Packt launched two new brands, Packt Enterprise and Packt Open Source, in order to continue its focus on specialization. This book is part of the Packt Enterprise brand, home to books published on enterprise software - software created by major vendors, including (but not limited to) IBM, Microsoft, and Oracle, often for use in other corporations. Its titles will offer information relevant to a range of users of this software, including administrators, developers, architects, and end users.

Writing for Packt

We welcome all inquiries from people who are interested in authoring. Book proposals should be sent to `author@packtpub.com`. If your book idea is still at an early stage and you would like to discuss it first before writing a formal book proposal, then please contact us; one of our commissioning editors will get in touch with you.

We're not just looking for published authors; if you have strong technical skills but no writing experience, our experienced editors can help you develop a writing career, or simply get some additional reward for your expertise.

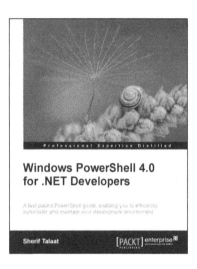

[PACKT] enterprise
PUBLISHING
professional expertise distilled

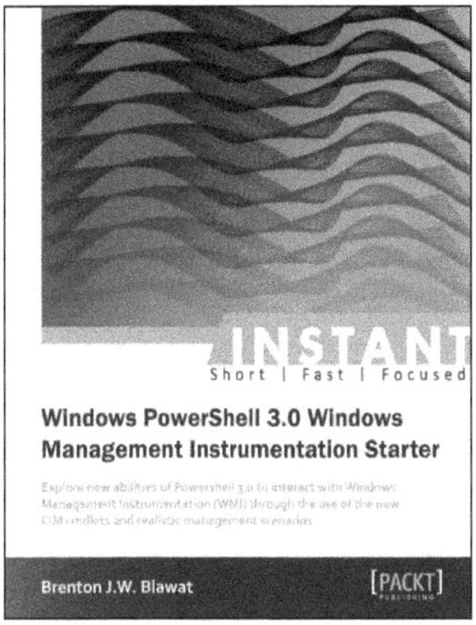

Instant Windows Powershell 3.0 Windows Management Instrumentation Starter

ISBN: 978-1-84968-962-5 Paperback: 66 pages

Explore new abilities of Powershell 3.0 to interact with Windows Management Instrumentation (WMI) through the use of the new CIM cmdlets and realistic management scenarios

1. Learn something new in an Instant! A short, fast, focused guide delivering immediate results.
2. Create CIM sessions to local and remote systems.

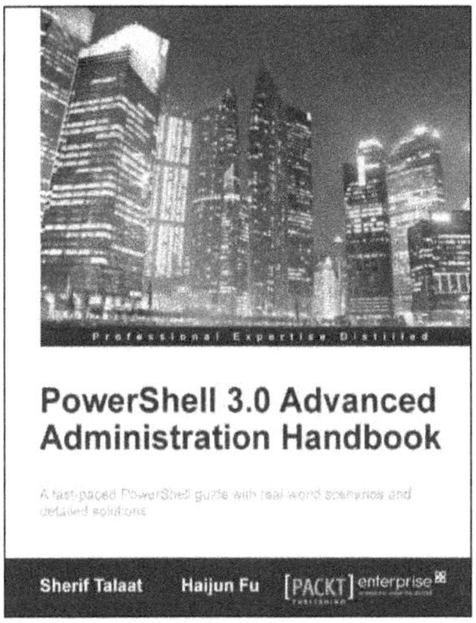

PowerShell 3.0 Advanced Administration Handbook

ISBN: 978-1-84968-642-6 Paperback: 370 pages

A fast-paced PowerShell guide with real-world scenarios and detailed solutions

1. Discover and understand the concept of Windows PowerShell 3.0.
2. Learn the advanced topics and techniques for a professional PowerShell scripting.
3. Explore the secret of building custom PowerShell snap-ins and modules.

Please check **www.PacktPub.com** for information on our titles

www.ingramcontent.com/pod-product-compliance
Lightning Source LLC
Chambersburg PA
CBHW060526060326
40690CB00017B/3401
* 9 7 8 1 7 8 2 1 7 3 5 5 7 *